Reader's Guide
to
THOMAS HARDY

Reader's Guide to THOMAS HARDY

Dr. Matt Bacak

CENTRUM PRESS
NEW DELHI-110002 (INDIA)

CENTRUM PRESS
H.O.: 4360/4, Ansari Road, Daryaganj,
New Delhi-110 002 (India)
Ph.: 23278000, 23261597

B.O.: No. 1015, Ist Main Road, BSK IIIrd Stage
IIIrd Phase, IIIrd Block,
Bangalore - 560 085 (India)
Tel.: 080-41723429
Visit us at: www.centrumpress.com

Reader's Guide to Thomas Hardy

First Edition, 2009
ISBN 978-93-80106-71-7

PRINTED IN INDIA

Printed at Salasar Imaging Systems, Delhi-110035 (India)

Contents

Preface

Thomas Hardy was born on Egdon Heath, in Dorset, near Dorchester on June 2, 1840. His father was a master mason and building contractor. Hardy's mother, whose tastes included Latin poets and French romances, provided for his education.

After schooling in Dorchester, Hardy was apprenticed to an architect. He worked in an office, which specialized in restoration of churches. In 1874 Hardy married Emma Lavinia Gifford. Thomas Hardy was equally eminent as a novelist and a poet and thus holds a unique place in English Literature.

The collection will be relevant and useful to both students and scholars of English literature as it brings into focus a wide spectrum of interesting sidelights on, and illuminating analyses of the various dimensions of Hardy's works; some of the papers are refreshingly original and perceptive in their approach to and treatment of the respective subjects.

As a 'great' writer Hardy has remained problematic, demanding that his readers wrestle with him. The present volume claims to have joined that unbroken wrestle—more than a century old—with the words and meanings of Hardy's works. Contributions from the eminent scholars in the field have enhanced the value of the collection.

Author

Chapter 1

Introduction

Thomas Hardy's long literary career witnessed and encompassed the most important artistic and literary changes of the modern era. Hardy was born in 1840 near Dorcester, England; before his death in 1928 at the age of 87, the genre of the Victorian novel had flowered and faded, and the erstwhile avant-garde movement known as modernism dominated the English literary landscape.

In his ornate, wordy style and his sensitivity to issues of class, Hardy seemed a characteristic Victorian novelist. But his writing increasingly revealed a sensibility and a moral code that seemed to discard the strict Victorian social and sexual mores, and that tended towards atheism and subjective morality rather than an absolutist Christianity. His philosophy was out of place in Victorian England, and presaged the coming social and cultural upheaval of modernism.

Trained as an architect, Hardy was at first unsuccessful in breaking through in the London literary world. His first poems and novels went unpublished or unappreciated. It was only after Hardy's return to his native Bockhampton that his novels began to attract attention and commercial success.

Far from the Madding Crowd, published in 1874, ushered in his most productive period; it was soon followed by many other novels, including The Return of the Native—published serially in monthly installments in an English magazine—in 1878. Controversy over the moral stance of his later novels Tess of the d'Urbervilles (1891) and Jude the Obscure (1896) led Hardy to abandon writing novels, and to concentrate on poems and—to a lesser extent—short stories, for which he also won deserved fame. It is not at all coincidental that Hardy's success as a novelist followed his returns home to Dorcester. Setting is of crucial importance in Hardy's novels, and his finest novels are all set in the region of "Wessex," which, while fictional, is based upon Hardy's own native corner of England. Wessex follows the geographical contours of Dorset, England, with only a few changes made by Hardy: it is not hard to see how the culture, language and geography of Hardy's home country shape his novels.

The Return of the Native takes as one of its central themes—and, arguably, as its central character—the tract of windswept upland in Hardy's Wessex known as Egdon Heath. The novel is deeply rooted in the folk customs of the residents of the Heath, and attempts to imitate their attitudes and even their patterns of speech. It is the return to the heath of the educated Clym Yeobright that supplies the novel's title and catalyzing crisis. This surely derives from the experience of Thomas Hardy himself, who only a few years.

The Victorian Era when Hardy lived was a time of great change. Queen Victoria ruled England from1837 until her death in 1901. During her 63-year reign, England became the most powerful and wealthiest country in the world through its colonial acquisition and by harnessing the power of the Industrial Revolution. The population in England doubled during Victoria's reign, and the economy of the country changed from agriculture-based to industry-based. More people were enfranchised (that is, given the right to vote) and, through this, gained influence in government. The Parliament passed labour laws that improved labour conditions, established universal schooling for all children, and reformed the civil service system. Britain ended restrictions on foreign trade, opening the way for the island to become a source for both raw materials and finished goods to an ever-increasing international market.

Victoria, interested in the welfare of her people, worked hard to pass meaningful reforms, and she earned the respect of her subjects. Her prime ministers were her greatest assets, and with them, Queen Victoria decreased the powers of the monarchy to empower the members of the prime minister's cabinet. As a result, the British monarchy has been able to endure, unlike the monarchies in most other countries. The changes that occurred during the Victorian era affected the lives of every person living in England in both great and small ways. As England quickly moved from an agriculture-based society to one that would produce many of the world's goods, factories replaced individual workshops, and people moved from small towns to large cities in search of work.

Mobility and the transport of goods were increased with the invention of steamships and the development of a railway system. The balance of traditional class distinctions shifted as more people prospered, amassing wealth and power that had been unthinkable in the years prior to this era. These tumultuous changes resulted in an examination of the traditional ways of thinking and acting, and the foundations of English society—family, religion, class divisions, and so on—came under increasing scrutiny.

One area that was particularly affected by the changes in England was religion. The Church of England was traditionally conservative and offered a literal interpretation of the Bible. During the Victorian period, however, as people began to see the church as an agent for social change as well as an agent for personal salvation, the question became how—and even whether—the church should best fulfill these missions. The result was a schism in the church that fostered three movements: the High Church movement, the Middle Church movement, and the Low Church movement.

The High Church movement was designed to align the Church of England with the "Catholic" side of Anglicanism. The thinking here was that traditional practices were the standard by which faith could be expressed and that supreme authority resided in the Church. The Middle Church movement cared less for tradition and believed that faith could be expressed in various ways, including through social action. The Low Church Movement believed that evangelicals were a force that could reform the church from within and without. Individual and biblical bases of faith were hallmarks of this movement. Evangelicals tackled serious issues of the day: housing and welfare of the poor, as well as social reform. They also believed in spreading the gospel around the world by any means necessary.

The growing reliance on science to explain the nature of man and his relationship with his world opened the doors for further examination of traditionally held beliefs. The publication of Darwin's Origin of Species (1859), which suggested that species evolved from common ancestors that could be found through scientific research, challenged the belief that God created each species individually and separately from every other species. The agnostic movement, which relied on scientific evidence and reason to find universal truths and which held that the existence of God could not be empirically proven, took hold and gained momentum.

From these ideological splits, religious liberals and conservatives battled over fundamental questions of faith and religious practice. In Hardy's work, we can see that this debate was one that he entered into. In Tess of the d'Urbervilles, Hardy's protagonist finds herself in a world where she questions religion, questions faith, looks for meaning in life, and searches for the truths that mankind has sought for centuries.

EARLY CAREER

By 1862, when he was 22, Hardy left for London to work as a draftsman in the office of Arthur Blomfield. While in London, Hardy was influenced by the works of Charles Swinburne, Robert Browning, and Charles Darwin (the author of Origin of Species, 1856).

Poor health forced Hardy to return to his native region in 1867, where he worked for Hicks again and for another architect, G.R. Crickmay. Hardy's education was interrupted by his work as an architect. He had wanted to attend the university and become an Anglican minister, but lack of funds and his declining interest in religion swayed Hardy away from that avocation and more toward a self-study of poetry and writing. Hardy tried his hand at writing when he was 17 and wrote for years while he was a practicing architect. His first novel manuscript, The Poor Man and the Lady (1867–68), was rejected by several publishers, but one editor, George Meredith encouraged him, and so Hardy set out to refine his style. A second story, Desperate Remedies (1871), was accepted and published.

His next novel, Under the Greenwood Tree (1872), demonstrates a more polished Hardy now coming into his own style. By 1870, Hardy was sent by his employer to begin a restoration project of the St. Juliot Church in Cornwall. Here he met his first wife, Emma Lavinia Gifford, whom Hardy married in 1874. Emma encouraged Hardy to write, and by 1872, Hardy left architecture to devote his time to his literary career.

LITERARY WORK

When Hardy left his career as architect, he did so with a contract for 11 monthly installments of a tale, A Pair of Blue Eyes, in the Cornhill Magazine. His reputation as one of England's newer novelists sustained the Hardy family from that time on. The next novel, Far from the Maddening Crowd (1874), introduced the Wessex area setting, which also is the setting for Tess. The next two novels, The Return of the Native (1878) and The Mayor of Casterbridge (1886), established Hardy as a formidable writer.

Hardy published two more novels, Tess of the d'Urbervilles (1891) and Jude the Obscure (1895), which were his last long fiction works. The last novels challenged the sensibilities of Victorian readers with situations that ruffled many a Victorian feather: immoral sex, murder, illegitimate children, and the unmarried living together. Heated debate and criticism over these two books helped Hardy decide that he would rather write poetry. In fact, so stung was he by the criticism of his works that Hardy did not write another novel.

Hardy wrote short stories, poems, and plays for the rest of his life. Two further volumes of poetry and short stories appeared, The Dynasts: A Drama of the Napoleonic Wars (1903–08) and Winter Words (1928), a volume of verse. Hardy was quite prolific during this period, writing some 900 poems on a variety of subjects. In 1912, Hardy's wife, Emma, died, ending 20 years of "domestic estrangement." In 1914, Hardy married Florence Emily Dugdale, with whom he lived until his death on January 11, 1928.

Hardy's body was buried at Westminster Abbey in Poet's Corner, while his heart was buried in Stinson, England, near the graves of his ancestors and his first wife, Emma. His second wife was later buried near her husband.

Chapter 2

Critically Analyse the "The Return of the Native"

THEME

In this novel, Hardy embodies the idea that we live in an indifferent universe. He also implies that the universe can be hostile, but he does not use this novel as a vehicle to remind us that "it's a jungle out there." Critics usually refer to Hardy's themes as fatalistic—a view of life that shows human actions being controlled by an impersonal force, perhaps called Destiny or Fate, which is independent of both humanity and its gods. The indifference of the universe, therefore, really describes what we see as we look about us or, perhaps, all that we can find when we are unable any longer to believe in the gods we created.

If it is said that we are created in God's image, it may also be argued that we create gods in our own images. The dilemma implied here is, of course, as old as humanity and perpetually without final answer, though historically there have been many attempted answers. Chance and coincidence are two ways in which this seeming indifference expresses itself in our lives. When we say an event has taken place by chance or coincidence, we are simply expressing our own view of the matter; it is simply all we are able to see at the level of events or plot.

POINT OF VIEW

Hardy's use of point of view is conventional for his time

in literary history. It can be described as a third-person or omniscient point of view, which means that events can be viewed through the eyes of whatever character at the moment suits the author's purposes. Usually, though not always, such a person is one of the main characters, although within Hardy's lifetime, F. Scott Fitzgerald made a minor character the principal point of view in The Great Gatsby. Such a point of view is normally confusing to the reader only when it is shifted frequently in a short space, as, for example, in the melodramatic scenes in chapters 7-9 of Book Fifth.

Following the example of Henry James, a contemporary of Hardy's, modern novelists ordinarily use a more restricted point of view, in part because of the greater reality it lends to a work of fiction. Hardy himself was no innovator of fictional techniques.

SETTING

Egdon Heath lends itself very well to the kind of story Hardy wanted to tell in the novel. It is meant as a tragedy, at least through the original five books, and the "gaunt waste" provides an appropriate setting. It is also a convenient microcosm, limited in physical extent and containing all types of human beings. Both its history and its character can be made meaningful parts of the story. Indeed, some critics go so far as to look upon Egdon as a character like any other in the novel. To do so, however, is to ignore the usual expectations the reader has of the nature of any novel.

The characters in Hardy's novel can be grouped by their attitudes toward the heath. Clym, Mrs. Yeobright, Thomasin, and Venn are products of Egdon and understand it: Clym is frequently shown, for instance, to have an intimate knowledge of its natural features; Thomasin, though well off after her husband dies, has no desire to leave it; Venn is shown to be so familiar with it that at night he can walk at full speed across it without losing his footing. On the other hand, both Eustacia and Wildeve look upon the heath as a place to leave with all deliberate speed, making it ironical and appropriate that both should die in a stream near Shadwater Weir.

Hardy has been criticized for his handling of plot. Like other novelists of his time, he often uses chance and coincidence to excess. This use, however, is sometimes for reasons other than simply furthering the story at a given point. Hardy also characteristically rushes his story along at times by using a series of short scenes rather than sacrificing variety or the interest that a fast pace can maintain to the detailed development possible in a longer or long scene. It may well be that here, as in the case of his adding a sixth book, his practice is influenced by the kind of readers he knew he would have in the serial publication of his books.

Hardy's habit of using melodrama in important scenes has also been pointed out. Modern critics and readers tend to complain about this, but Hardy was doing nothing very different from contemporary writers. Compare the melodrama with Hardy's use of realism, which is effective by today's standards and still effectively evokes the physical and emotional landscapes Hardy wanted to convey to his readers.

STRUCTURE

The structure of a novel is the shape given to its plot or series of events. The structure of Hardy's novel has been said to be described by a curve of expectation which traces the changes in the relationship between, and the aspirations of, Clym and Eustacia from waiting in anticipation and hope to the defeat of any possibility for happiness. This curve also reflects the changes in the relationship between the less important characters of Wildeve and Thomasin. The structure of the novel reaches its logical completion by the end of Book Fifth; Book Sixth is an extension not accounted for by it.

SYMBOLISM

Hardy uses a number of symbols in the novel: Egdon Heath, Rainbarrow, the moon, Paris, gambling, physical impairment (eyesight), a storm, water are those singled out for comment. Many of these are aspects of the setting. Like any symbol, these are both facts and representatives of certain meanings or significance. Symbols are appropriate to a work of fiction if they can be both at the same time. They are successful if they enable an author to convey meaning without forcing it. Most of the above symbols are appropriate and successful; those which are not are connected with the melodramatic scenes at the end of Book Fifth. Symbols are useful guidelines that can help to demonstrate an author's theme.

IRONY

Irony is a literary device in which the difference between intention and performance is shown. It is an effect that figures heavily in Hardy's novel. The theme itself contains irony, because man can never know just what sort of universe he lives in. If a man is convinced, for example, that the gods are indifferent to his aspirations and his life, he may be wrong. Eustacia's despair may well be caused by a mistaken view of what life is like.

As a consequence, her view of things becomes one of the causes for her despair, though she looks upon it rather as a symptom. To take an extreme case, Hardy himself may have been quite wrong in his way of looking at life. Indeed, any view of humanity in relation to the universe is susceptible of irony.

STYLE

Much has been said, pro and con, about Hardy's style in his fiction. It is easy to say he has a clumsy style or an adequate style or an intermittently effective style. A demonstration of some particular aspect of his style is perhaps more useful. Hardy's narrative style makes use of several kinds of imagery, including a number of figures of speech using analogies drawn from the setting of his story.

Consider such a sampling as the following: "Eustacia's journey was at first as vague in direction as that of thistledown in the wind"; "the party had marched in trail, like a traveling flock of sheep; that is to say, the strongest first, the weak and young behind"; "[Grandfer Cantle] also began to sing, in the voice of a bee up a flue"; "Grandfer Cantle meanwhile staring at [Christian] as a hen stares at the duck she has hatched"; "in her winter dress, as now, [Eustacia] was like the tiger-beetle, which, when observed in dull situations, seems to be of the quietest neutral colour, but under a full illumination blazes with dazzling splendor"; "[the settle] is, to the hearths of old-fashioned cavernous fireplaces, what the last belt of trees is to the exposed country estate, or the north wall to the garden"; "[Clym] longed for death, as a field laborer longs for the shade"; "Fairway gave a circular motion to the rope, as if he were stirring a batter"; "[Eustacia] had entered the dance from the troubled hours of her late life as one might enter a brilliant chamber after a night walk in a wood"; "the leaves of the hollyhocks hung like half-closed umbrellas."

In the first of these, the term carrying the analogy comes from nature; in the second, from the characters' daily activities on the heath. In short, Hardy's imagery is appropriate to the world of his story and effective in conveying what, at a given moment, he wishes to show, not merely say.

Chapter 3

Intended Audience and Serial Structure

Addressing himself initially to magazine readers rather than the book-buying public and the memberships of lending libraries, Hardy is writing outside the traditions of London society and university education. The somewhat headstrong but virtuous female protagonist and the villainous man of education and substance seem to be derived more from the conventions of the contemporary theatre rather than from the Victorian novel prior to 1870, although one sees affinities between Hardy's characters and those of Wilkie Collins.

Although a voracious reader and consumer of ideas, Hardy was still very much a countryman when his first critical success, Far From the Madding Crowd, was published in the pages of London's respectable Cornhill Magazine, edited by a man of letters (Leslie Stephen), in 1874.

Hardy, wanting desperately to give up architecture and become a professional writer, desired, as he told his editor, "to be a good hand at a serial." Thus, each monthly 'part' (anything from three to five chapters, but of roughly the same number of pages) moved towards a climax and a cliff-hanger, the "curtain" (ending of one instalment and opening of the next) both implicitly posing and answering a question of suspense in the reader's mind.

For example, at the close of Part One of Far From the Madding Crowd (Chapter 5), one is left wondering what will become of Gabriel Oak after the younger of his dogs has destroyed his flock and bankrupted him. This implicit question

Hardy immediately addresses at the start of Part Two (Chapters 6 through 8): what question does he similarly pose then answer at the close of Part Two and the opening of Part Three (Chapter 9)

PHYSICAL SETTING

Hardy's handling of physical setting is unparalled in English fiction, although in the verse of the Lake Poets and Robert Burns one has a similar sense of a specific topography and landscape. But, when Hardy is at his best, as in The Return of the Native, the natural backdrop becomes another person in the picture, so to speak. Egdon Heath is not described sop frequently and in such detail merely for the sake of "local colour." Indeed, such rural settings were outside the range of experience of the primarily urban readership that purchased the periodicals such as Belgravia in which Hardy originally published his "Novels of Character and Environment."

How does Hardy convey the numinous, atavistic sense that pervades the glade where Tess encounters the dying pheasants, for instance? Egdon in The Return of the Native is an objective correlative for the forces of tradition and environment that condition the actions of its denizens, and ultimately destroy the lives of the outsiders Eustacia Vye and Damon Wildeve. How is the tragic ending of Tess of the D'Urbervilles, then, both similar to that of The Return of the Native and yet a departure? Prior to The Return of the Native,in such lesser novels as Under the Greenwood Tree and The Hand of Ethelberta Hardy brought his stories to closure by marrying off his heroines.

Although one might argue that Ethelberta's being outsmarted by Lord Mountclere represents a dimunition of the feminine principle, it is hardly as extreme as the execution that brings Tess of the D'Urbervilles to a close. Had only Alec died, the book might well be categorised as a Victorian melodrama translated from the stage to the page: what motivated Hardy to kill off a heroine he genuinely admired? And why does he have Angel marry Tess's younger sister, Liza Lu, when in Far From the Madding Crowd he is content to dispose of Gabriel's rivals in a single shot, leaving Bathsheba free to marry the self-taught, resilient rustic who has stood by the quixotic heroine through thick and thin?

CHRONOLOGICAL SETTING

Unless Hardy gives the reader specific clues such as "before the nineteenth century had run one-third of its span" at the beginning of The Mayor of Casterbridge, the reader should presume that the chronological setting is roughly contemporaneous with the year of publication. But Hardy is not always direct in his presentation of chronological setting; for example, only by certain internal references and a conspicuous lack of railway travel is one to deduce that The Return of the Native, published serially in 1878, is set thirty years earlier.

Life in rural Dorset and the surrounding counties that make up Thomas Hardy's "Wessex of the novels and poems" moved more slowly than in metropolis of London or the industrial north, so that a novel such as Under The Greenwood Tree may seem to be set much earlier than it actually is. To a certain extent, the world of Hardy's peasantry is timeless, their lives determined by the natural rhythms of planting and harvest rather than by clocks and railway timetables, so that the movement of most Hardy narratives is through seasons rather than through months. Hardy's Wessex is generally pre-industrial and agricultural, its society close-knit and traditional.

Figures such as Donald Farfrae in The Mayor of Casterbridge and the Baron in The Romantic Adventures of a Milkmaid who are associated with technological progress (the seed drill and the steam yacht, respectively)and "the ache of modernity" are outsiders, marked by their clothing and speech as contrary to the traditional usages of the Wessex folk. It is not difficult, therefore, to spot these interlopers, whose arrival often bodes trouble for the story's principals—Sergeant Troy in Far From the Madding Crowd (1874) and William Dare in A Laodicean pose a threat to the security of the society, the stability of industrial employment and the traditional servant-master relationship; hence, their symbols and past-times are sordid, violent, and disruptive. What activities and symbolic objects represent Dare and mark him out as "modern"? How is Troy's sword indicative of his role as a womanizer and seducer? How are Alec D'Urberville's smoking, dressing fashionably, and racing about in a dog-cart intended to comment upon his "outlandish" (and morally out-of-bounds) nature

NARRATIVE VOICE

If Hardy's handling of the plot mechanisms seems derived from the pot-boiler and Sensation Novel, his handling of narrative voice is highly sophisticated in diction, allusion, syntax, and tone, largely as a result of his modelling his narrative voice on that of the mid-Victorian Sage, George Eliot. A modern reader unused to the lengthy, carefully subordinated sentence that is the hallmark of Hardy's prose style may encounter some difficulty in comprehending the overall effect and meaning of the sentence. For example, the opening sentence of Far From the Madding Crowd requires that the reader distinguish the principal clauses from the subordinate elements in order to focus on the subject (Farmer Oak's face) and the narrative intention (the revelation of Farmer Oak's character): "When Farmer Oak smiled, the corners of his mouth spread till they were within an unimportant distance of his ears, his eyes were reduced to mere chinks, and divergent wrinkles appeared round them, extending upon his countenance like the rays in a rudimentary sketch of the rising sun." Wisely, editor Stephen has formatted this complex sentence as a paragraph by itself.

After the initial subordinate clause (when...smiled), the sentence rushes by, the principal clause being a mere six words (the corners...spread),the remainder being the consequent effects of that smile. The closing of the sentence, actually a simple simile ("like the rays...sun"), identifies the force and vigour of Farmer Oak's genial nature with that of the morning sun, the source of the cornland's strength and fecundity. The tone behind the sentence suggests satire rather than straight exposition, an impression that the remainder of his physical description reinforces, for as a farmer he is unfortable and awakward in his Sunday best. The narrative voice is, in fact, working two ways at once, mildly satirizing Gabriel Oak inn his best clothes and yet praising him as "a young man of sound judgment" on "working" days.

To the urban Victorian reader, the sort of person who purchased The Cornhill Magazine month by month, such a protagonist would have been a conundrum, for he is not clearly middle-class, andcertainly not professional. Gabriel is a rustic, often a figure of fun on the London stage, but he is also the single character with whom Hardy wishes us to identify ourselves now and throughout the novel.

Despite the complexities of the syntax, the narrator through direct analysis leaves us with an impression of congeniality, physical strength, massive size, diligence, and developing intellect. On the other hand, instead of presenting the heroine, Bathsheba Everdene, directly, Hardy has others (Gabriel and the toll-booth operator) comment upon her and has the reader judge her from her actions and from others' responses to her. Thus, the narrator does not commit himself to unqualified approval of the heroine. Even though the undoubtedly amused, tolerant masculine narrator enjoys her beauty and vigour, he does not entirely approve of her willful nature.

COMPARING IMAGERY IN CONRAD AND HARDY

Part 3 of the author's "Tartarus and Promethean Symbolism in Conrad and Hardy: The Return of the Native and The Nigger of the 'Narcissus'". In-text citations refer to the linked bibliography of selected readings. Writing shortly after the death of Joseph Conrad, Richard Aldington credited the impressionistic novelist with both a "brooding poetic fire" and "powers of evocation" greater than those of another senior British novelist, Thomas Hardy.

Aldington's casual dismissal of Hardy as merely a regional novelist (recording characters and customs fast becoming extinct, but unable to tell a good story) seems somewhat surprising from a late twentieth-century perspective.

However, since Conrad began to publish fiction at the very time that Hardy ceased, Aldington was doubtless responding to the biases of his own generation against the tastes of the previous generation. Aldington finds Hardy's chief defect to be his style, which he pronounces "never particularly beautiful and... sometimes almost clumsy". In contrast, he feels that Conrad's prose is of a higher quality—'wondrous' and 'mysterious'—because of its power to make the reader visualise the scene described. In other words, he evaluates Conrad's imagery as being of a higher denotative as well as a higher connotative quality than Hardy's.

While Aldington's essay may be categorized as something between an appreciation or eulogy for Conrad and a depreciation of Hardy, Aldington's method is largely anecdotal; he makes little rational justification for what amounts to a purely personal preference. In contrast, in the next decade Richard Gordon Lillard addressed himself to the question of "Irony in Hardy and Conrad" more analytically, concluding that "Hardy's irony is more objective, more systematic, more dramatic, Conrad's more introspective, more reflective, more psychological."

Lillard observes that Hardy works from a formal, logical, almost architectonic plan, Conrad from feeling and connotation. Put another way, Hardy was by nature a story-teller and observer of human nature; "Conrad's vision," as Arthur Kay remarks, "was instinctively symbolic."

In their applications of the techniques of symbolism and imagery Hardy and Conrad are likewise different. Hardy enriches his descriptions and narrative commentary with allusions to great deeds, thoughts, and persons, to music, art, philosophy, and mythology to create a sense of the eternal lurking behind the aspirations and passions of his Wessex characters, whose significance as individuals Time works to diminish.

Conrad's method is quite different, more recognizably Romantic and less Classical than Hardy's. For the most part,

Conrad couples the general symbol with a straight-forward simile: his symbolic patterns draw their energy from the very nature of things, from the ancient elements of earth, air, fire, and water, from darkness and light and all the colours in between, from the great chain of being itself, connecting the lowliest beast and tormented devil to the noblest man and the enigmatic creator of all.

Whereas Hardy is overt in his use of images and symbols, Conrad in his speaks what Shakespeare terms "a kind Of excellent dumb discourse." In his novels, Hardy attempts to state a meaning through his symbols; in his novels, Conrad is content to imply rather than define. Hardy's symbolism is neither so elemental nor so readily apprehensible as Conrad's; often Hardy's symbols are oblique, shrouded in garments which only informed readers may see through, a legacy in narrative technique that Hardy received from his reading the works of the erudite George Eliot.

Like Conrad, Hardy attempts to produce impressions through an orchestrated pattern of allusions, similes, metaphors, and images, investing certain characters, objects, and elements with powers not inherently their own. A case in point is the Tartarean imagery of The Return of the Native (1878) and The Nigger of the 'Narcissus' (1897). Whereas Hardy builds his symbols upon associations with Egdon Heath, its inhabitants, and vegetation, Conrad works with connotations from the sea, its ships, and its men. Hardy confines his stage to the Heath, which, like the Rainbarrow that approximates its centre, is a accretion of generations of humanity, animals, and plants, age piled upon age.

... all things merge in one another—good into evil, generosity into justice, religion into politics, the year into the ages, the world into the universe. With this in view the evolution of species seems but a minute and obvious process in the same movement.

In Hardy's terms, the action of the first five books of The Return of the Native occurs not in a year and a day, but in a fraction of the time that humanity has inhabited the planet. As Dale Kramer remarks, Hardy dwells upon the "contrast between the profound permanence of Egdon Heath and the transitory importance of its human inhabitants [, and thus] points to an analogous correlation between nature's and man's notions of time." Like his persona of the Heath, Hardy views human actions in a continuum, so that future and past are connected immediately in the present.

The Hardyan paradox that what is past and dead still impinges upon the present and the living is well illustrated by his poem "The Moth Signal," in which the lovers' passions are doomed to the brief existence of the insect that in the novel Wildeve employs to signal Eustacia. While Hardy's characters egocentrically believe that their emotions are important and that their works will endure, they themselves are as easily "burnt and broken" as the moth in the poem.

The grinning Ancient Briton, serving a chorus and commentator from one side of the stage foregrounded with the business of the living, applies a second narrative perspective as he points out that the human condition is immutable, that people love "In these days as in mine!" In the novel the moth signal must be appreciated in the context of the fire imagery, which, as John Paterson notes in "The 'Poetics' of 'The Return of the Native'," is "by inference Promethean." For Paterson the novel's furtive lovers, Eustacia and Wildeve, are "Consumed in the flames of their own passion and in effect by their own aggressive humanity" drawn by their overweening desires and a fatal attraction analogous to the that of a moth for a flame.

The fires that illuminate the darkened form of the "Titanic" Egdon Heath at the opening of the novel are at first associated with the life force, the "Festival fires to Thor and Woden" that demonstrate humanity's eternal rebellion against the dark. At the opening of the story the heath-dwellers light bonfires which "are rather the lineal descendants from the jumbled Druidical rites and Saxon ceremonies than the invention of popular feeling about Gunpowder Plot".

Egdon joins with the menacing darkness to become representative of "the eternal natural forces which control the destiny of man" and the standard by which the reader is to judge the struggles, desires, and passions of both the individual and the human species: though different in temperament and life- span, the Heath and humanity are alike in their changeless natures.

Where once Celts constructed a burial pyre for a chief, now Grandfer Cantle and his cronies dance around a blaze of furze. The dead are trampled under foot; their monuments and works, the Rainbarrow and the Roman via, are neither venerated nor understood. Man is as unknowing, as insentient as nature. The barrow is "but as a wart on [the Heath's] Atlantean brow", and a human being is as of little consequence relative to the whole universe.

As the Romans conquered and subdued the ancient Britons, so too does the Heath overwhelm their puny works; where once, as Hardy remarks in the lyric "The Roman Road," "Helmed legionaries" marched, a mother and her child now walk, oblivious to the road's origins and significance.

The Heath becomes, then, both change agent and symbol, the sum total of decay and rebirth, of past, present, and future, affecting humanity but apparently unaffected by it.

The Nigger of the 'Narcissus' demonstrates how differently Conrad uses symbolism from Thomas Hardy. Conrad constructs his symbols not on this tension of past and present, but on that of binary opposites such as day and night, life and death, dream and reality. His symbol is the poetic equivalent of a Hegelian concept: thesis plus antithesis equals synthesis.

In this early Conrad novel visible reality is a juxtaposition of opposites—the crew, for example, contains both Singleton, devoted to his craft, and Donkin the shirker. Oxymoron abounds:

"Life seemed an indestructible thing.... It was bright like the twisted flare of lightning, and more full of surprises than the dark night," and "the sky [was] like a triumphal arch of eternal light, thrown over the dark pathway of the earth". In both the instances cited Conrad utilizes the light-dark dichotomy to suggest that all experience is a fusion of diametrically-opposed opposites: "white, symbolizing the pure abstract virtue and ideality, and black, symbol of material reality and evil."

While time in Hardy moves forward through seasonal cycles and human epochs, Conrad redefines time as a stream whose currents wash images up on the shores of human consciousness. As no two people perceive the world in the same way, so in Conrad no two persons' conceptions of time's passing can be identical.

What is and what seems to be exist in the same proportion as the visible and unseen parts of an iceberg. Man's participation in Ideality may be far more "real" to him than his participation in the material world; and so the [Conrad] novel works extensively with the paradox that the real is unreal and dead, whereas the unreal is alone real and alive.

Such an apprehension of material reality as unreality is a reflection of the fundamental pessimism of the latter part of the nineteenth century. This Arnoldian frame of mind, which Conrad and Hardy share, is apparent in their choice of symbols, and in the relationships they establish between these symbols and their characters. Acccording to Paterson's Making of "The Return of the Native", Hardy "persistently identifie[s]" Egdon Heath "with the Tartarean underworld of the ancients" to reinforce Eustacia's conception of the Heath: "Egdon was her Hades". Whereas the female protagonist in Hardy's novel has arrived in Hell prior to the story's opening, in Conrad's novel the 'Narcissus' is a vessel bound thither.

Through an accumulation of images Conrad renders the voyage from Bombay to London as a Dantesque, Virgillian, or Homeric descent. As they complete their initial muster in Bombay harbour the crew are confronted by James Wait, emerging from the darkness beyond the ship; gradually for his fellows he becomes "a symbol, not of death but of fear of death" to which each member of the crew must reconcile himself. James Wait is significant (indeed, is real) only insofar as he influences his fellows and they perceive him. "He is merely as Conrad put it, the centre of the psychology and action".

In this voyage of inner exploration the elements through

which the 'Narcissus' passes reflect the conflicting emotions and ephemeral moods of the crew: "As with the sea, so with the universe; and so with ourselves". Conrad's crew constitute a "minute world", a microcosm of humanity that carries within itself visions of hell and heaven, visions that are ever- present in each man's mind and therefore more real to him than the ship's physical destination. Thus, Conrad renders the experience of the crew of the 'Narcissus' Tartarean through a series of images that play upon the reader's subconscious rather than, in the manner of Hardy, through specific, 'learned' allusions.

As in Lord Jim and Heart of Darkness, Conrad here imparts a nebulous glow to elements of his setting and his characters in order to develop his symbolic patterns. Conversely, through clearly-defined similes and metaphors Hardy works from the outset to endow the inanimate Heath with superhuman attributes, breathing poetic life into "its Titantic form" through classical allusions and images.

It is intended from the first to remind the reader of that region where in Virgil's Aeneid "the breed of Titans, who / Were hirled down by Jove's lightning writhe" because they refused to acknowledge Jupiter's supremacy over the universe. Hardy associates the Heath with the classical underworld as a whole rather than with any particular set of occupants. It is "the home of strange phantoms" where with "Promethean rebelliousness" the denizens, "fettered gods of earth"), light bonfires to dispel the anarchic gloom of night.

Both Homer and Virgil mention the suffering in the outer darkness of the Titan Tityos, and the earlier poet Hesiod recounts how a vengeful Zeus punished Prometheus for having stolen fire to comfort his creatures, shivering humanity. Although Hesiod places the chained Titan on a rock upon Mt. Caucasus, his Prometheus suffers the same torture as that which Zeus imposed upon Tityos. Since later Greek poets tended to confuse the rebellious giants with the warring Titans, the same figure is likely the subject of all three poets from classical antiquity: "He lay more than nine measures long / And two vultures, perched on both sides, rent at his liver /

Plunging into the caul." The giant's perpetual torment is analogous to Eustacia's on Egdon, the liver being held to be (appropriately enough) the source of sexual and reproductive energies. In that Prometheus has come to represent a pagan Christ, suffering in order to redeem feckless humanity, Eustacia's sufferings are hardly Promethean since they are the direct consequence of her egocentricity.

However, in his image of the heath-dwellers as shackled Titans at the opening of the novel Hardy is attempting to demonstrate the futility of humanity's age-old struggle against the natural, environmental forces arrayed against it.

The denizens of the heath are the product of ages of natural selection: like their ancestors, they have survived on the heath because they have adapted to it rather than, as is Eustacia's case, struggled against it. Consequently, her suffering is not totally unmerited since, by refusing to adjust her ambitions and desires to her environment, she wilfully brings her suffering upon herself.

"Like Oedipus," as Charles E. May observes, "Eustacia meets the destiny she unknowingly created in the very process of trying to escape that destiny Like Oedipus' father Laius in his attempt to cheat the Delphic Oracle and the divine ordinances, Eustacia's vying (true to her name) with circumstance in an attempt to escape it leads ironically to her destruction.

However, since it is her character and not unknown deities who shape her fate, Eustacia is responsible for her own downfall in a way that Sophocles' Oedipus is not: through her determination not to adapt to life on the heath through her willing herself to be unhappy and unfulfilled on Egdon, she suffers, schemes, rebels against social norms, and drowns.

Chapter 4

Compare Imagery in Conrad and Hardy

Part 4 of the author's "Tartarus and Promethean Symbolism in Conrad and Hardy: The Return of the Native and The Nigger of the 'Narcissus'". In-text citations refer to the linked bibliography of selected readings. Michael Millgate in his chapter on The Return of the Native in Thomas Hardy: His Career as a Novelist is highly critical of the classical context, the allusions and language, through which Hardy attempts to aggrandize Eustacia, to render her character noble and her struggle ennobling. Millgate finds that "The classical apparatus is... obvious and indeed obtrusive, the frame it provides both too heavy and too ornate".

In particular Millgate finds fault with the nexus of Promethean allusions and the hyperbolic language surrounding the heroine, whom Hardy described to his Belgravia illustrator Arthur Hopkins as "wayward and erring" rather than tragic. Millgate feels that the sustained "allusions are... excessive in themselves and [tend to draw] attention to precisely those features in the novel which prove recalcitrant to analogical cross-referencing: the inappropriateness, for example, of any serious application of the term "Promethean" to the self- consuming passions of Eustacia Vye". Her suffering, after all, is the consequence of neither a Christ-like self-sacrifice or a violation of unjust dictates. Rather, it is the result of her inability to adjust to circumstances and accept an unequal marriage.

Although the progress of Eustacia from alienated romantic

to outcast Titan is hardly logical, it is poetically and connotatively effective. Hardy connects her to the Tartarean heath by speaking of her first as "the raw material of a divinity" exiled from Olympos (the beau-monde represented by the provincial resort of Budmouth) and cast through the whim of her grandfather into the cultural and social gloom of Egdon Heath, which has affinities with the Shakespearean heaths of King Lear and Macbeth, and more proximately with the setting of Wuthering Heights.

Hardy endows her with "Pagan eyes, full of nocturnal mysteries", which, with her tendency to "utter oracles of Delphian ambiguity", render her a sort of Cumaean Sibyl, the priestess whom Hecate, Goddess of the Underworld and Witchcraft, appointed to superintend the Avernian grove, according to Virgil in The Aeneid, Book Six, line 564.

Hardy's description of her soul as "flame-like" suggests the torment that the fraudulent counsellors Ulysses and Diomedes suffer in Limbo, "as viewed from the brink by the sublime Florentine," Dante Alighieri, in his Inferno. However anguished, her language is hardly Sibylline. Her passions may be unruly; her temperament may chafe against the bonds of her liminal social status; but her utterances, conceived of by a male writer, do not emanate from any wild zone.

Although the series of images is coherent, that they should literally apply to the daughter of a bandmaster in south-west England in 1842 makes a large demand upon the reader's credulity, as Millgate has suggested. How, then, does Hardy intend his reader to interpret these images and allusions? By conjuring up visions of that grim region of the Underworld where spirits such as those of Prometheus and Ulysses suffer eternal agony for their opposition to the laws of the universe, Hardy makes the reader respond imaginatively to Eustacia's torment.

However, to suggest that Hardy means these allusions to constitute a sort of external reality is specious. As Charles E. May points out in "The Magic of Metaphor in The Return of the Native," critics in the twentieth century have made the mistake of approaching fictional characters from literary works of the nineteenth "as either psychologically-motivated real people acting within a novelistic social similitude or as mythically- motivated archetypes acting with a psychologized allegory code".

Hardy was hardly a modern symbolist; although, as his notebooks suggest, he "was aware of the problem of the novel-romance dichotomy", as May asserts, he was interested in synthesizing the two, so that the reader may have in Eustacia both a naive, romantic nineteen- year-old and a would-be pagan deity. Only her death can resolve this tension between her anomalous natures:

The eternal rigidity of death freezes her into a transitional state between the fervour of her psychological character and the resignation of her archetypal position in the fable of her own making.

Eustacia's conflict with the spirit of the heath is an aspect of her rejection of the community and her changed circumstances; however, she does not reject only what it symbolizes or stands for in her mind. Through the mechanism of allusion, association, and metaphor "the psychological passes into the mythical". Supplementing Eustacia's spiritual and physical opposition to the Heath as place of residence, as home, is her conflict with the denizens of the place, who sincerely suspect her of being a witch who is employing her dark powers against them.

Throughout the course of the story, Eustacia senses that, no matter how she tries to avert it, her end will come as a victory not only for Egdon Heath but also for the community that has imbibed its spirit.

Her death in the Narcissistic pool of Shadwater Weir reinforces her 'marginalized' witch-identity: attempting to escape her socially-sanctioned union, she drowns in the "boiling caldron"—total immersion being by tradition the test for one accused of practicing witchcraft. That which brings life to the Heath extinguishes her flame-like soul. Although such Pateresque effusions as that which opens the "Queen of Night" chapter are rare in the book, they leave their mark, partly through their exuberant exoticism, and partly through the sheer accumulation of images and allusions. Eustacia Vye was the raw material of a divinity. On Olympus she would have done well with a little preparation. She had the passions and instincts which make a model goddess, that is, those which make not quite a model woman. There is the hallmark of Hardy's style: even in the midst of an effusion, he cannot resist the ironically humorous, undercutting parenthetical remark. Her extended tresses may render her Sphinx-like, and her "Pagan eyes" may be "full of nocturnal mysteries," but with gentle raillery Hardy sums her up with the litotes "at times she was not altogether unlovable".

The new moon behind her head, an old helmet upon it, a diadem of accidental dewdrops round her brow, would have been adjuncts sufficient to strike the note of Artemis, Athena, or Hera respectively, with as close an approximation to the antique as that which passes muster on many respected canvases. Again, the colloquial "passes muster" has a deflating effect, as if the narrator cannot take his own effusion seriously, but must poke fun at such language and such a heroine.

Her classical lineage proves but another practical joke by Hardy's 'purblind doomsters', the rulers of the Darwinian universe, for "celestial imperiousness, love, wrath, and fervour had proved to be somewhat thrown away on netherward Egdon" Possibly a consciousness of his own hyperbole prompted Hardy after serial publication to cut the line: "She differed from Demeter's daughter as a queenly bondswoman differs from a bondaged queen".

It is certainly inconsistent with the ironic equipoise of the narrative voice in these paragraphs, which are in a sense an elaboration of the proposition that "Egdon was her Hades".To make her a suitable antagonist for the spirit of the Heath, Hardy adorns Eustacia with the golden trappings of classical myth.

She becomes a Greek princess with "true Tartarean dignity", a descendant of "Alcinous' line, her father hailing from Phaeacia's isle," being "a Corfiote by birth", although in the original version of story, as serialised in the magazine Belgravia, "She was the daughter of the bandmaster of a regiment which had been quartered there [at Budmouth]; a Belgian, who met his future wife during her trip thither.... Hardy's process of transforming Eustacia from a Bovaryesque adolescent to a Sophoclean heroine is thus laid bare if one compares the final text with the serial version at this point.

The likeness of Hardy's heroine to female deities from classical myth is present in the text from the first, when Hardy describes her beauty as a painterly commodity, as is indicated in the visual emphasis of such expressions as "her general figure," "The new moon behind her head, an old helmet upon it, a diadem of accidental dewdrops round her brow," and "respected canvases".

If the reader dismisses the narrator's jocular tone, "Egdon was her Hades" may be taken as implying an analogy to Persephone, but Hardy nominates no one goddess for Eustacia's Olympian counterpart: she may an Artemis (goddess of the moon, virginity, and hunting), Athena inappropriately for Hardy's heroine, goddess of wisdom and handicrafts—although in her capacity of sponsor of military strategy Athena may be a suitable analogue for the scheming Eustacia), or Hera (the temperamental Queen of Olympus and patron of marriage and statecraft).

The similes and metaphors implying a connection between Graeco-Roman goddesses, then, cannot be taken literally; rather, these constitute an artistic similitude, a context, a 'canvas' of the pseudo-antique designed to stir the reader's emotion and evoke a certain quality of feeling for this dark heroine. As we have seen with respect to Hardy's endowing Eustacia with Homeric rather than merely Belgian antecedents in revisions conducted after the serial version, Hardy employs his allusions consciously to give his heroine's plight universal significance.

The accretion of classical allusions heightens the novel's tragic effect, giving Hardy's Egdon the feel of Sophocles' Thebes. By comparing Eustacia to no particular classical deity, Hardy makes her a synthesis of the quintessence of four. Eustacia is virgin huntress, patron deity of the chase, the vengeful goddess who transformed the careless Actaeon, violater of her privacy, into a stag to be attacked and slain by his own hounds.

She will allow herself to be mastered by neither man nor the rugged, masculine environment of the heath. Then, too, for Hardy she is analogous not to the patron goddess of crafts or common sense, but of wiles and strategies, fond of disguise and deviousness. She, like the Homeric Hera, is queenly, fond of power, and chafing under male domination; however, Eustacia is unable—unlike Collins' Magdalen Vanstone in No Name or Conan Doyle's Irene Adler in "Scandal in Bohemia" — to utilize her deviousness to assert herself against such domination. Finally, she is in emotional bondage, confined to Egdon as Demeter's daughter was to the kingdom of Hades; Eustacia suffers the fate (life in death) with which Coleridge's Ancient Mariner was threatened not for violating natural but patriarchal law. No marriage of the heart can save her as it does Collins's wayward heroine in No Name: Wildeve proves no Kirk, for he encourages rather than rescues her from her own duplicity in order to exploit her, and does not have her welfare at heart when he arranges to carry her off.

To her the heath is a version of "Homer's Cimmerian land", a desolate plain at the ends of the civilised world, a desert place "surrounded in mist and cloud". She deems the place fit only for such worshipers of Dionysus, such "Maenades" as Grandfer Cantle, Susan Nonsuch, and Olly Dowden to tread their "demoniac measure." Dissatisfied with the savage surroundings and crude society in which she finds herself entrapped but from which by herself she believes herself unable to escape, Eustacia dreams of the gaiety of the outer world, as represented by Paris and Budmouth.

And again Hardy provides a classical analogy: "her moods recalled [the] lotus-eaters" whom the hero Odysseus encountered, a people wholly given over to fantasy, daydreams, and avoidance of hardship, striving, and responsibility. Like Tennyson in the celebrated dramatic monologue, Hardy intends that the Lotus-eaters connote a desire to escape from duty and an unwillingness to face workaday reality:

Hateful is the dark-blue sky, Vaulted o'er the dark-blue sea. Death is the end of life; ah, why Should life all labour be?

In Homer's Odyssey, some of the hero's crew, desiring release from the rigours of their arduous homeward voyage, respond to the narcotic influence of the African lotus fruit by shunning their loyalty to their craft and their fellows. In pleading to be left among the Lotus- eaters, they abandon all hope of seeing their homes and families again. Daunted by the terrors of sea, they settle for less than their proper goal. Hardy thus implies that the Lotus- eaters are a fit emblem for Eustacia's emotional state.

Her hero has not only failed to release her from her Hades, but has also attempted to chain her further, in bonds of social obligation, of marriage, and of patriarchally-determined respectability. Clym has forced upon her a mature, adult role for which she is emotionally unprepared and ill-equipped, and now deprives her of even her dreams of release. Her only escape, as forecast by her earlier dream of drowning, is in the oblivion of death.

Whereas Egdon Heath is the classical Hell for Hardy's tragic heroine, Conrad's 'Narcissus' (its very name signifying the sin of self-love, its self-deluding and fatal consequences) is a piece of a different sort of Hell, a microcosm of European society, travelling towards the greater Hell of London. While Hardy employs classical allusions for their visual, poetic, and rhythmic effects and emotional connotations, Conrad uses such references and images to create a sensuous and sensory appeal for concrete and perceivable objects.

In The Nigger of the 'Narcissus', Lord Jim, and Heart of Darkness Conrad is not merely a spinner of yarns but also an Impressionist painter working with sounds and images conjured up by sounds to make the reader (as he remarks in the well-known "Preface" to The Nigger of the 'Narcissus') "hear," "feel," and "before al, see". Conrad does not rely on the intellectual cognition or decoding of mythological references in the way that Hardy does, although with the later novelist, too, a knowledge of the classics will furnish the reader with the necessary mental bank of images to "see" as Conrad would have him do. However, one needs neither a specific and detailed knowledge of Bulfinch's Mythology to mediate between his consciousness and Conrad's text, nor even a general acquaintance with the classics to feel the power of Conrad's imagery. Since Conrad would have his reader hear and, above all, see, he fashions his symbols with images that appeal to the senses first, and to the intellect second.

The Conrad tale is a "shadowy" reminiscence of a ship "manned by a crew of Shades". To begin with, the reader apprehends an image of these men that has been rendered vague and amorphous by the passage of time; then he sees them as ghosts on a spectre barque. These men Conrad deems to be "about as wicked as any ship's company in this sinful world", and, as such, suitable representatives of humanity on this 'earth in microcosm', the 'Narcissus', "a fragment detached from the earth,... [going] on lonely and swift like a small planet". Thus, the symbolic level of Conrad's images of ship and crew proves to be a confusion of the classical underworld ("Shades"), the Christian Hell ("wicked," "sinful'), and the ship of fools ("ship's company," "a small planet").

In the midst of the storm that nearly destroys the 'Narcissus' and her human cargo, the ship becomes a second Noah's Ark, "the last vestige of a shattered creation..., bearing an anguished remnant of sinful mankind". Although both visually and connotatively effective, these images seem to lack any coherent, central design or intent. In fact, in this last image Conrad has inverted the pattern found in biblical and classical flood stories (the saving of the innocent and the concomitant punishing of the wicked)—in Ovid's retelling of the Deucalion and Pyrrha myth, for example, the couple are spared because "both had served the gods, and done no ill"—by floating on the flood those who are damned.

Fit representatives of the worst elements in humanity are Donkin, a Cockney from London's East-end slums, and James Wait, a Black seaman from St. Kitt's in the British West Indies. The former is a lesser devil, a Beelzebub or Mephistopheles, who "looked as if he had known all the degradations and all the furies" and, as one of the crew initially remarks, appears "a blamed sight worse than a broken- down fireman". Wait, on the other hand, seems to represent a higher order of evil; his dramatic appearance, for example, so startles the rest of the crew that the cook exclaims, "I thought I had seen the devil". An analogue for Wait is the polluting tug that tows 'Narcissus' out of harbour, "an enormous and aquatic black beetle... [that] left a lingering smudge of smoke on the sky,... an unclean mark" (an Impressionistic image) that is similar to the "smudge" of Wait's name on the ship's roster.

A visual analogue for Wait and Donkin's towing the ship towards a moral hell is J. M. W. Turner's "'Fighting Temeraire' Tugged to Her Last Berth To Be Broken Up", the evil pair represented by the smoke- and cinder-belching tug in the foreground. Sails furled, the 'Fighting Temeraire' is drained of all colour, in contrast to red and black, twin paddle- wheeled tug, its reflection, and that of the painting's discordant, blood-red sky.

What is touching in Turner's painting is the loss of the romance of sail, the passing of a way of life and its being replaced by more efficient but less attractive modern technology; what we sense in Conrad' novel is the concomitant loss of faith, of fidelity to the craft, so that Wait and Donkin, like Turner's devilish, little tug, are symbols not merely of the new technological age but of a new (and hardly better) morality that attends making men extensions of a machine.

From Wait's arrival on board Conrad figures the Negro as a devil or the Devil, to whom the currish Donkin pays strange homage. Like Milton's Satan regarding his fallen cohorts in the first book of Paradise Lost, Wait sweeps a glance domineering and pained over his shipmates, "like a sick tyrant overawing a crowd of abject but untrustworthy slaves". In return, the crew serve him "as though [they] had been the base courtiers of a hated prince".

After Belfast's theft of a pie from the ship's galley, the cook announces "that wickedness flourishe[s]... [and] that Satan [is] abroad amongst those men", and singles out Charley "with a patch of soot on his chin... [as] a brand for the burning".

Charley's blackened chin associates him with the polluting

tug and the smudged name on the roster; it is also a mark of Cain, an emblem of the betrayal of the brotherhood of the craft. Wait's "infernal spell" gradually overwhelms the spirits of more and more of the sailors until nearly all shirk their duties and make him obeisance. "He became the tormentor of all our moments; he was worse than a nightmare", recalls Conrad's narrator.

Although physically it was Wait who took "enough [paregoric] to poison a wilderness of babies" — a suggestion of demonic rites and the worship of Moloch–it is the crew who suffer the malignant effects of a far stronger opiate, self-pity. As the narrator concludes, "he tainted our lives", sapping the men of rectitude and loyalty to the craft. Even when the ship is in peril during the storm, the crew misdirect their energies to "trying to keep life in that poor devil".

As the foregoing paragraph implies, Conrad's allusions are far more oblique, fragmentary, and disconnected than Hardy's; indeed, only when connected in the manner demonstrated do they begin to suggest a symbolic pattern. Viewed individually in context, these allusions seem to be nothing more than evanescent impressions. Viewed collectively and out-of-context, however, they combine to create a network of meaning, which for example in The Nigger of the 'Narcissus' endows Wait with Satanic qualities and renders the voyage a purgatorial experience. Whereas Hardy states similarities in clear similes, although Conrad works at both realistic or conscious and metaphorical or unconscious levels of meaning, he tends merely to imply.

As she approaches her destination, the 'Narcissus' becomes closely associated with fire imagery. For instance, after the storm had subsided, the becalmed craft stood out with its masts and rigging, with every sail and every rope distinct and black in the centre of a fiery outburst, like a charred ship enclosed in a globe of fire. The image recalls both the spectre ship of Coleridge's The Rime of the Ancient Mariner and the Flying Dutchman legend, but also suggests the exhaustion of the crew's energies. "That's how them firemen do in steamboats," explains the sweating cook about their efforts to save the vessel; "Did you ever see them down the stoke- hold?" he enquires of Wait. "like fiends they look—firing—firing—firing—down there". As one who works the topmasts, Wait may not have had the experience of seeing firemen working in a stoke-hold, but the implication is that, as a Satanic figure, he has witnessed many a time the agonies of the damned.

Later the cook warns the crew of the torments that await them for their current sins: "Hot! Did I say? The furnaces of one of them White Star boats ain't nothing to it". The furnaces on Pacific and Orient and Cunard vessels would be suitable analogues also, but for Conrad would lack the connotations of fate, destiny, and doom with which "White Star" is freighted. As Kay points out, as a symbolist Conrad selected details from actual experience, including the names "Wait" and "Narcissus," and employed them in a way both "integrated and pervasive as we contemplate the structure of the novel, its characters and theme". The centre of these images of fire, heat, and furnaces is Wait's cabin, "hot as an oven".

The Hell in store for Wait may be that of Judeo-Christian tradition, for physically he is dying; that in store for the rest of the crew is the outbreak of mutiny, for spiritually they have been perverted by the influence of Wait and Donkin. Even Allistoun, who is convinced that the crew are essentially hardy-working and trustworthy, concedes that they possess the capacity to be "Worse than... down-right, horned devils". When they rebel, they sin against the principles of order and discipline, and are metamorphosed from being "a troop of wild beasts" to "forlorn souls," agents and subjects of the Devil and Beelzebub, Wait and Donkin, self- love and disobedience. The ship has unmistakably become a hell: "At night, through the impenetrable darkness of earth and heaven, broad sheets of flame waved noiselessly".

Also contributing to Conrad's symbol of the passage of the 'Narcissus' as a voyage to the realm of the dead and damned are abundant images of ghosts and the grave. At the outset, Conrad describes the berths in the forecastle as "resembl[ing] narrow niches for coffins in a whitewashed and lighted mortuary", and Donkin as "a startling visitor from a world of nightmares", Wait being expressly identified later as "worse than a nightmare". The port of Bombay, from which the 'Narcissus' sails, proclaims evil through its electric lamps, which pierce the dark "with a glow blinding and frigid like captive ghosts of some evil moons". While Conrad presents the crew's quarters as their grave, he implies that the city that marks their point of departure is the entrance to the classical Underworld.

Ironically, Conrad expresses his admiration for these common seamen in moribund metaphors: the sailors are "men who knew how to exist beyond the pale of life" and cities, men who perished at sea and "died free from the dark menace of a narrow grave" on land. Wait's ominous arrival silences the lively hum of conversation on deck; as he shakes before them "the bones of his bothersome and infamous skeleton", reminding them of their own mortality, Wait blights the crew's spirit of fellowship. Later, "singers became mute because Jimmy was a dying man".

The imaginations of the crew begin to weave a spell of gloom about the ship as they are unnerved by their own hung-up oil suits, which assume the aspect of the "reckless ghosts of decapitated seamen dancing in a tempest", and by Archie's great coat, "resembling a drowned seaman floating with his head underwater" The scene may be borrowed from vestry scenes in Dickens's Martin Chuzzlewit and Collins's Woman in White, but Conrad has made it his own through its marine context and psychological realism. Envisioning themselves as dead, the sailors lose their vivacity and morbidly dwell on death, serving the death's head of James Wait.

"They clustered round that moribund carcass, the fit emblem of their aspirations", which they place upon the shoulders of a dying man who is "becoming immaterial like an apparition". As Wait has cowed each man into submission through his counterfeiting the dread image of death, so the crew's passions run highest when he becomes a living corpse, his "fleshless head resembl[ing] a disinterred black skull". "For what the crew see reflected in their black mirrors is the face of their own Todenangst, a fear of death so obsessive that, clinging to the preservation of the self's identity, it negates the spirit of life itself".

Appropriately enough, off the island of Flores, true to the patriarchal Singleton's prediction, Wait dies and is buried at sea. Almost reluctantly, his remains go to their final rest off "a sombre ruin [lying] upon a vast and deserted plain", as if it were not an island at all, but rather the ruins of some ancient citadel such as Troy or Sodom, laid low by human pride and folly. "The word 'wait' can be a noun meaning 'a delay', and the ship appropriately makes increasingly slow progress until his death, upon which the vessel spurts for home".

Freed of the burden (the homophonous 'weight') which Wait's "name itself suggests", its idol of self-love gone to the bottom like the self-obsessed body of Narcissus in the Ovidian myth, the 'Narcissus' returns to normality when it encounters the British coastal steamers, "migrating and amphibious monsters". Is Conrad here suggesting the world has been purged of evil with Wait's burial at sea as it was by the great flood in Genesis, or is he merely creating a striking image? Either interpretation is viable.

The connection between 'Narcissus' and Britain Conrad subsequently clarifies when he compares the island to an ark, a huge "ship carrying the burden of millions of lives". As the great island-fortress harbours within its stronghold such decadence and corruption as one finds in London, so the 'Narcissus' has sheltered the corrupting Donkin, whom Wait reviles as "East-end trash".

As the tug takes her in tow, 'Narcissus' is "Shorn of the glory of her white wings", a possible allusion to the dove that Noah sent out to find land in the Genesis flood story. Now the nexus of images shifts as, following the tug "through the maze of invisible channels", like Theseus following the thread to the heart of the Cretan Labyrinth, the ship passes buoys pulling "at their chains like fierce watch-dogs", suggestive of Hades' watchdog Cerberus. Further up river, factory chimneys seem to leer down at her as if they are "a straggling crowd of slim giants", like the Titans whom Zeus consigned to Tartarus as punishment for their rebellion.

Once 'Narcissus' has been docked and chained, Conrad adds with a note of finality, she has "ceased to live". Her voyage to Hades is complete when her melancholy crew disembark to re-group later for their pay. And to the right of the dark group the stained front of the Mint, cleansed by the flood of light, stood out for a moment dazzling and white like a marble palace in a fairy tale.

If this place is not London but Hades, the central feature is not the Mint but the Palace of Dis. The ritual of signing names and in return receiving notes and coin is like a funeral's, each man paying his respects and contributing to the post-mortem of a voyage like that of the short story "Youth," a voyage fitted to be an illustration of life. Now that 'Narcissus' has died, the crew ceases to exist as a corporate entity. The sailors drift off on their separate ways, and belong to 'Narcissus' no longer. "The sea took some, the steamers took others, the graveyards of the earth will account for the rest"; their end, like Eustacia's, is oblivion.

Of course, this final succession of images need not be absorbed into the novel's symbolic pattern. As Cedric Watts remarks in A Preface to Conrad, "the dominant conventions of Conradian fiction are secular and realistic", so that London need not be the classical underworld, the tug a Charon's ferry, the buoys a multiple-headed Cerberus, the lowering chimneys incarcerated Titans, or the Mint Pluto's palace.

Conrad makes no specific identifications because such are not necessary to the creation of the appropriate feeling and visual effects. Although we may attribute the gradual deterioration of the crew's morale through "sentimental pseudo-sentimentality" to the same cause as that of Narcissus, unwitting self-love, we need not make any such connection to realize that the physical deterioration of James Wait is intimately bound up with the spiritual wasting away of the crew. Conrad makes no special demands on his reader in terms of a priori knowledge, only in terms of imaginative sensitivity.

Hardy, on the other hand, assumes his reader to be a member of a 'fit audience though few' which possesses the background knowledge necessary to comprehend and interpret his classical allusions. Only one who has read Virgil's Aeneid, for example, can properly savour the irony of Hardy's likening Eustacia's appearing before Clym in the guise of a mummer to that occasion "When the disguised Queen of Love appeared before AEneas" to send her son to seek Dido, the Carthaginian Queen whom he loves passionately, then abandons at the behest of the gods and destiny.

Virgil's story of love and betrayal becomes a metaphor for the ill-founded affair between Eustacia and Clym, the flame of which is as intense but also as brief as that of the affair between Dido and AEneas. "His passion for Eustacia had been a sort of conserve of his whole life, and he had nothing more of that supreme quality to bestow", so that Clym never re-marries, for after the death of Eustacia he finds himself drained of emotion. While Virgil's heroine does not want her lover to answer the promptings of fate by leaving her to found Rome, Eustacia implores Clym to renounce his plans for becoming a country schoolmaster.

However, as Hardy often quotes Novalis as remarking, character is fate, so that Clym can no more renounce his unrealistic schemes than Eustacia can abandon hers. "Hardy's fictive world [is] composed of an indifferent nature, irresponsible fellow travellers, and exquisite twists of circumstance" intimately connected with the accidents of time and place.

Eustacia on this desert heath, which is like something out of King Lear or Macbeth, yearns to escape across the water, but instead achieves release through drowning. Unlike the conclusion of a Shakespearean or Attic tragedy, the end of Eustacia's fitful drama coveys little catharsis, no ambivalence of reaction, and no dual sense of mourning for the passing of a great one but elation at the hero's final triumph over circumstance. Classical and Elizabethan similitudes seem out-of-place on Egdon; thus, Hardy's employing grand allusions to characterize Eustacia only heightens "the cruelty of illusions" that such hyperbolic comparisons as those to classical myth and legend embody.

She has created for herself an unattainable, unrealistic

ideal as a shield against surroundings which she feels are not merely mundane, but horrible. The repeated allusions, then, convey Eustacia's state of mind, her sense of apartness from the world of Egdon, as well as her sense of kinship with the beau monde of Paris.

By unknowingly attempting to severe Eustacia's emotional affiliation with that ideal Clym is unwittingly attempting to assault her sense of herself. She has cherished an illusion of what she is as well as what she is not, and chooses to risk all rather than abandon her ideal. In that she cannot bring herself to part with a spiritually-sustaining illusion, Eustacia comes very close to Conrad's Lord Jim, who deliberately chooses death with honour over a life of "inherent opportunities for failure".

In Conrad, as in Hardy, ideas come to have a strange power over the concrete, so that the mistake of Eustacia and Jude is also the mistake that the crew of the 'Narcissus' make, a failure to value the practical and the real (the solidarity of the craft) over the sentimental ideal. In accordance with the genre that he had chosen for his story in The Return of The Native and the language in which he had couched his descriptions of his dark heroine, Hardy gradually transformed her into something she is not: a tragic heroine in the Greek manner.

As a result of her refusal to compromise her unrealistic aspirations and adjust herself to normality, Eustacia is a pathetic but hardly a tragic figure. Hardy becomes the victim of his own allusive framework, making Eustacia so compelling a figure by virtue of the images with which he associates her that the reader identifies with her despite her folly.

Conversely, as Gerald Morgan points out, in Conrad consciously controls how characters and things acquire their symbolic meanings, "by reason of the clarity, rather than the obscurity of their perceptible aspect". To see as Conrad would have us see, with the mind's eye, is quite enough to apprehend his meaning. Despite the classical tale of destructive self-love alluded to in its title, The 'Nigger' of the Narcissus defies the sort of rational decoding that one might apply to The Return of the Native, and yet Conrad never puts the reader in jeopardy of misapprehending his central figure. The standard of manly conduct and single-minded determination, Singleton, is clearly juxtaposed against the deviousness of Donkin and "the duplicity of the ambiguous James Wait".

As specific, concrete, and visually appealing as Conrad's images may be, they do not lend themselves to a point-by-point correlation to myth, legend, history, and the Bible that Hardy's do; nor, however, do they engender ambiguity. For instance, the story of Narcissus and his reflection as found in Ovid's Metamorphoses has relevance to Conrad's novel only in so far as the ship's name is a fitting emblem for the self-love that captivates and nearly destroys the crew.

That Wait dies off a real island named Flores is symbolically convenient, but his doing so might be literally true in light of its actual position relative to the Bombay-to-London shipping lanes.

Hardy's images possess a very different sort of obliqueness in that he gives his reader no indication as to how far to interpret them, although certainly his images may generally be assimilated into clearly perceived and readily analyzed symbolic patterns. Like Conrad's less explicit, more painterly images, Hardy's defamiliarize the landscape and persons of the fiction. The heath upon which the action of The Return of the Native transpires, like the very actors on this rural stage, thus acquires universal significance through the pattern of classical imagery surrounding Eustacia.

Similarly, Conrad transforms the common realities of British nineteenth- century culture, ships and sailors and ports, into forms and figures of universal significance by enveloping them in a heightened form of language drawn from the realms of myth, legend, and archetype.

Since the docking of 'Narcissus' is gradually stripped of that additional level of meaning, it constitutes an exodus for the quasi-allegorical tale. A return to reality as the reader knows it, Conrad's ending changes the representatives of humanity back into common seamen. Hardy, in contrast, loses his recounting of his characters' "erratic histories with a catastrophic dash" redolent with pathos for the yearning, entrapped heroine.

The Nigger of the 'Narcissus' is more poetic and evocative throughout, its ending being pessimistic rather than tragic. Because of its cultural backdrop — the many voices of the ancients and their mythology speaking through Hardy's novel — and Hardy's permeating sense of history in the present, The Return of the Native surpasses the potential of its story. Its artistry lies within the language that shapes the character of Eustacia Vye; the artistry of The Nigger of the 'Narcissus' lies beyond the characters, in the interplay of language, actions, and settings.

Chapter 5

Aristotelian Tragedy and the Novels of Thomas Hardy

Writing in The Poetics about 330 B. C. E., the philosopher Aristotle sought to analyse the structure of Athenian tragedy using as an example his favourite play, Sophocles' Oedipus Rex. He held that the essence of drama was action, which took place in one situation, in one place, at one time (i. e., within 24 hours). There would be no change of scene, no stage violence, and no mixing of comic and tragic elements.

Of course, Aristotle would have objected to Hardy's being a writer of prose rather than a dramatist or playwright. The origin of that very English conception of the dramatic writer alerts us to the fact that an acting company's resident writer revised and revamped existing texts as well as wrote new ones. The story of Tess, in particular, smacks of an oral tradition, the seduction of a maid in a great house...or, the rape victim bringing her attacker to justice. Can we experience Aristotelian catharsis in our armchairs as opposed to seats in a theatre?

HARDY'S MICHAEL HENCHARD AS AN ARISTOTELIAN TRAGIC HERO

According to Sidney Lamb in Tragedy, although the form of tragedy written in Elizabethan England differs somewhat from that written in ancient Greece, in both eras tragedy was a reflection of a hierarchical society. Even late in the twentieth century with the tragedy of the average man well-established critically, we still tend to think of a tragedy as "the story of the fall from greatness of an exalted personage"—a king

(Sophocles' Oedipus or Shakespeare's Lear), a general (Aeschylus' Eteocles or Shakespeare's Macbeth), or a man of great wealth, rank, and social prestige (The Old Testament's Job or Shakespeare's Romeo).

Consequently, the fall of Michael Henchard from prosperity and power to obscurity and alienation is certainly the stuff of Aristotelian tragedy. Even though the French tragedian Beaumarchais argued that "The nearer the suffering man is to my station in life, the greater is his claim upon my sympathy" (Essay on the Serious Drama, 1767), whether there can be a truly tragic middle-class hero is highly debatable. Aristotle in The Poetics (330 B. C.) required two things of the tragic protagonist: he must be noble (whether in spirit or social status), and he must be responsible for causing his own suffering (not necessarily death).

Making references to his favourite tragedy, Oedipus Rex by Sophocles, the Greek philosopher proposed that a tragic hero usually is

- A leader in his society, exemplifying both the good and bad elements of that society ('a person neither wholly good nor bad').
- Disclosed to the audience at the height of his prosperity, power, and influence in that social group so that his fall from its favour will seem that much greater (and, therefore, more tragic).
- Driven to his fall (social alienation, suffering, death, or exile) by some innate flaw (Greek: hamartia) in his nature, yet appear to have the ability to alter his course. (In other words, he should appear to possess free will, and yet be a victim.)
- Made a scapegoat for the sins or errors of his people—and accordingly be exiled or punished by them in such a way that his suffering is irreversible (since Oedipus is blinded, his suffering cannot be reversed).
- The cause of his own punishment through his own pride (hubris).
- Ready to take upon himself the burden of his

society's (and hence the audience's) sense of guilt, shame, or short-coming.

- Grander and more noble as the result of his futile struggle with fate.
- Through his suffering instrumental in the resolution of a problem that plagued his society at the outset, and in the restoration of a harmony that was not present at the opening of the play. Our grieving over the destruction of the hero but our relief over the restoration of social harmony produces in the audience what Aristotle termed "catharsis" or "tragic satisfaction" through the purgation of pity and fear.

Despite the fact that The Mayor of Casterbridge is not a drama in which we vicariously participate by watching an action and identifying ourselves with certain characters on stage, we may argue that Michael Henchard satisfies many of the Aristotelian requirements for the tragic hero.

His physical power and strong-willed determination to succeed, to expiate his sin, and to do what he feels is best for Elizabeth-Jane are consistent with the usages of his society—as are his impulsiveness, quick temper, and manly pride. Hardy reveals Henchard first as itinerant hay-trusser burdened by a wife and child as a sort of prologue; this antecedent circumstance renders his corporate and municipal rise all the more impressive, but also reveals how tentative this outward success is.

As the suffering outcast whose daughter cannot reciprocate his affection, Henchard is far grander—and far more sympathetic—than the leader of the town council at the King Arms' dinner. As he falls socially, we tend to accept his sullenness and temper as part of the emotional makeup of this complex character. I am never sure as I re-read the novel's conclusion, however, as to whether Henchard satisfies the eighth point, except that his fate enriches Elizabeth-Jane's understanding of the human condition.

In order that he appear to have the illusion of free-will in determining his fate, Michael Henchard's fate does not seem "inevitable," but the result of a very Victorian series of coincidences that result in his poverty, exile, and alienation. Like Shakespeare's King Lear, even in his youth Henchard is one who but scantily knows himself (Hardy's phrase is "introspective inflexibility"), and permits his passions, especially the desire to save face in the furmity vendor's tent, to overwhelm his common sense.

His is a pathological tragic flaw, for he makes much the same mistake when he fires Farfrae out of jealousy. Hardy himself seems unclear about the nature of Henchard's hamartia when he quotes Novalis: "Character is fate"—certainly a useful aphorism for a Victorian novelist, though something about which Aristotle in The Poetics does not address.

To the Greek critic, the catastrophe is the result of those external forces which he called "Fate," and which we might call "determining psycho-social contexts." Still, among Hardy's would-be tragic heroes Henchard is rare; as the title page announces, he is "A Man of Character," a local economic leader as well as the town's mayor whose initial social and economic eminence render him more properly an Aristotelian tragic hero than Giles in The Woodlanders or Tess.

However, in terms of emotional response, the ultimate fate of Tess, scion of once-proud aristocratic family brought low by Hardy's twin enemies of humanity (Time and Chance), arouses more pity and fear in a modern reader than does Henchard's.

Somewhere between the two on my emotional response scale lies Eustacia in The Return of the Native, for her fate results from the very twentieth-century error of marrying entirely the wrong person. A dazzling figure from the beau monde of the Parisian boulevards, Clym is gradually diminished in her estimation as he pursues the goal of becoming a rural schoolmaster. Yet Eustacia herself remains worthy of our interest from beginning to end because she never abandons her dream.

Chapter 6

The Power of "No" for Hardy's Heroines

"The Power of 'No' in Hardy's Heroines: 'Her Confession' and 'Her Reproach' as 'Before' and 'After' Companion Poems"

Throughout his fiction, whether it be in so slight a creation as Lizzie Newberry in "The Distracted Preacher" (1879) or so thorough an exploration of the female psyche as that afforded in Eustacia Vye in The Return of the Native (1878), Hardy seems to have been fascinated by the one power 'respectable', middle-class women had in nineteenth-century Britain, the power to say "No" to a prospective suitor. Setting his fiction several generations before the date of composition, Hardy explored the relative powerlessness of such women, noting that society gave them one currency only: beauty.

For example, in The Mayor of Casterbridge (written in 1886, but set in the early 1840s), Lucetta worries that her "currency" is nearly expended and that she is no longer "marketable": "How many years more do you think I shall last before I get hopelessly plain?" she asks her young companion, Elizabeth-Jane, who astutely replies, "... with a quiet life, as many as ten. With no love you might calculate on ten" (Ch. 24). The irony here is that Lucetta wants it all — long-term beauty and passionate romance — and she wishes to choose without regard for social constraints and proprieties:

"I will love him!" she cried passionately; "as for him — he's hot-tempered and stern, and it would be madness to bind myself to him knowing that. I won't be a slave to the past — I'll love where I choose!" (Ch. 25)

Given the limited availability of divorce for much of the century and the paucity of married women's property rights, one can well appreciate her vexation. How does a woman know when to accept and when to reject, to say "No," is an issue that concerns the whole line of Hardy heroines, from Fancy Day in Under The Greenwood Tree (1872) to Ethelberta Chickerel in The Hand of Ethelbertato Anne Garland in The Trumpet-Major to Sue Bridehead in Jude the Obscure.

In a number of his poems, too, particularly in "Her Confession" (which he penned in 1865-67, before beginning his career as a professional writer of fiction), Hardy studies the mentality of negation, of a woman's exerting what little power she has by waiving the "proffered kiss" (line 6) and by shifting the topic conversation away from her feelings and towards an emotionally- neutral, "safe" subject such as the "scenery nigh" (line 7).

Cruelly, however, and certainly not in a manner consistent with the "proto-feminist" tendencies he manifests in his novels, Hardy ascribes such evasive behaviour to a desire on the part of the female speaker "to enhance [her] bliss" (line 8). Since the poem is a supposed "confession" (if not an out-and-out apology), the speaker insists that apparent lack of ardour and avoiding giving her lover any sign or token of emotional commitment stemmed from feigned or "false uneagerness" (line 13).

Only when it seemed that she would lose his romantic overtures did she "falter" in this noli me tangere pose — posture that so many of Hardy's fictional heroines (Paula Power in A Laodicean [1881], for instance) adopt toward their admirers, as if they are not quite ready to abandon the only freedom society has permitted them.

This falsity of outward demeanour and the heroine's disguising of her true feelings to play the only role that Victorian society has given her are raised pertinently by Andrew Clinton in "'She Stopped Like a Clock': Science and Artificiality in The Hand of Ethelberta and The Cornhill Magazine"in The Thomas Hardy Journal 18, 2 (May 2002).

"Her Reproach", a lyric written in the same period as "Her

Confession" (text) and likewise taking the form of a more-or-less regular English sonnet (except that the sestet is divided into a quatrain and a couplet, perhaps to emphasize the closure afforded by the last two lines), presents the converse situation, after commitment has been made and marriage vows taken.

Here we do not have an Atalanta-esque Ethelberta or Paula fending off the advances of an ardent suitor, but a miserable and thwarted Eustacia, bound in holy matrimony to a man obsessed with conning "the dead page" (line 1) of some scholarly tome rather than the nuances of her face. While her erstwhile lover pursues a knowledge of "Cold wisdom's words" (line 2), she feels herself wasting away.

While he attempts the ascent of "Fame's far summits" (line 5), she in the valley of domesticity is subject to the "biting blasts" (line 4) of a Time-controlled climate, losing her "currency" like Lucetta, concerned that her cheeks appear worn and her once bright eyes dim. If this persona could but accede to Elizabeth-Jane's advice and avoid the anguish of love she would not be withering in the male carelessness that inevitably (the poem implies) is the aftermath of the lover's winning his race and claiming his prize.

She reproaches her lover, not merely for neglecting her to pursue "worldly" Fame through such a masculine endeavour as career, but for failing like a good gardener and husbandman "To water love." His wrong-headedly making the choice determined by patriarchal society is ironic, she contends, because such a "glory-gleam" is soon enough eclipsed by later [male] strivers, only the "kindliest" (line 13) of whom will even momentarily concede that her beloved achieved anything noteworthy: "He, too, had his day."

As Tennyson remarks in In Memoriam A. H. H., "Our little systems have their day; / They have their day and cease to be" ("Prelude," lines 17-18). In the context of this Hardy sonnet, "had his day" implies the "15 minutes of fame" concept: ephemeral public recognition and acclaim, followed by oblivion (or, as Housman says in "To an Athlete Dying Young," "the name died before the man"). Such is masculine achievement outside the domestic sphere.

The persona's "reproach," then, is that her lover mistook what was valuable (their love) and what was dross (worldly renown), and that he failed to "seize the day" by ignoring her, by an "absence" which may be mental rather than physical, as Clym's attitude towards his wife in The Return of the Native suggests. Neglecting one's obligations to foster a relationship does not necessarily entail the physical absence or apartness of Angel Clare in Brazil.

In The Woman Question, Vol. 3 (1983), Helsinger et al. single out the heroines of Olive Schreiner, George Gissing, Thomas Hardy, Henry James, Theodore Dreiser, and Virginia Woolf as "New Women" far different from their sisters in the works of earlier novelists in that these modern heroines are not, like George Eliot's Dorothea in Middlemarch (1871-72), long-suffering angels. Rather, as independently minded, fully-realised characters they have departed from the unrealistic ideal epitomised by poet Coventry Patmore's Angel in the House (1854-56); however, as Helsinger et al. note, such fin de siècle New Women as Sue Bridehead and Tess Durbeyfield "emerge as sympathetic characters who will not or cannot find happiness, despite their possession of both strong minds and womanly virtues".

Behind their lack of fulfillment lies the old dictum "A woman might work, but a lady does not." Furthermore, Hardy seems to have shared with Schopenhauer and others a notion that women, by virtue of their physiological organisation and their biological or social roles as mothers, were closer to the operative forces of evolution, natural and (more particularly) sexual selection.

In Tess this will develop into an almost Zolaesque naturalism, when the girl workers at Talbothays are to be found in sultry high summer writhing "feverishly under the oppressiveness of an emotion thrust on them by cruel Nature's law, their individuality extinguished into "portion of one organism called sex" (p. 174).

While unmarried middle-class women earlier in the century were relegated to becoming their married sisters' companions (as first Mary and then Georgina Hogarth were for Catherine Dickens), those who engaged in gainful employment such as domestic servants (for example, Tess in Hardy's novel) or governesses (for example, Tom Pinch's sister, Ruth, in Dickens's Martin Chuzzlewit [1843]) virtually lost their social status.

A middle-class woman's only means of securing status and economic security was marriage — hence, the desperate competition between the village beauties for the hand of eligible bachelor Tony Kytes in Thomas Hardy's farcical short story "Tony Kytes, the Arch-Deceiver" (first published in March 1891 in Harper's New Monthly Magazine as the first of what would become the frame-tale collection A Few Crusted Characters in Life's Little Ironies (1894).

In the jeux d' espirit that parodies with a gender reversal the romantic situation in Far From the Madding Crowd (1874) — that is, a heroine wooed by three suitors, Hannah Jolliver exercises the only control she can grasp over the exasperating situation under her father's watchful eye by rejecting the young carrier as a prospective husband, even though she is apparently his first choice: "I have spirit, and I do refuse him!" (Collected Stories 522), casting her refusal in a positive form. "I would sooner marry no — nobody at all!"

Hardy does not mention whether the proud beauty ever does marry, or whether, like the hapless Phyllis Grove, the doctor's daughter in the tragic "Melancholy Hussar of the German Legion" (first published in The Bristol Times in January 1890), she lives to regret losing her sole chance for domestic stability, if not exactly domestic bliss. Such aging spinsters constituted a kind of Malthusian "surplus population" who were regarded as redundant because they could not fulfill their divinely sanctioned roles as wives and mothers as Nature (in the Darwinian sense of biological imperative) seemed to have dictated. William Rathbone Greg reflected a commonly held opinion when he argued against employing middle-class women in "Why Are Women Redundant?" in Literary and Social Judgments (1873).

The only acceptable alternative to marriage for Victorian women of the middle class was entering one of a limited number of professions, including teaching (like Hardy's Fancy Day in Under the Greenwood Tree, although she is not driven by economic necessity, but, as Boumelha notes, uses teaching as "a means of filling in time until marriage", nursing, social work, and (despite the limited number of subjects that society expected them to deal with) journalism and writing (like Hardy's poetess, Ethelberta, and romance-writer, Elfride, respectable women in droves became novelists in fin de siècle Britain).

In the 1880s and 1890s, younger middle-class "New Women" were able to take advantage of the social trail-blazing of their sisters in the previous generation, including Florence Nightingale (and of the late nineteenth-century technological revolution), and enter the burgeoning Civil Service and other white-collar and service sectors of the economy without loss of social status.

"Her Reproach"
CON the dead page as 'twere live love: press on!
Cold wisdom's words will ease thy track for thee;
Aye, go; cast off sweet ways, and leave me wan
To biting blasts that are intent on me.
But if thy object Fame's far summits be,
Whose inclines many a skeleton overlies
That missed both dream and substance, stop and see
How absence wears these cheeks and dims these eyes!
It surely is far sweeter and more wise
To water love, than toil to leave anon
A name whose glory-gleam will but advise
Invidious minds to eclipse it with their own,
And over which the kindliest will but stay
A moment; musing, "He, too, had his day!"
Westbourne Park Villas, 1867.
"Her Confession"
As some bland soul, to whom a debtor says
"I'll now repay the amount I owe to you,"
In inward gladness feigns forgetfulness
That such a payment ever was his due
(His long thought notwithstanding), so did I

At our last meeting waive your proffered kiss
With quick divergent talk of scenery nigh,
By such suspension to enhance my bliss.
And as his looks in consternation fall
When, gathering that the debt is lightly deemed,
The debtor makes as not to pay at all,
So faltered I, when your intention seemed
Converted by my false uneagerness
To putting off for ever the caress.

Chapter 7

The Implicit Theme in the Works of Thomas Hardy

In Hardy, theme (a unifying observation about the human condition) is generally implicit (understood) rather than explicit (overt or stated). Rarely is a Hardy theme as easily stated as "The virtuous though humble will inevitably triumph over the corrupt, greedy, and oppressive of the middle and upper classes," a statement that would be satisfactory for Victorian melodramas such as Black-Ey'd Susan; or, All in the Downs and The Rent Day. The triumph of Dick Dewey over his higher-class rivals Farmer Shiner and the minister for the hand of Fancy Day in Under the Greenwood Tree, although it is one of Hardy's simplest prose narratives, cannot be stated so simply, for example, because personal as well as class issues occupy the minds of the young lovers.

Although it is almost axiomatic that the briefer a work, the simpler its theme, and that the longer the work the greater the number of themes it is likely to embrace, even a relatively short Hardy poem such as "The Channel Firing" is likely to communicate a number of observations about or insights into human nature: "The dead regret their inability to advise, correct, or reprove the living," "God, knowing all, cannot help but be a little cynical about human morality," and "Nominally Christians, by the early twentieth century, Europeans had permitted militant nationalism to overwhelm any recognition of Christ's teachings" are but three possible statements of theme that logically arise from several readings of "The Channel Firing."

Conversely, in a short story considerably longer than the poem, "A Tradition of 1804," Hardy is ironically observing that, when one has the chance to seize a significant opportunity (here, the assassination of Napoleon), he may well lack the means (a suitable firearm). However, before we can accurately examine any Hardy text for its themes, we must first determine the meaning of the term "theme."

Since a student's knowledge of literary terms should gradually become more sophisticated over the secondary grades, studying a novel such as Tess of the d'Urbervilles in the senior year a student cannot appraise the themes of the novel with the limited definition of "theme" given in The Concise Oxford Dictionary:

N. Subject on which one speaks, writes, or thinks; school composition, essay, on given subject; (gram.) Stem of noun or verb, part to which inflexions are added; (mus.) Melodic subject usu. developed with variations; (hist.) any of 29 provinces in Byzantine empire; ~song, recurrent melody in musical play or film. [Middle English, from Latin from Greek thema -matos (tithemi set, place); partly through Old French].

Junior secondary English students often tend to think of the theme of a literary work as a single word, such as "War," "Friendship," or (at best) a phrase such as "The anxieties of romantic love."

In fact, in formulating the theme of a literary work, the student should pick the central insight—for example, in "The Channel Firing," Hardy uses the dialogue among the dead and God to point out that the world hasn't changed fundamentally because humanity, despite its technological sophistication, has not developed morally or spiritually and still relies on violence to solve its disputes because all too often it is blinded by anger and hatred, as suggested by "all nations striving strong to make Red war yet redder."

Words such as "war" or "hatred," however, are mere motifs, frequently recurring elements or ideas that may form the basis for a statement of theme. As Laurence Perrine explains in Story and Structure (1959), The Theme of a piece of fiction is its controlling idea or its central insight. It is the unifying generalization about life stated or implied by the story. To derive the theme of a story, we must ask what its central purpose is: what view of life it supports or what insight into life it reveals. To illustrate the concept, Perrine offers the following joke:

"Daughter, your young man stays until a very late hour. Hasn't your mother said anything to you about this habit of his?" "Yes, father. Mother says men haven't altered a bit."

Consider how many themes (or, more properly, how many statements of theme) we might generate if we each wrote down what we thought the joke-teller was driving at:

- As men grow older, they tend to grow more conservative.
- Fathers of daughters are apprehensive about the kinds of young men their daughters date.
- Fathers tend to scold their children for doing the very things they themselves once did.
- Women see men more clearly than men see themselves, and judge them more acutely.

Although it is impossible to determine which of these remarks most accurately reflects the intention or narrative purpose of the joke (or, if you subscribe to hegemony of the author, of the jokester), we recognize that all of the above share certain features:

- Each is statement, a complete sentence with subject and predicate.
- Each accounts for the principal elements in the joke, the censorious tone of the father and the witty rejoinder of the daughter.
- Each is less amusing and far more dry than the joke itself.
- Each statement is implied by the final line of the joke.
- No detail within the joke contradicts any of the statements.
- None of these statements relies upon details not furnished by the joke itself.
- None of these statements is some familiar adage, proverb, or gnomic remark.

- Each statement ratifies the opinions of teenaged daughters about their fathers!

Theme, then, is neither a cliched moral nor a framework on which to hang the other elements of the work; rather, it arises naturally from an interaction of all the other elements of the work: characters, setting, conflict, atmosphere, imagery, symbolism, ad even narrative perspective. It is not a preachment such as "people from different social backgrounds and with different career aspirations and life goals should not marry" (Jude the Obscure). Tempting as it may be to bring in such biographical details as Hardy's unhappy marriage with Emma, the student must not permit such extraneous matters to colour his or her statement of theme.

Even though such a jaded relationship as that of the Henchards at the beginning of The Mayor of Casterbridge may be related to the Hardys' marital problems, one should not assume that the persona or narrative voice is that of the historical Thomas Hardy himself. Therefore, it would be unwise to say that in The Mayor of Casterbridge the theme concerns the impossibility of finding personal fulfilment inside a conventional marriage–after all, Elizabeth-Jane's and Donald Farfrae's is a conventional marriage, but (insofar as the narrator describes it) it seems happy since the partners are intellectually and emotionally well- matched.

The central theme of the novel The Mayor of Casterbridge may be as enigmatic as "anything [is] possible at the hands of Time and Chance, except, perhaps, fair play" (Ch. 1). However, the novel's subtitle, A Study of a Man of Character, suggests that it must be related to Henchard's capacity for suffering, since for Henchard—in part owing to his failure to communicate his true feelings and to his tendency towards "introspective inflexibility" (an inability to understand his own motivations)—"happiness [is] but the occasional episode in a general drama of pain" (Ch. 45), for that is the lesson that the youthful Elizabeth-Jane apparently learns from her step-father. And yet the "unbroken tranquility" she enjoys in maturity, as Farfrae's wife, forces her "to wonder at the persistence of the unforeseen...."

Thus, Hardy's essentially gloomy, nihilistic view of the human condition colours even the conventional "happy ending" in a second, better marriage that Hardy may have derived from Dickens's David Copperfield. Certainly, neither Henchard nor Lucetta realizes any satisfaction from an existence (and, apparently, a pleasant existence socially and materially) founded on a lie. Both characters' fates illustrate the pattern of a secret in the past unexpectedly being brought to light and blighting present happiness. Lucetta refuses to "be a slave to the past" (Ch. 25), and determines to bury the secret of her former relationship with Henchard (and, therefore, her social obligation to marry him) in order to satisfy her present passion.

Similarly, Henchard's lieing to Newsome about the death of Elizabeth-Jane is directly responsible for her rejection of him. Elizabeth-Jane and Farfrae both escape the tragedy because, although they too are guilty of minor duplicities, they are essentially altruistic and "single-hearted." It is not enough, Hardy seems to imply in this novel, to meet the vicissitudes of life heroically or defiantly—one must do so with love, compassion, and charity.

Again, in Tess of the D'Urbervilles, there are a number of themes, but a single unifying principle of (or observation about) human existence emerges from the relationships of the principal characters. Although suffering and death are inevitable, Angel Clare through his lack of empathy for Tess on their wedding night and his apparent rejection of her (as suggested by his trip to Brazil) brings upon Tess more suffering than she deserves and unwittingly drives her towards the final catastrophe, the murder of Alec D'Urberville. Only after it is too late does Angel, realising Tess's true worth, accept responsibility for his own actions. Tess is an odd combination of contraries: a fatalistic who nevertheless struggles for happiness and fulfilment in a world bent on denying her both. This attitude is summed up in her remarking at Stonehenge "This happiness could not have lasted" (Ch. 58).

Like Tess, each of us is defined by our past, which (together with our upbringing and social pressures) limits our choices and conditions the kind of people we become. And yet, Tess struggles against the past and believes she has the power to overcome it; this belief may be a phantasm, but holding fast to it is what makes Tess worthy of our sympathy, for it lies at the core of her personal heroism..

In brief, then, theme must be a statement with a complete subject and predicate, and it must be a generalization about life or human nature that is clearly supported by the text and that contains the unifying and central concept of the work. While this thematic statement should account for all the major details of the text, it should not be contradicted by any of these major details and should not rely upon supposed facts. For example, if a student, having read Hardy's "The Three Strangers," were to say that "From the first for the Fennels' visitors the 'hangman's horror' hovers about the mysterious stranger in cinder-grey," the student should not go so far as suggesting that the other visitors immediately realize that the second stranger is the hangman from Casterbridge Gaol.

Although there is never just a single correct statement of theme, various critics' statements of theme may isolate certain common features, such as the economic hardships that have resulted in Timothy Summers' becoming a criminal in "The Three Strangers."

Finally, students should avoid making thematic statements that tend reduce theme to some familiar saying, such as (with respect to Summers' appearing to be a countryman rather than a middle-class urbanite because of his fustian clothing and hobnailed boots) "You can't judge a book by its cover."

THOMAS HARDY — NOVELIST OR POET

Thomas Hardy — Novelist or Poet?, a title which Bill Morgan has quite justly termed "unfortunate," is nonetheless a fascinating book. It is at once rich and thin, expert and amateurish, informed and ignorant. Privately printed in Philadelphia in 1929, the book is clearly a labour of love: large format, hard covers with cloth spine and glassine wrapper, 19 pages of text and 23 pages of reproductions of Hardy's letters.

Although its author at one point refers to it as an "essay," it is something more — and less.

The author was not a critic, but a bibliophile, A(lfred) Edward Newton of Philadelphia. He owned an electrical business in Philadelphia, but spent most of his adult life collecting first editions, manuscripts, and ephemera. Newton built a huge library of 10,000 volumes, called "Oak Knoll"; after his death in 1940, "his famous 'Oak Knoll' library in Pennsylvania was auctioned and for that purpose an elaborate catalogue of three volumes was printed."(Schweik) One of his possessions, as he describes in the text, was the manuscript of Far From the Madding Crowd.

Newton was more than a collector, however. He was the founder of the Trollope Society and the president of the (Samuel) Johnson Society—positions which explain references to both of these authors in his book. In 1935-36 he was the Rosenback Lecture Fellow in bibliography at the University of Pennsylvania. Finally, he published several books on book collecting, and was a frequent contributor to The Atlantic Monthly.

For all his bibliographical experience, Newton does not seem endowed with a particularly sophisticated literary palate. Reading Thomas Hardy—Novelist or Poet?, one is struck by his tastes. He was clearly put off by Hardy's tragic muse. Tess barely makes his list of Hardy's top five novels; on some days Two on a Tower beats out The Mayor for number six; and of Jude, "personally I dislike it exceedingly." Indeed, Newton's eponymous question becomes no question at all when he remarks, "Now the bald fact is that gloom and pessimism, relieved only here and there by flashes of sardonic humour, is not the stuff out of which the finest poetry is made."

Given all his reservations, it is fair to ask why Newton admires Hardy as much as he clearly does. Some of the attraction is probably related to Hardy's stature as "the grand old man" of English letters in the first quarter of the twentieth century. Anyone with any pretension to catholic biblophilia would have to make much of the chronicler of Wessex. Another reason may lie in Newton's affection for Trollope and his explicit comparison to Wessex and Barsetshire. Both Hardy and Trollope "peopled [an 'imaginary county'] with characters which are as real to [their] readers... as any people of their acquaintance." Certainly this is a logical connection. Hardy corresponded with Trollope, asking advice on matters of the writer's business, and Michael Millgate suggests that he may have modeled his use of the Wessex locale on Trollope's series.

THE TEXT

The text of this book has been scanned by a text reader from one of the original copies. Scanning is still an imperfect science, expecially when the type is small, but I have tried to proofread carefully. Formatting HTML is also difficult. I have tried to suggest the typography of letters and news articles with font size changes and indentation, but perfect reproduction is not possible in this medium. On several occasions I have typed material which appears only in a facsimile reproduction. In those cases, I have enclosed the material within brackets, to indicate it is not part of the typeset.

The front matter and the typescript of the final letter appear with "horizontal rule" lines separating the pages. I have not, however, indicated the breaks between pages of text. The book consists of 8 blank pages at the front and the back. The front matter consists of 8 pages. There are 19 pages of text, interspersed with 23 pages of reproduced letters, all in Hardy's hand. None of these illustrations is numbered, and the pagination is imperfect; as a result the final page of text is numbered 31. Page 31 is followed by 8 pages of the letter mentioned above.

Chapter 8

"Hardy's Romanticism in The Woodlanders"

By the time Hardy came to write The Woodlanders (1887 — his eleventh novel) his emotional impulse towards Romanticism, hitherto strongly expressed in his fiction, had been replaced with the acceptance that Romanticism had failed to survive in the second half of the nineteenth century. Paradoxically, though, as Hardy matured, Romanticism became increasingly important to him, as a touchstone in the midst of a society in which rural values were declining.

In The Woodlanders, even though Romanticism generally has become more important to Hardy, it is the Darwinian elements in nature which seem more visible - harsh proof that Romanticism has had its day. So in The Woodlanders the tone is one of gloom, in keeping with Hardy's melancholy vision, a vision in which Darwinism was becoming more prominent than Romanticism.

Extracts from The Life of Thomas Hardy (published under his second wife's name, but written by Hardy himself) bear testimony to this despondency and depression. The entry for November 17 1885 reads, "In a fit of depression, as if enveloped in a leaden cloud". Other entries made around this time are portents of gloom, including a "sick headache" on November 21-22; "'Everything looks so little - so ghastly little'" (December 9); "The Hypocrisy of things. Nature is an arch-dissembler" (December 21); sadness (December 31); fears for the reception of The Mayor of Casterbridge (January 2). And upon finishing The Woodlanders, Hardy writes: "February 4 [1887] 8.20 p.m.

Finished The Woodlanders. Thought I should feel glad, but I do not particularly, — though relieved."

So it is no wonder that The Woodlanders is enveloped in gloom and despondency, and is often described as elegiac. Aside from Hardy's sombre journal entries, which help explain the tone of the novel, there are several entries concerning art which are useful in ascertaining Hardy's intention in writing The Woodlanders. Hardy writes, "January 3 [1886]: My art is to intensify the expression of things...so that the heart and inner meaning is made visibly visible." One year later (January 1887), as he neared the end of writing The Woodlanders, he wrote,

After looking at the landscape ascribed to Bonington in our drawing-room I feel that Nature is played out as a Beauty, but not as a Mystery. I don't want to see landscapes, ie., scenic paintings of them, because I don't want to see the original realities — as optical effects, that is. I want to see the deeper reality underlying the scenic, the expression of what are called abstract imaginings.)

These passages are revealing, as they show that Hardy is now less interested in re-creating Romantic beauty in the landscape than in searching for the "intention" within nature. This "intention," which Hardy is most explicit about in the famous "Unfulfilled Intention" passage in The Woodlanders, incorporates a Romantic and a Darwinian meaning: the word intention suggests the Darwinian impulse for change and progression, as well as implying the Romantic sense of the word, the hidden meaning at the heart of nature. So even though Hardy is no longer attempting a re-creation of a Romantic landscape, his intention still lies within the Romantic tradition, because like the Romantic poets, he is seeking a presence within the landscape, as opposed to merely trying to describe nature itself. I will argue, then, that Hardy's depiction of nature in The Woodlanders relies upon him discovering this "intention," either Romantic or Darwinian, within nature.

Bound up in this division between the Darwinian and the Romantic in Hardy's view of nature, is the division, so overt in The Woodlanders, between Hardy's nostalgic love of the past, and his acceptance that change is inevitable. From this split comes Hardy's affection for the Romantic view of nature, yet his acceptance of change and progress dictated by Darwin's evolutionary theory of nature, and loss of faith in an anthropomorphic God.

Hardy's 1883 essay "The Dorsetshire Labourer" (written only three years prior to the serialisation of The Woodlanders is evidence of how keenly Hardy felt the eroding of traditional rural societies. The Dorsetshire labourers, argues Hardy, "are losing their peculiarities as a class" because of their increasing mobility which results in "a less intimate and kindly relationship with the land [the labourer] tills". So this new nomadic tendency is resulting in less individuality, less stability, and a weaker relationship with the land and with the labourer's employer. Hardy argues that such changes are leading to the loss of the previously strong morality typical of the labouring class.

Many critics have recognised this elegy for a past age, including Dale Kramer who argues that Hardy "was at odds with the way of life he saw developing around him.... The world of rural Dorset, which he loved, was eroding". Kramer continues, arguing that "disillusionment raised in Hardy a discontent with what seemed to be the causes for the unsatisfactory conditions of existence and the imbalance between what ought to have been and what were the possibilities of achieving happiness". Glenn Irvin describes Hardy's love for the past as appearing strongly throughout The Woodlanders.

He argues that in this novel, Hardy presents the new order as "malignant and depraved," and that "Even with its limitations and inflexibility, the old order is preferable to the new, but impossible, of course, to preserve". Peter Casagrande captures well the painful tension within Hardy between past and present: "There is simply no way to reconcile the conflict between loving loyalty to the past and obedience to the heartless ongoingness of things. What the novel invites in its powerful close is that the reader contemplates the beauty of the sad truth that things decay".

Perhaps Mary Jacobus sums up Hardy's position most forcefully and concisely, in her statement, "Hardy laments... the rape of the woods by rootless predators from the modern world".

The characters in the novel are divided along the lines Jacobus suggests, between the woodland characters, who are closely connected to the land, and the "rootless predators," who irrevocably change the lives of the land characters. Edred Fitzpiers is the central "rootless predator" in the novel, and I believe the power of, and interest in, his character results from him being created in a Shelleyan mould. It is an obligatory feature of Hardy's novels to include a Shelleyan-influenced character, a character who idealises his (or her) beloved rather than loving the beloved directly, for what she (or he) is.

In previous novels, these Shelleyan lovers have been portrayed sympathetically, as tragic figures whose ideals are out of place in their hostile environment. But Hardy's portrait of Fitzpiers is unsympathetic: proof of the strength of Hardy's disillusionment with the practical application of Romantic ideals. Although his portrait is unsympathetic, it is, nonetheless, strongly Shelleyan: Fitzpiers quotes Shelley at length on several occasions; Fitzpiers idealises the women in the novel, attributing to them the ethereal qualities of Shelley's women in poems such as "Epipsychidion;" and Fitzpiers' interests, ideas, and even appearance resemble Shelley's.

The influence of Wordsworth is also important in The Woodlanders. Wordsworth's poetry was powerful for Hardy because it served as a monument to the past, as a guarantor of the memory of previous feeling. As William Buckler suggests, towards the end of Hardy's novel-writing career Hardy used Wordsworth "as a sort of critical correspondent, testing his own way of looking at creative problems with Wordsworth's way." Like Wordsworth, Hardy's motive was poetic, and also like Wordsworth, Hardy drew on the "dense fabric of details" maintained "in the storehouse of memory." So Buckler sees Hardy's fictional world as "a created, not a copied world".

Buckler's ideas tie in with the thoughts of other critics, that for Hardy, The Woodlanders was an act of memory. Ian

Gregor writes that The Woodlanders is based on "recollection, the remembrance of things past, a concern to render a consciousness increasingly susceptible to the tensions of the present". Hardy had the idea for the story in mind after completing Far from the Madding Crowd, but put it aside. So over a period of twelve years the story had time to develop. Michael Millgate, in his biography of Hardy, adds weight to the idea that The Woodlanders was an "act of memory," explaining that Hardy did not visit North-west Dorset (the setting for The Woodlanders) while he was writing it: "he wrote at a deliberate distance from the scenes being recreated in fictional terms, chiefly in order to preserve the freshness and vitality of the emotionally charged impressions already fixed on his imagination".

The two main ways, then, in which I see The Woodlanders as a Romantic novel are as follows. Firstly, Hardy's vision of nature combines a Romantic with a Darwinian view. In this novel Hardy searches primarily for the intention behind nature, whether this intention be beautiful or grotesque, Romantic or Darwinian. As such, nature comes across as both Romantic and Darwinian, although the Darwinian predominates, perhaps owing to Hardy's despondency at the time of writing.

And secondly, the character of Fitzpiers is strongly influenced by Shelley, although as I mentioned earlier, this Shelleyan character is crueler and more self-seeking than characters in the earlier novels, causing misery in the lives of all around him, in his pursuit of the elusive ideal. My concluding comments will briefly consider the novel as an elegy, which I also see as aligning the novel to Romantic poetry, remembering that an elegy is typically a mode of poetry.

As I suggested in my introductory comments, the lasting impression one takes away from The Woodlanders is the gloom and decay which exist in the natural world, and which is mirrored in the lives of the woodland characters. This overwhelming feeling of pain and decay results from Hardy's insistence on the Darwinian struggle for survival within the woods, built up through numerous references throughout the novel.

At times, this sombre view gives way to a real celebration of the beauties in nature, particularly in the progression of the seasons and their influence on the productivity of the natural world. But this jubilee is not to last: just as Grace's joy and discovery of her love for Giles will not come to fruition, so the Darwinian element in nature remains dominant. Another way in which I believe Hardy's depiction of nature is most powerful, and most Romantic in The Woodlanders, is in his creation of a close relationship between the woodland characters and the natural world.

There are many examples of unity between character and landscape, as well as times when a character's feelings are imitated by nature. By examining Hardy's natural world in this novel, I will show the presence of both Romanticism and Darwinism, as well as the interdependence of character and natural world.

The most obvious reason why the Darwinian aspects of nature dominate the Romantic occurrences in The Woodlanders, is that the characters, with the exception of Fitzpiers, are doomed to unhappiness, and Hardy translates their unhappiness into pain in the natural world. From the outset, we are overwhelmed with images of decay and destruction in the woods, and this unconsciously prepares us for the similar struggle in the world of the characters (in particular I have in mind the conflict between the aggressive, modern Fitzpiers, and the passive, traditionalist Giles, who recognises his weakness and gives in to his stronger opponent).

Hardy's use of ivy, the plant notorious for its poisonous and parasitic qualities (its habit of winding itself around other plants), quickly comes to symbolise the brutal struggle for survival between plants in the woodlands: "In the hollow shades of the roof could be seen dangling and etiolated arms of ivy which had crept through the joints of the tiles and were groping in vain for some support, their leaves being dwarfed and sickly for want of sunlight". In the famous Unfulfilled Intention passage we learn that, "the ivy slowly strangled to death the promising sapling", a succinct and poignant evocation of the struggle between the plants. And further on, the points of the ivy leaves "scratch [their] underlying neighbour restlessly". These references capture exactly the nature of the ivy plant, fighting ruthlessly for survival.

Often the decay and struggle in the woods is explained by the sounds of the struggle between two trees, and their pain is shown by the wounds resulting from this battle. For example, Marty's three a.m. excursion to deliver her spars is made fearful by "the creaking sound of two over-crowded branches... rubbing each other into wounds".

Similarly, towards the end of the novel, Grace views the woods as being in a battle: There were "trees close together, wrestling for existence, their branches disfigured with wounds resulting from their mutual rubbings and blows". Hardy also pays attention to the decay and disfigurement in the woods.

The grotesque description of the walking sticks is a striking image: "the chief [pattern] being corkscrew shapes in black and white thorn, brought to that pattern by the slow torture of an encircling woodbine during their growth, as the Chinese have been said to mould human beings into grotesque toys by continued compression in infancy". The human comparison makes the description all the more disturbing. Much later in the novel Hardy gives us a magnificent image of the decayed woods: "Dead boughs were scattered about like ichthyosauri in a museum, and beyond them were perishing woodbine stems resembling old ropes".

Also present in this grotesque description are "rotting stumps... rising from their mossy setting like black teeth from green gums" With all of these descriptions, it is the personification of the woods which makes the images so vivid and hideous. And the ichthyosauri fossils in the museum cannot but invoke Darwin. This connection between the human and the natural world emphasises the point Peter Casagrande makes that things inevitably decay, including the hopes and lives of the characters.

This idea is marvellously made by Hardy himself, in the card-playing scene at Giles' Christmas party:

Each card had a great stain in the middle of its back, produced by the touch of generations of damp and excited thumbs, now fleshless in the grave; and the kings and queens wore a decayed expression of feature, as if they were rather an impecunious dethroned dynasty hiding in obscure slums than real regal characters.

Elsewhere personification is taken even further, perhaps, as Wiliam Matchett suggests, "as a means of extending throughout the universe the same sufferings [Hardy] sees in man". Marty feels akin to the fir trees she plants because "'It seems to me...they sigh because they are very sorry to begin life in earnest - just as we be'".

Lost in the woods, Grace and Felice hold each other, "while the funereal trees rocked and chanted dirges unceasingly". And most disturbing of all is Hardy's description of the victims of the barking process: "Each tree doomed to the flaying process was first attacked by Upjohn... an operation comparable to the 'little toilette' of the executioner's victim." The trees "stood naked-legged... as if ashamed". By describing the trees as preparing for execution Hardy evokes powerful images of human sacrifice, making the fate of the trees human and universal. Kramer sums up well this connection between the natural and the human world, explaining that "The sufferings that the trees of the title inflict upon each other in their natural setting parallel those inflicted by one well-meaning human on others in the story".

Hardy's view of the Darwinian struggle does not stop at nature, but extends into the human and the animal world. The best image to show the chain of being in the animal kingdom comes in the fourth chapter. The chapter begins with an ominous and distinctly un-Romantic description of morning: "the bleared white visage of a sunless winter day emerged like a dead-born child." With the coming of morning, "Owls that had been catching mice in the outhouses, and stoats that had been sucking the blood of the rabbits" cease their activities. The animals and plants also interact in struggle and this is demonstrated by the rabbits nibbling bare the bases of some of the small woodland trees. And in the human world, the strong and arrogant Fitzpiers dominates and destroys the weaker (both in terms of will and physical endurance) Giles, who abandons his suit for Grace with the coming of a rival.

The intense struggle in the natural (and animal) world seems to sap energy from the earth, and Hardy portrays this exhaustion several times in the novel. One example is Grace's observation of a sunrise: "It was even now day out-of-doors, though the tones of morning were feeble and wan.... The tree-trunks, the road, the out-buildings, the garden, every object, wore that aspect of mesmeric passivity....

Helpless immobility seemed to be combined with intense consciousness; a meditative inertness possessed all things". Gregor identifies this passivity as a new condition of Hardy's natural world. He goes on to say that the woods emphasise "a sense of passive exhaustion and melancholy... there is a mood operative in [The Woodlanders] more deeply pessimistic than anything else in Hardy's fiction".

And this pessimism can be easily attributed to a man whose need for solace in an increasingly unfamiliar world, is matched with his acceptance that solace cannot come from Romanticism, which has no place in this new world. By showing the helplessness and inertness of the landscape, and by describing so vividly the violent struggle endured by plants in the woodlands, and animals in the Melbury homestead, Hardy insists upon the unpleasantness in nature. This point is reinforced by Hardy's juxtaposition of elements of beauty (descriptions which at times come close to a Romantic view of nature) which temporarily bring hope, but are often destroyed by brutal reality.

At times in The Woodlanders, Hardy presents the Darwinian and Romantic elements of his vision simultaneously. For example, when Melbury and Grace drive away from the woods, "their wheels silently crush... delicate-patterned mosses, hyacinths, primroses, lord-and-ladies, and other strange and common plants". The description of the plants is fine and detailed, but ultimately pointless because the gig destroys them. And so here, as is usual in The Woodlanders, the Darwinian element in the woods dominates and the surface beauty of the landscape is destroyed. Another example of the dominance of Darwinism occurs when Grace and her father walk through the woods to the auction. Hardy gives a beautiful description of nature's bounty in some of the sheltered hollows, their sheltered nature giving the idea of a "mixture of the seasons... in some of the dells they passed by holly–berries in full red growing beside oak and hazel... and brambles whose verdure was rich and deep as in the month of August". The landscape then changes "from the handsome to the curious," and then leads into one of decay:

On older trees... huge lobes of fungi grew like lungs. Here, as everywhere, the Unfulfilled Intention, which makes life what it is, was as obvious as it could be among the depraved crowds of a city slum. The leaf was deformed, the curve was crippled, the taper was interrupted, the lichen ate the vigour of the stalk, and the ivy slowly strangled to death the promising sapling.

Here, the power of the description overrides the beauty previously described, leaving the reader with the image of destruction in mind. It is also interesting to note in this passage that the decay and deformity is purposely linked to the human world (the city-slum), pre-empting the ruin that will befall the characters. These descriptions mark a turn in vision. In previous novels, Hardy saw more readily the beauties in the landscape.

Now, in The Woodlanders, most of his descriptions of nature are full of decay, disease, and Darwinian struggle. Hardy is so unable to abandon the Darwinian view that his attempts to describe beauty are overshadowed by his new admission that all things will pass. Only when Grace's love for Giles awakens does Hardy see, unadulterated, the beauty of the season. Having said this, however, there are other instances of Hardy's Romantic view of nature to be found in The Woodlanders.

A Romantic view of nature is, in fact, presented in the opening pages of the novel, from Barber Percomb's perspective as he is travelling to Little Hintock: "though there might be a sombre beauty in the scenery, music in the breeze, and a wan procession of coaching ghosts in the sentiment of this old turnpike road, he was mainly puzzled about the way".

These ideas are unmistakably Romantic — Wordsworth's idea of sombre beauty features in many poems (The Prelude is full of the darker side of beauty), while the music in the breeze may be a reference to the Aeolian harp, an instrument symbolising inspiration in many Romantic poems (Coleridge's "Aeolian Harp" and "Dejection," for instance).

And Percomb's being "puzzled about the way" of finding these beauties in Little Hintock is surely Hardy's view: where and how can one enjoy the Romantic glory of nature when so much is changed, when all around is struggle and ruin? The Woodlanders, then, from the opening pages, seeks to explore this puzzle, and Hardy reaches no real conclusion.

That the book ends with an elegy, however, suggests that Hardy has accepted that nature must struggle for survival as Darwin claimed, and that we must look beyond the surface to find beauty. This is what the Romantics themselves did, in landmark poems such as "Tintern Abbey," where Wordsworth couples imagination and memory with the landscape in order to find meaning.

With the change in the seasons, from Summer to Autumn, comes Hardy's most Romantic description of the glory of nature. Melbury's excursion to Highstoy Hill lends him a Keatsian view of the cider district showing "the miles of appletrees in bloom. All was now deep green". At the beginning of the cider season Hardy unsparingly describes the orchards of Little Hintock: "beyond the yard were to be seen gardens and orchards now bossed, nay encrusted, with scarlet and gold fruit, stretching to infinite distance under a luminous lavender mist".

Hardy then quotes the marvellous Autumn description from Chatterton's "Song to Aella," the source for Keats' later description:

When the fair apples, red as evening sky,
Do bend the tree unto the fruitful ground,
When juicy pears, and berries of black dye
Do dance in air, and call the eyes around.

Everything in these pages reverts back to the beauty of the season. There are lengthy descriptions of Giles and the process of his cider-making, and Grace's thoughts of Giles and his cider press. The power of Autumn is captured in the description of "the blue stagnant air of autumn which hung over everything [and] was heavy with a sweet cidery smell".

Even the villainous Fitzpiers, on his way to see Felice, is immersed in the beautiful Autumn landscape, travelling "through the gorgeous autumn landscape of White-Hart Vale, surrounded by orchards lustrous with the reds of apple-crops, berries, and foliage, the whole intensified by the gilding of the declining sun".

All in the natural world is burgeoning, and nature is at its most bountiful. The narrator explains that, "The earth this year had been prodigally bountiful, and now was the supreme moment of her bounty". Grace also thinks along these lines, but embellishes the meaning of nature to include Giles, her fertility God, within it, as shown in these thoughts: "Nature was bountiful....No sooner had she been cast aside by Edred Fitzpiers than another being... had arisen out of the earth ready to her hand".

With Grace's realisation of her love for Giles comes Hardy's most exquisite and Romantic description of nature in the novel. Giles, coming along the road, is seen by Grace in the following way:

He looked and smelt like Autumn's very brother, his face being sunburnt to wheat-colour, his eyes blue as corn-flowers, his sleeves and leggings dyed with fruit stains, his hands clammy with the sweet juice of apples, his hat sprinkled with pips, and everywhere about him that atmosphere of cider which at its first return each season has such an indescribable fascination for those who have been born and bred among the orchards.

The similarities between Hardy's description of Autumn, and Keats' description in his Ode to that season, are obvious. Both include the natural bounties of Autumn (apples, pips, kernels, juices, cider) in their descriptions; both imagine the sweet juices from the Autumn fruit and so use adjectives such as clammy, sticky, sweet, juicy, swell, plump; and both figure Autumn as a person — while Keats' personification is general, Hardy describes Giles himself as the season. The tone and atmosphere of both pieces of writing are also similar. Keats evokes a feeling of drowsy calm with his long vowel sounds and sibilance, while Hardy's adjectives prolong the description, and add a gentleness to the scene.

In his description of Autumn, Hardy is writing in a Romantic mode, focussing on the sensuality of the scene — the smell of the ripened apples, the sweet taste of cider, the sticky, clammy residue left on the hands, the feeling of the warm sun ripening the Autumn fruit — as well as the glorious spectacle of Giles as a fruit God. The union (although brief) between Grace and Giles is confirmed in Romantic language: Giles and Grace "could see far into the recesses of heaven as they mused and walked, the eye journeying on under a species of golden arcades" (xxviii 156).

And as if to affirm the legitimacy of the union, Grace's senses are finally awoken, and she abandons herself "to the seductive hour and scene," "her senses revelled in the sudden lapse back to nature unadorned," and she experiences "revolt for the nonce against social law" and a "passionate desire for primitive life". For a moment, we (and Hardy) are convinced that the power and the beauty of a Romanticised nature can win; but this is not so, as Grace cannot undo her marriage to Fitzpiers, and the Darwinian struggle in nature, though Hardy showed it as being temporarily outweighed by harmony, must return. There is also the pragmatic reason why Grace cannot live by her feelings and consummate her love for Giles: the reaction to the slight sexual content of Hardy's previous novels had been hostile, showing that Victorian England was not ready for moral or sexual liberation.

The close connection between the natural world and human nature has been seen in this great Autumn scene. Just as the natural world burgeons and blossoms, so too do Grace's feelings and senses unfold, and Hardy makes this link obvious in the simile that Grace applies to her own situation of unhappiness in marriage. Contemplating the bounty of the season, Grace realises that "some kernels were unsound as her own situation, and she wondered if there were one world in the universe where the fruit had no worm, and marriage no sorrow". Grace's aspiration is towards an impossible, pre-Lapsarian world – but Hardy's writing here is again Romantic, recognising the close connection between human feeling and the natural world that the Romantic poets sought.

The emotional state of the other woodland characters, too, is mirrored by the woods, which again reveals Hardy's debt to the Romantics and their mode, the pathetic fallacy (here I will take the pathetic fallacy to mean the attribution of human emotions to inanimate objects).

When Melbury goes to solicit Giles' advice on Fitzpiers' infidelities, Hardy's description of the evening is symbolic of the illness Giles has been plagued by, and which will eventually kill him: Melbury "set out to look for Giles on a rimy evening when the woods seemed to be in a cold sweat; beads of perspiration hung from every base twig; the sky had no colour, and the trees rose before him as haggard, grey phantoms whose days of substantiality were passed" A similar parallel is made on one of Fitzpiers' visits to Felice.

Felice has shut herself up in her boudoir, with the curtains closed and candles burning, ostensibly to shut out the gloom of the outside world: "'the world is so dreary outside!'" Felice's exclamation arguably echoes the early Tennyson poem "Mariana," with its refrain of "'My life is dreary,'" for "Mariana" is a meditation on Romantic loss. And Felice goes on to speak of "'Sorrow and bitterness in the sky, and floods of agonised tears beating against the panes'".

But we learn that these emotions, attributed to the weather, are in fact the feelings of Felice herself, since Hardy's subsequent description makes clear that she is mingling the weather and her emotions: "her constitutional cloud of misery, the sorrowful drops that still hung upon her eyelashes". Fitzpiers presently draws the curtains to let in "the flood of late autumn sunlight," confirming that Felice's picture of the storm outside is really a portrait of her emotions.

So in Hardy's depiction of the natural world in The

Woodlanders, he is both writing in a Romantic tradition, and also rebelling against it. His view of nature is Romantic in that he is resolute on seeing the intention behind nature, as the Romantic poets were. And yet this propensity for "truth" often reveals a Darwinian struggle, not a Romantic gleam. His recognition of a declining rural society also contributes to the despondent way in which he sees the natural world in this novel. His union of character with landscape, however, is quite Romantic, and his two main woodland characters, Marty South and Giles Winterborne, are Hardy's outstanding figures of the goodness of rural values in a world gone wrong because of progress.

Despite their goodness, however, they are not rewarded, and by the end of the novel Giles has died, and Marty is broken-hearted. It is, ironically, the villainous urban-invader Fitzpiers who reaps the rewards at the end of the novel. In his portrait of Edred Fitzpiers, Hardy's debt to Shelley is obvious. This influence extends beyond the abundance of Shelleyan quotations Hardy provides him with to aspects of his character.

Fitzpiers is given Romantic characteristics: his carrying of an eyeglass to spy on Grace symbolises Romantic vision; and later on in the novel he is explicitly compared to Prometheus. Even his appearance is Shelleyan (or Byronic), particularly the description of his eyes, which are "dark and impressive, and beamed with the light either of energy, or of susceptivity." There is a hint here, though, that Fitzpiers is not a thoroughly good character, as the narrator wonders "whether his apparent depths of vision were real, or only an artistic accident of his corporeal moulding".

The narrator says, "nothing but his deeds could reveal" whether this depth of vision is real, and Fitzpiers' deeds confirm the falsity of his character. This falsity is connected with his selfishness, which David Lodge alludes to when describing Fitzpiers as a "third-rate Shelley... an idealist, a dabbler in science, philosophy, literature; [but one who is] idle, fickle, egocentric, selfish as a child". Fitzpiers' cruelty is shown, for example, after discovering Grace's social status: "Instead of treasuring her image as a rarity he would at most have played with her as a toy. He was that kind of man". He is thus a study in the extremes of Shelleyan tendencies, and in his character are to be found the attributes of idealising and egocentricity, without the goodness of some of Shelley's heroes.

It is appropriate that Hardy should create a villainous Romantic character at this point in his career, as The Woodlanders was written at the height of Hardy's distress (yet acceptance) that Romantic values, in this society, no longer had merit. Jacobus argues that Hardy's portrayal of Fitzpiers is "ambivalent," and that this ambivalence "lies in [Hardy's] involvement with the ideas he parodies". Hardy was personally attached to poems such as "Epipsychidion," and "The Revolt of Islam," which instilled in him a desire to be faithful to his vision and pursue the truth of any experience. In The Woodlanders, however, these poems are used ironically because they are quoted by the selfish and egotistical Fitzpiers.

Several critics see Fitzpiers as moulded on Shelleys "Alastor," the Spirit of Solitude. The hero of "Alastor," however, is disappointed in his search and dies an early death, whereas Fitzpiers, although failing to discover the ideal, marries and lives on at the novel's conclusion. The ending clearly shows the author's post-Romantic gaze. By the time he wrote The Woodlanders Hardy had become all too aware that the likes of Fitzpiers would not die during their search for the ideal, but corrupt their values, in typical evolutionary style, in order to survive and dominate.

Fitzpiers' initial optimism at his belief that "'Nature has at last recovered her lost union with the Idea!'" is proven to be false, but this issue, rather than leading to Fitzpiers' demise, is abandoned and Fitzpiers remains dominant. Fitzpiers' chameleon-like quality, his ability to adapt to different circumstances, is how Hardy perceived life in the new Darwinian society, a society in which faithfulness to one's vision would no longer be rewarded.

Fitzpiers combines his interest in science, with a desire for philosophy and romantic poetry: "Fitzpiers was in a distinct degree scientific, being ready and zealous to interrogate all physical manifestations; but primarily he was an idealist". His interest lies largely in this combination: his scientific investigations into, among other things, John South's brain, his readings of metaphysics and transcendental philosophy (particularly the works of Kant and Spinoza) and his pursuit of Romantic idealism which vents itself in his obsessive quoting of Romantic poetry. Fitzpiers' scientific and philosophical interests are conveyed by the narrator as passionate, and yet pretentious, adding to the ambiguity of his character.

Fitzpiers "had lately plunged into abstract philosophy with much zest", but this passion is combined with self-importance, as evidenced when he tries to explain idealism to the illiterate Grammer Oliver. Grammer reports this to Grace: "'Ah Grammer,' he said at another time 'let me tell you that Everything is Nothing. There's only Me and Not Me in the whole world. Grammer would find such ideas nonsensical, and Fitzpiers should have realised how inappropriate it was to talk philosophically to the old woman.

It is significant that Fitzpiers should be so influenced by Spinoza's ideas, because Wordsworth and Coleridge discussed Spinoza too. Spinoza's system of God and Nature was similar to the views of the Romantics: Spinoza writes, "By the government of God I understand the fixed and unalterable order of nature and the interconnectedness of natural things", and the Romantics constantly sought to see life as interconnected (for example, Wordsworth writes in "Tintern Abbey" of the all-pervading "presence" which "rolls through all things").

But it is in keeping with Hardy's ambiguous portrayal that Fitzpiers' actions are in complete opposition to Spinoza's recommendation for happiness, that "It is by goodness and piety that man reaches perfect happiness: virtue is its own reward". We have only to think of Fitzpiers' initial insistence that his and Grace's wedding take place at a registry office, to see his lack of piety and his unkindness to Grace, who reacts "with real distress" to this idea. Ironically enough, Giles and Marty unwittingly live their lives according to Spinoza's creed, but their virtue goes unrewarded. Platos influence on Fitzpiers is also readily observed, especially in his exclamation to Grace that "'Nature has at last recovered her lost union with the Idea!'", which refers to Plato's belief that an idea was a perfect and eternal pattern of which reality is no more than an imperfect copy.

Bruce Johnson describes Fitzpiers as a Platonic idealist, one who addresses the relationship between the ideal and the material in a way "characteristic of his sentimentalism and Romanticism in general" The second generation of Romantics were particularly interested in this idea, seeking transcendence of the real world in favour of an ideal realm of immortality. They longed to discover the ideal forms, as evidenced in poems such as "Ode on a Grecian Urn," "Ode to a Nightingale," and Wordsworth's explicitly Platonic "Intimations Ode."

Fitzpiers philosophical musings relate directly to what I see as his Romantic idealism. This idealism is first revealed in the narrator's description of him as a "dreamy 'ist of some sort, or too deeply steeped in some false kind of 'ism". That Fitzpiers "much preferred the ideal world to the real, and the discovery of principles to their application" not only reveals his idealism, but also reveals Hardy's view of him as impractical: his preference for principles over their application is surely absurd.

His ideas about the subjectivity of love, although presented pompously, are, however, quite close to the Romantics' ideas. Fitzpiers reveals his belief that love is a subjective projection while talking to Giles, and so Fitzpiers seems pretentious because Giles, like Grammer Oliver, is ignorant of such an idea. Fitzpiers contradicts Giles's supposition that he is in love with Grace:

'Human love is a subjective thing — the essence itself of man, as that great thinker Spinoza says — ipsa hominis essentia; it is a joy accompanied by an idea which we project aga nst any suitable object in the line of our vision, just as the rainbow iris is projected against an oak, ash, or elm tree indifferently. So that if any other young lady had appeared instead of the one who did appear, I should have felt just the same interest in her, and have quoted precisely the same lines from Shelley about her, as about this one I saw.'

What Fitzpiers describes here is his pursuit of the essence of love, or the ideal, which he believed resided within one woman. Shelley's influence is again present here, as his protagonist's pursuit of the ideal is the subject of both "Epipsychidion" and "Alastor." Hardy enlarges this theme in his final novel, The Well Beloved, which presents Jocelyn Pierston's pursuit of the ideal in three generations of women. Fitzpiers also pursues the ideal, for it does not remain with Grace, but moves from her to Felice Charmond.

The first meeting between Grace and Fitzpiers furthers Fitzpiers' interest in Grace, since he believes that she has visited him in a dream. He explains to her that owing to the "dose of Idealism" he received, from reading transcendental philosophy the previous evening, he was "scarcely able to distinguish between reality and fancy".

After this meeting, Fitzpiers fancies himself more in love with Grace than ever, although his "love" of Grace is not an individualised desire to be with her alone, but a manifestation of his need to project his feelings onto another. Fitzpiers' humorous explanation of this to Giles indicates that Hardy is critical of Fitzpiers' indistinct love: "'people living insulated, as I do by the solitude of the place, get charged with emotive fluid like a Leyden jar [an apparatus for storing and discharging electricity] with electric, for want of some conductor at hand to disperse it'".

In line with his view that love is subjective, is the idea (hinted at here, but given a little more attention in The Well-Beloved) that Fitzpiers' love is a form of narcissism: Fitzpiers admits that "'I am in love with something in my own head, and no thing-in-itself outside it at all'". Because he is pursuing the "ideal," Fitzpiers never views Grace as herself, but always as part of an ideal form. She is "a piece of live statuary", or a shrine: Fitzpiers says to her, "'God forbid that I should kneel in another's place at any shrine unfairly'".

Initially, Fitzpiers has no intention of marrying Grace because of her lower social standing, and is merely using her "as an object of contemplation for the present... to keep his soul alive, and to relieve the monotony of his days". Perhaps because of the presence of a rival, though, Fitzpiers' feelings for Grace last longer than they would have ordinarily. At times, for example, he is under the impression that "the Idea had for once completely fulfilled itself in the objective substance - which he had hitherto deemed an impossibility".

This is, however, not the case. He is soon thrown into the path of Felice Charmond, and, as her name suggests, he is immediately charmed by her, feeling the same emotions as when he first saw Grace: "While the scene and the moment were new to him and unanticipated, the sentiment and essence of the moment were indescribably familiar. What could be the cause of it? Probably a dream". Indeed it was a dream, the dream induced by the study of transcendental philosophers at the time of his first meeting with Grace. He is quickly enamoured with Felice Charmond, who he recognises as his psychidion, his soul mate: "He gazed at her in undisguised admiration. Here was a soul of souls!"

The language used to convey this new interest suggests Fitzpiers' Romantic, and also philosophic and scientific, interest: "The intersection of his temporal orbit with Mrs Charmond's for a day or two in the past had created a sentimental interest in her at the time." But finding her now, "in these somewhat romantic circumstances, magnified that bygone and transitory tenderness to indescribable proportions".

That the ideal has moved from Grace to Felice is confirmed when Fitzpiers, on his way to see Felice, quotes the following lines from "Epipsychidion:"

Toward the load-star of my one desire
I flitted, like a dizzy moth, whose flight
Is as a dead leaf's in the owlet light.

At this point in Shelley's poem, the poet is excitedly tracking the ideal figure, oblivious to the fact that he will soon lose sight of the ideal: "But she... Past... Into the dreary cone of our life's shade". So Hardy makes it apparent that Fitzpiers' idealised love for Felice will also pass — what he sees as the essence of love, is not permanently housed in Felice Charmond. This is why Fitzpiers is so easily able to resume his marriage to Grace at the end of the novel.

Fitzpiers idles away much of his time in dreamy contemplation. This is hardly surprising, as we are early told that he prefers the ideal world to the real, and he has little to do in Little Hintock. He is, therefore, strongly imaginative, but in keeping with Hardy's somewhat negative presentation of him, his imagination is more fanciful than imaginative in a Romantic sense.

After learning Grace's identity, "his whole attention was given to objects of the inner eye, all outer regard being quite disdainful" and "he constructed dialogues and scenes in which Grace had turned out to be the mistress of Hintock Manor-house, the mysterious Mrs Charmond, particularly ready and willing to be wooed by himself and nobody else".

The fact of her social class, however, means for Fitzpiers that "personal intercourse" could only take place in "the world of fancy". After he has tired of Grace and become infatuated with Felice, Fitzpiers indulges in similar fanciful musings: "the two or three days that they had spent... above the Neckar were stretched out in retrospect to the length and importance of years; made to form a canvas for infinite fancies, idle dreams, luxurious melancholies, and pretty alluring assertions which could neither be proved nor disproved".

One very humorous, and distinctly Romantic episode occurs when Fitzpiers, after visiting Felice, has been thrown from his horse. Melbury offers him a lift, and Fitzpiers, not recognising his father-in-law, accepts the ride, as well as the proffered rum, which "flew to the young man's head and loosened his tongue". His monologue is both revealing and insulting to Melbury, who eventually throws him from the horse. But not before Hardy has thrown in several Shelleyan allusions. Fitzpiers begins by alluding to himself and his education, "'the poets and I are familiar friends; I used to read more in metaphysics than anybody within fifty miles'". He then describes Felice in lyrical terms "'A passionate soul, as warm as she is clever, as beautiful as she is warm, and as rich as she is beautiful'". Then comes the reference to Shelley: Melbury, angry at Fitzpiers, has begun to clasp him too firmly and Fitzpiers complains: "'I say, old fellow, those claws of yours clutch me rather tight - rather like the eagle's, you know, that ate out the liver of Pro- Pre- the man on Mount Caucasus'". The reference, although to Prometheus generally, is most likely to be to Shelley's verse drama Prometheus Unbound in light of Fitzpiers' close knowledge of other of Shelley's poems: upon seeing Grace he is able to quote nine lines of "The Revolt of Islam".

So what does Hardy intend by this eclectic mix of characteristics, and the ambivalent, half-mocking, half-earnest, presentation of them? Clearly, as a follower of Shelley, Hardy does not encourage us to accept Fitzpiers as a Shelleyan figure. By filling him with quotations, with philosophical ideas, and then making him a thoroughly selfish, unlikeable character, Hardy seems to suggest that the Romantics were flawed. But this is not the case.

A more committed Romantic would have pursued his vision, even if unpractical, rather than compromise in the way Fitzpiers does. Fitzpiers' faults lie in his anti-Romantic qualities — his changeability and his nonchalance. He cannot sustain his ideals, and abandons them when they are no longer practical or profitable.

His marriage to Grace owes much to her dowry and the convenience of living off the Melbury family. His abandonment of Grace is easy when he finds a better object, and his return to her is just as convenient when this object is no longer available.

While creating Fitzpiers largely in order to comment on his flawed Romantic qualities, Hardy also uses Fitzpiers as a type-character, the urban invader, showing how this type perceived rural life. The rest of the novel, however, shows that Fitzpiers' perception is far from accurate. A good example of Fitzpiers' idealised view of rural life occurs in the incident where he observes the woodlanders barking the trees. Fitzpiers is enchanted by their activities, thinking of them in terms of his own entertainment, rather than as people earning a living.

Hardy makes this point explicit, at one point having Fitzpiers look up from his book "to observe the scene and the actors".

This line of thought continues, and Fitzpiers imagines "that he might settle here and become welded in with this sylvan life by marrying Grace Melbury" Once the woodlanders have departed, Fitzpiers lingers: "He dreamed and mused till his consciousness seemed to occupy the whole space of the woodland round, so little was there of jarring sight or sound to hinder perfect mental unity with the sentiment of the place" He again ponders settling in Little Hintock, referring to the "calm contentment" and the "quiet domesticity according to oldest and homeliest notions." His immersion within, and meditation upon, the natural landscape seems Wordsworthian, in that both men are lost in thought while observing the beauty and power of the natural world. But there are grave ironies present in Fitzpiers' meditations: Fitzpiers is blind to the reality of the woods, the violence and struggle going on around him, which everyone but he is aware of. His preconceptions dictate the calm, sylvan appearance of the woods, but as the narrator is at pains to point out, this is not the reality.

To conclude this discussion of The Woodlanders, I will now discuss the elegiac nature of the novel, and why I think this elegiac note contributes to its Romanticism.

As I have just shown, Fitzpiers' effect on Little Hintock is largely negative, and is one factor which contributes to the elegiac feeling of the novel. In marrying Grace, he not only ends her hopes of happiness (Hardy makes it clear that she is happiest when following her natural instincts), but also destroys the hopes of Giles (by forcing him to abandon his own suit for Grace), and Marty (whose love for Giles can never come to fruition because of Giles' death, for which Fitzpiers is partially responsible).

It is appropriate that Hardy should choose to write an elegy at this point of his career. Not only is The Woodlanders written at a time when Hardy's Romantic faith is at its lowest ebb, but his previous novels (A Pair of Blue Eyes and The Return of the Native in particular) have hinted at elegy, and his later novels will reinforce it in a more overt way than this.

The elegiac strands of The Woodlanders are a natural progression in Hardy's career as a novelist.

There are many elements of elegy in The Woodlanders, including the tone, the "funereal dirges" sounded by the trees in the woods, and the poetic quality of the language. The opening paragraph, which sounds the note of nostalgia with mention of the rambler travelling near Hintock "for old association's sake," and the closing scene of Marty's poignant elegy over Giles' grave, frame the tale. Marty's elegy is particularly important. As the final word in the novel, it makes a lasting impression. It also encapsulates Hardy's position, that Giles was "'a good man, and did good things'" but that such goodness is no longer esteemed in modern society.

The mournful goings on in the woods also contribute to the sombreness of mood. In The Woodlanders, Hardy clearly shows that nature can no longer be seen as an idyllic retreat from the urban world (which is the way nature is depicted in Coleridge's "Frost at Midnight," in which Coleridge describes himself as having grown up "in the great city pent 'mid cloisters dim").

Hardy's poem "In a Wood," which he describes as a companion piece to The Woodlanders, clearly contrasts this Romantic view with the Darwinian view.

In the poem, Hardy firstly presents the idea of nature as Romantic idyll. He comes to the wood,

As to a nest;
Dreaming that sylvan peace
Offered the harrowed ease -
Nature a soft release
From men's unrest.

This Romantic view gives way to the actuality, that nature can no longer promise a refuge from the city. The trees, far from content, jostle and destroy each other:

Sycamore shoulders oak,
Bines the slim sapling yoke,
Ivy-spun halters choke
Elms stout and tall.

Another poem, also written for The Woodlanders, again

strikes an elegiac note. "The Pine-Planters," subtitled "Marty South's Elegy," presents Hardy's despair both for the human condition and the condition in the natural world. The newly planted tree,

In this bleak spot,
...will grieve here
Throughout its time
Unable to leave here,
Or change its clime;
Or tell the story,
Of us to-day
When, halt and hoary,
We pass away.

But the most important sense in which I see the novel as an elegy is in its highly poetic quality (an elegy, remember, is generally thought of as a mode of poetry, not prose). William Buckler's article describes the poetics of The Woodlanders, drawing attention to its "organic, verifiable, critical" nature.

The poetic quality of Hardy's language and his poetic vision, not to mention the novel's organicism, its symmetry, and Hardy's impressionistic view of characters, all add weight to the argument for elegy. As Hardy neared the end of his novel-writing career and prepared himself for a life of poetry, it makes sense for him to have thought in increasingly poetic terms, and to have relied more on tone and mood to create atmosphere in his story-telling. The move towards elegy was perhaps initiated by Hardy's increasing disability, in the face of a Darwinian and highly industrialised world, to recapture his early Romantic views of nature. I have earlier demonstrated just how keenly Hardy felt the pain of industrialisation, in my discussion of his essay "The Dorsetshire Labourer."

Not only was Hardy troubled by industrialisation, but the more mature Hardy refused to compromise his poetic vision, and insisted upon revealing the "heart and inner meaning" of whatever he was describing. This "heart and inner meaning" was to become even more intensely elegiac in his final tragic novels, Tess of the d'Urbervilles and in particular Jude the Obscure.

Chapter 9

The Medievalist Impulse of Thomas Hardy

While it is impossible to classify Thomas Hardy as a medievalist in the spirit of the Pre-Raphaelites or Tennyson, it is clear that he maintained an intellectual and literary interest in the period throughout his career. References to matters of medieval interest are evident in his letters and notebooks and his career very nearly begins and ends on a medieval theme. However, in keeping with his unique position as a novelist closing the Victorian period and opening the modern, Hardy's interpretation of the medieval period takes on an urgency and somber tone expressive of the "ache of modernism" his later characters experience.

In Hardy's Wessex, a nostalgic longing for a glorious past becomes a destructive urge that prevents characters from adjusting to the present and, therefore, from evolving into the future. Conversely, a false embrace of "modern" thought cannot stand the strain of everyday life. In the end, characters who do not question the world, neither forcing the premature birth of a new world, nor longing nostalgically for one long dead, are all who emerge unscathed.

In the interest of time, I will focus exclusively on Hardy's final two novels, Tess of the d'Urbervilles and Jude the Obscure. Outside of these two novels, Hardy's chief interest in things medieval can be generally summed up in his architectural background. While he did participate in restoration projects as a young man, it is important to note briefly the contempt in which he later held such efforts. In his

1906 essay, "Memories of Church Restoration," Hardy decries the furor to restore, as such work has denied England the opportunity to mark the passage of history in a proper manner: ".. if all the mediaeval buildings in England had been left as they stood at that date, to incur whatever dilapilations might have befallen them at the hands of time, weather, and general neglect, this country would be richer in specimens to-day than it finds itself to be after the expenditure of millions in a nominal preservation during that period."

In Jude, he introduces this very subject and makes his views bluntly clear and, more importantly, marks just such a passage of time through human history symbolically in the characters of Jude and Tess. Both novels, in very different ways, symbolize the clash between modernity and medievalism and the pain that clash produces in the lives of the individuals.

Tess, in fact, even appears to embrace the pre-Christian elements of Wessex as the very means, perhaps of moving into the future. In Jude, similarly, there is a leaning toward a classical pagan past. However, neither viewpoint is necessarily antithetical to medievalism as pagan religions and rituals lingered in Britain far into the medieval period and classical literature was rediscovered at the close of the Middle Ages.

Tess of the d'Urbervilles presents a dual critique of society, for the clash between worlds is not only the temporal one of pagan, medieval and modern mindsets, but the economic one of class. In Tess, newly- minted middle class aristocracy rapes rural England, now stripped of its prior grandeur. Later, modern socialist thought seeks to remake the rural into a purely idealized illusion, one that has little foundation for success. In the end, one part of this rural ideal is sacrificed, but there is hope for salvation for those who remain, now chastened and stripped of illusions. However, while Hardy was obsessed in both his professional and personal lives with issues of class, this is only one aspect of the dilemma the novel presents. It is over this backdrop of economic conflict that the clash of past and present is played out.

The most basic medieval element of Tess concerns her

descent from an ancient and fallen family, a circumstance that lies at the root of all of Tess's troubles. In fact, every decision and sacrifice Tess makes is for her family's benefit; hence, it seems only natural that family, past and present, should form the foundation of her downfall. The novel opens with Parson Tringham, "the antiquary," and his explanation of Jack Durbeyfield's connection with the ancient line of d'Urbervillie. Involving no money, land, or power, the d'Urberville name is useless.

But its mystique gives the dissipated Jack a reason to celebrate ostentatiously and sets the wheel of Tess's fate spinning forward. It is their mighty connections—and the tangible rewards they hope it brings—that prompt the Durbeyfields to send Tess to "claim kin" with the Stoke-d'Urberville family of Trantridge. While Jack seeks cash, Joan seeks an advantageous marriage for Tess. In other words, Jack's goal is economic while Joan's is emotional and connected to fertility and the earth, an important pagan aspect of the novel.

In her relationships with Alec and Angel, Tess's name becomes a source of shame and, even worse, of destruction. Alec asks her not to use the d'Uberville name, realizing his own false pretensions and trying, in the defensiveness of guilt, to underline the difference between them. Yet, despite her social inferiority, her inherent gentillesse rings true: "'I wish for no better, sir,' said she with something of dignity". For her father, that dignity is ironically most powerfully felt under the influence of Rolliver's brew. As such, spent and probably imagined glory returns to harm the innocent descendants, reiterating Hardy's message that the past has no practical use in the modern world and is only a romantic notion best left to artists and poets.

Tess herself realizes the incongruousness of the distant past in relation to her own present as she scorns her ancestors and "the dance they had led her". In her disdain of her ancient history, she also vows to forget her recent past and to move forward with her life, and so "[s]he dismissed the past—trod upon it and put it out as one treads on a coal that is smouldering and dangerous". However, the honesty of her love for Angel drives her to confess all and her revival of the past becomes her downfall. Angel is unable to assimilate an actual modern situation into his weakly-held modern principles and so he reverts to medieval morality.

In rejecting Tess, he has forgotten his own earlier revelatory observatious of her natural philosophy—one which was as old as the earth, but seemed new when transfigured into modern vocabulary. He is surprised to find the ache of modernism in one so sheltered and "is bewildered to find such a sophisticated consciousness in so simple a nature." Yet, Hardy points out deliberately that what they both feel are "sensations which men and women have vaguely grasped for centuries". Their ache becomes an artificial one, as the unknown future has always stood before humanity, filling them with a confusion of hope and dread.

Despite her rejection of her ancestors, Tess does experience a superstitious hope that their presence may somehow bring her luck at Talbothay's in the first chapter of "The Rally." The mourning for her lost innocence nearly past, "she wondered if some strange good thing might come of her being in her ancestral land...". However, her modern turn of mind soon scoffs at such foolish notious. Her father's ridiculous attachment to his lost glory make it obvious to her that there is nothing for her in the shrouded past of her family. "'Pooh—I have as much of Mother as Father in me!' she said. 'All my prettiness comes from her and she was only a dairymaid.

Hardy had made this very point himself earlier in the novel, remarking that "the personal charms which Tess could boast of were in main part her mother's gift, and therefore unknightly, unhistorical," and Joan even remarks to her husband that Tess's trump card is her face, not her ancestry. Indeed, so useless are the d'Urbervilles that they do not even manage to secure Angel as a dance partner for Tess at the May Day club walking. The irony is later revealed in Angel's romantic fascination with old families which stands in opposition to his philosophical loathing of their past oppressiveness. Hardy's implicit point is that, had Tess the money to stand out from the crowd, she could. have better utilized her ancestry, even with the socialist Angel Clare.

When first she realizes her attraction to Angel, Tess fears her lineage will reduce her in his eyes. She understands that it is her "supposed untraditional newness" that attracts him to her. Yet, for his own part, Angel feels an unexplained sense of nostalgia when he sees her, while simultaneously thinking she is "fresh" and "virginal". His nostalgia is two-fold as he has, in fact, seen her face before at the club walking so many years before. However, he is also feeling a symbolic longing for things past, for things lost—namely, the mystique of Tess's virginity and the pristine name of her forbearers.

His nostalgia becomes a powerful reality once Angel learns of Tess's past. He had, until their wedding night, expressed nothing but delight in her ancestry, even deciding to spend their honeymoon in a d'Urberville mansion. He is fascinated by the contradiction Tess represents to him. She is a child of the soil, a fresh and modern bloom of a girl, but her lineage is older and nobler than his own. Despite his philosophical dislike of such families, he revels in the aura of romance attached to her name. This is an essential contradiction in Angel himself and only an imagined one in Tess.

It is this very fragile philosophical foundation of which Hardy is most critical, so much so that he returns to it in Jude the Obscure. Angel's weakly-held ideals disappear when confronted with the reality of Tess, one which he believes conflicts with his image of her. He immediately blames her much-vaunted ancestry. In his hypocrisy,. he even wonders why, "[w]hen he found out that Tess came of that exhausted ancient line and was not of the new tribes from below, as he had fondly dreamed, [he] had not stoically abandoned her in fidelity to his principles?". Angel conveniently forgets that, in reality, lineage has very little to do with who Tess is. Much later he recants again and reexamines the differences between practical and romantic notions of ancient lines.

In essence, Angel's behaviour is a condemnation of the entire repressive morality of the Victorian period itself; a morality that stood in conflict with the needs of a modem world. A society that would condemn an innocent girl for being raped, as Angel does, is out of step with the natural order, one which Hardy sees as the only viable order for the world. Tess is, in essence, a condemnation of medieval Christian moralities artificially imposed on a modem world.

It is only in the medieval pagan world that woman and nature properly conjoin; Victorian society, not cognizant of woman's role as anything beyond an idealized exemplary one, condemns all that does not conform and is, therefore, in opposition to nature. Hardy continually equates women with the pre-Christian, pagan world of mother earth, while men rule the artificial (and hypocritical) realm of society. Throughout, men condemn Tess—her father, the parson, Angel—while women accept her for who she is. It is no accident that the sole participants in the May Day dance are women, an event that is clearly a pagan celebration.

Hardy later remarks that "women whose chief companions are the forms and forces of outdoor Nature retain in their souls far more of the Pagan fantasy". Tess loses touch with this essential inner voice when she allows herself to be overwhelmed with unfounded shame in her own "ruin." Although "she looked upon herself as a figure of Guilt intruding into the haunts of Innocence... she was quite in accord. She had been made to break an accepted social law, but no law known to the environment in which she fancied herself such an anomaly". The "moral hobgoblins" she fears are connected to the "God of her childhood", implying that Christian religion—with its attendant morality—and Nature are not compatible, a point reiterated by Angel Clare's rejection of Tess. The irony is compounded by their marriage, a Christian regulation of natural urges, in which Angel has vowed to take Tess "for better, for worse."

Tess is last seen in the pagan temple of Stonehenge, another pre-Christian symbol, albeit a man-made one. Tess feels at home here and remarks that not only were her mother's family shepherds, but Angel had often called her a pagan. Tess's conclusion is inevitable and she sleeps upon the stone of sacrifice, despite Angel's efforts to urge her onward. Having urged Angel to marry her sister, she is able to answer the policemen in the affirmative, "'I am ready'". She is indeed ready, for the restrictive and flawed Victorian world with its medieval morality is no fit place for Tess, who remains a pure woman.

While tragic, Tess's fate is expected. The clash of the time she represents with the one she inhabits makes her death almost a relief to the reader. In the hypocritical modern world of Hardy, what Tess represents is antithetical to so-called progress. Yet, there is some hope on Hardy's part that the marriage of modernity—released from the bonds of medieval morality—and pagan medieval pastoralism will give birth to a unified, perfected future.

No such hope remains at the end of Jude the Obscure. In this final novel of Hardy's, only callous modernity emerges unscathed, while those who consciously search for answers are brutally crushed by a hypocritical society. As in Tess, there are empty dreams in bygone things. For Jude, it is the medieval city of Christminster and his romantic perception of what it represents. As noted, Hardy himself had his own romantic attachments to medieval architecture. However, Jude's undoing is his insistence on acting on such attachments—of making romantic notions practical realities. Jude's own medieval Christian temperament suits the ancient Christminster but the town—like the world—has moved on.

Sue Bridehead, on the other hand, is a curious mixture of Classical paganism and free-thinking modernity. Unfortunately, like Jude and Angel Clare before him, her attitudes are tenuously held and fragilely defined. Under stress, she experiences a reversal of Jude's own reaction—he becomes modern, rejecting Christianity, while she embraces religion with hysterical fervor. In and out of their lives passes Jude's wife Arabella, who emerges from an apparently sheltered rural background to represent the true modernity in the novel.

Not uncommonly for Hardy, the most looming presence in Jude is the town of Christminster and the secondary other towns through which Jude passes. These towns not only give Hardy an opportunity to make use of stone masonry—and hence Gothic restoration—as Jude's profession, but also to employ settings as symbols of the useless romanticized past. The first old town that fails to meet Jude's needs is Marygreen. Though rural and backward, the town was no stranger to Hardy's despised enemy, radical restoration. Being artificially gothic, Marygreen clashes with Jude's sincerely medieval temperament.

He pines instead after the city "veiled in mist"—his Avalon, Christminster. Every decision that Jude consciously makes from the moment he first sees the town is calculated to place him inside the city gates. He learns Latin and Greek and apprentices as a stone mason so that he can be near the colleges. Hardy deliberately uses Jude's training, and his expertise in every kind of masonry, to further illustrate Jude's complete blindness to the reality of Christminster. Trained to know better, he ignores the signs of falsehood, signs that go deeper than the false faces of buildings.

Approaching the first "mediaeval pile," Hardy remarks, "[w]hen he passed objects out of harmony with its general expression he allowed his eyes to slip over them as if he did not see them". Jude does realize that mainly "copying, patching, and imitating went on here," but he attributes it to a "temporary and local cause". Blinded by his dreams, "[he] did not at that time see that mediaevalism was as dead as a fernleaf in a lump of coal; that other developments were shaping in the world around him, in which Gothic architecture and its associations had no place".

In this particular passage, Hardy finally makes completely explicit the lesson he symbolically presented in Tess. "The deadly animosity of contemporary logic and vision towards so much of what he held in reverence was not yet revealed to him" Like Tess, Jude represents an earlier time, one which is incompatible with Victorian modernity. However, Tess's medieval paganism is Hardy's own answer to modernity, the only salvation he can find to society's hypocrisy. Jude, on the other hand, initially represents Christian medievalism, which is antagonistic to future social progress in two ways. Firstly, the revitalization of lost and probably illusory ideals is impractical in Hardy's view.

It is akin to Gothic restoration, as to do so is to artificially halt the natural passage of history. So contradictory are the two that Hardy emphasizes the "rottenness" of Christminster's buildings, writing "[it] seemed impossible that modern thought could house itself in such decrepit and superseded chambers". Secondly, Hardy obviously finds Christian society to be repressive, hypocritical and dangerously patriarchal.

It is through the character of Sue Bridehead that Hardy confronts the issue of religion and the related one of marriage. She lacks respect for Christminster and what it represents as she does for most institutions. Sue rearranges his Bible chronologically and later, she pushes him to reject Christminster itself as outdated and old-fashioned. "'An intellect at Christminster is new wine in old bottles. The mediaevalism of Christminster must go, be sloughed off, or Christminster itself will have to go'". She admits to a grudging nostalgic fondness for what it represents, but her practicality outweighs such sentimentality for a romanticized past. For Sue, such a past includes pursuit of the holy orders Jude hopes to take, in her eyes another outmoded tradition. Yet, her rejection of what Jude holds sacred is too strident, nearly hysterical and, ultimately, untenable. Like Angel Clare, she has defined herself in opposition to the world, believing herself to be modern. But a negation does not a philosophy make and under stress the foundation crumbles.

Sue is deliberately antagonistic to the hypocritical Middle Age mentality she must endure in the society she inhabits. Hardy illustrates the essential incompatibility of medieval and modern when Jude and Sue quarrel over her promise to marry Phillotson. While he longs to sit in a cathedral for comfort, while she turns to the railway station. Jude marvels at her modern attitude, yet Sue sees herself as a negation rather than a creation of civilization, remarking "'I am not modern, either. I am more ancient than mediaevalism, if you only knew'". She sees herself as a Classical pagan, in her mind the antithesis of all modern culture represents. Yet her efforts to flaunt her paganism are childish and ineffectual. She impulsively buys the statues of the god and goddess of sexual desire but keeps them hidden within her very Christian room. Her purchase has made her feel daring, but her secrecy negates the negation she believes she is achieving.

Sue's other attempts at negating modemity are equally destructive. Her views of marriage are extremely liberated in one sense, but her repressed sexuality makes her liberation illusory. Marrying Phillotson she sees as a show of her freedom. Her inability to consummate the marriage, however, imprisons them both in repressed tension.

When she leaves Richard for Jude, an extremely modern action, her continued repression causes similar anguish. When she eventually agrees to sleep with Jude, her timidity and regrets run counter to the very free-thinking modern concept of pre-marital sex. Rather than a positive urge to revitalize a dynamic pagan philosophy, Sue instead sees a negative; an absence of action, morality, and structure. In the end, she is reduced to a paranoid fear of the very thing she has fought against through the entire book. In essence, she has negated herself. Jude, on the other hand, finally sees a truth in Sue's abandoned philosophy, but in so doing, he also negates the self he has always been. The two characters who survive the philosophical clash are the erstwhile spouses, Arabella Donn and Richard Phillotson. While the character of Phillotson is difficult to categorize so simply, both are perhaps the only true moderns in the novel.

Arabella personifies all that is negative in the modern world, yet ironically she passes though it unscathed. She is from a rural background, much like Tess, but has worked in a tavern before she meets Jude and returns to this occupation to support herself after she ends her bigamous union in Australia. A woman preferring work to the support of a man is a modern enough concept, but her chosen occupation underlines her extreme liberation. As physical desire personified, Arabella embodies the ultimate freedom of the modern woman—earthy, capable, and independent—but her heartlesssness makes her modernity distasteful. Like Arabella, Richard Phillotson represents modernity. Their positions in the novel are parallel in that they are both ill-chosen and unwanted spouses. However, Phillotson's role is in opposition to Arabella's own as he is the voice of modern progress. He is an older man, a victim of the same disappointment Jude experiences in Christminster. Unlike Jude, he does not allow his dreams to defeat him. He is stable, responsible, caring; philosophically, however, Richard is very progressive. He weighs Sue's happiness against his own and allows her to leave him for Jude, even at the expense of his own professional and social reputation.

As Arabella seems to represent the individual negativity possible in modern thought—the selfishness and callousness too much individuality can engender—Phillotson is the positive side of the coin. Unfortunately for him, his modernity is not the sort rewarded by his repressive society with its medieval standards of morality. He has made his personal dealings in an open and honest way, as had Tess, and he pays. As his own reward, however, Phillotson survives. The resolution of both novels is bleak, yet Hardy offers a small glimmer of hope; one which requires the abandonment of medieval Christian principles. The repression and hypocrisy such ideals naturally engender in modern society constitute a force of destruction, one which crushes the individual will, resulting in misery. Like the falseness inherent in radical restoration or in a modern enthusiasm for Gothic architecture, medieval morality is a force that has survived past its time.

For Hardy, there is a great deal to admire in the distant past. But, beautiful as it may be, the natural order is toward progress. As renewing crumbling medieval edifices robs humanity of true knowledge of its past and the opportunity to move forward architecturally, so the act of clinging to outmoded moralities denies society the ability to progress intellectually. Through sloughing off the Christminsters of the world and all they represent, the wine of human experience can be uncorked and free to age, spilling over fruitfully into the living world.

Chapter 10

View of Life Through The Return of the Native

The Return of the Native, by Thomas Hardy, begins with personification of a majestic heath, the setting for this novel: "The face of the heath by its mere complexion added half an hour to evening; it could... retard the dawn, sadden noon, anticipate the frowning of storms... and intensify the opacity of a moonless midnight to a cause of shaking and dread."

Yet these emotionally intense descriptions are extremely misleading, for in reality the heath is an inanimate object which possesses no feelings, opinions, or biases. It is an immortal place, and continues to exist as its inhabitants live their lives and die. In contrast with the heath is man himself: mortal and vulnerable, selfish, and always looking to advance his place in the world. This novel shows the dominance of nature over man, stressing man's impermanence against the infinity of nature.

This belief, also known as fatalism, is emphasized throughout the novel. This view is shared by the character of Clym Yeobright, who survives at the end of the story, but is contrasted by Eustacia Vye, who rebels against these ideas, leading to her own downfall.

The views of these characters are emphasized through their own actions, their interactions with other characters in the book, allusions to biblical references, and the use of motifs. Fatalistic views can best be illustrated through Clym Yeobright's character and relationships with the other characters of the novel. On his own, Clym believes that everyone's lives are predetermined, and that fate will direct what will happen to a person. Because of this, Clym is able to constantly revise his lifestyle to adapt to what his life brings to him.

He takes all of his successes and failures in stride, because he knows within his life there is an underlying reason and plan for what is happening. His first big life change occurs when he decided that life in Paris was not for him, and that he must return to his native land, and live his life on the heath. This is almost like a birthright, for although he is an extraordinary person, shown through his description, at heart he is a man of the heath.

Clym is again forced to make a modification in his lifestyle when he is blinded. This is a major set-back to Clym's plans of setting up a school to educate the people of the heath. But, instead of being devastated by it, as Eustacia is, Clym decides to continue on with his life as best he can in spite of this new obstacle.

Although he is an exceptional person, Clym finds no shame in becoming a furze-cutter, the typical job of a heathsman. He even enjoys the job, as, "the monotony of his occupation soothed him, and was in itself a pleasure... [his] effort offered homely courses." Clym's enjoyment of his new work shows that he is at peace with physis, and he sings songs of delight while working. This flexibility that Clym shows in his lifestyle exemplifies his notion of fatalism, and shows how he survives life on the heath.

During the novel, there is an allusion to Oedipus, "[Clym's] mouth had passed into the phase more or less imaginatively rendered in the studies of Oedipus." This allusion is really the mention of Clym's partial parallel, as he is very much like Oedipus in numerous ways. In the tale of Oedipus, he gouges his eyes out when he finds out that he married his mother; Clym's equivalent is that he is blind.

When Oedipus first came back to the town of his birth, the people lauded him as a hero and gave him the gift of the queen; later, however, when the truth was discovered that the queen was really Oedipus' mother, it caused much harm and bad happenings. Likewise, everyone on the heath is very happy to have Clym return from Paris, but after a while, his return causes disturbances on the heath, and leads indirectly to the deaths of Mrs. Yeobright, Eustacia, and Wildeve.

In addition, it is suspected that Clym has an Oedipus complex, and that name is derived from Oedipus' marriage to his mother. This shows fatalism because the entire story of Oedipus is based on a series of omens (which told of his fate), and miscommunications. Because Oedipus is a partial parallel to Clym, Clym's return to the heath can be seen as being predetermined, as Oedipus' life was based on fate as well. Fatalism is also shown through the people of the heath.

The people who live there are innocent and simple, trying to cope with their day-to-day struggles as best they can. Their dialect, which is simple and softly accented, illustrates their naturalness, "'Twas to be if ëtwas, I suppose.'" These people lead menial lives; still they accept, and are content with, whatever comes their way. This is a part of what makes them so innocent. It is this fatalistic approach that allows them to survive live on a place like the heath, and to be happy and at-one with nature.

One way they try to cope with this harsh, rustic lifestyle is through rituals. Their annual November 5 bonfire introduces the heathfolk into the story. This bonfire is their way of trying to lighten the darkness of the coming winter, which could be symbolic of the dismal lives they lead. They enjoy dancing around the bonfire in a circle, and, even after the fire goes out, they continue with their dance, showing of their untold peace with nature.

Dancing seems to be a common practice at most other special events: "'You be bound to dance at Christmas because ëtis the time o' year; you must dance at weddings because ëtis the time o' life. At christenings folk will even smuggle in a reel or two...'" These dances help to put hope and good times into the heathfolks' lives and to be together as a community.

Thomasin could also be considered as a person of the heath, for she is simple and natural, and abides by the laws of nature. Thomasin is first described as possessing, "A fair, sweet, and honest country face... reposing in a nest of wavy chestnut hair... The grief had... abstracted nothing of the bloom. The scarlet of her lips had not had time to abate..." These numerous references, (country, nest, chestnut, bloom, scarlet (as in berries)), illustrates how Thomasin was very much in accordance with nature.

Thomasin reveals her fatalistic views when dealing with her relationship with Wildeve. Although she knows that it is not truly in her best interest after their non-marriage, Thomasin agrees to marry Wildeve again. She realizes that if she does not marry Wildeve that the heathfolk will gossip about her and Clym will be ashamed.

This self-consciousness helps her stay on-track with her fate. She accepts Wildeve's second marriage proposal with the following view: "'I agreed to it... [because] I am a practical woman now. I do not believe in hearts at all. I would marry him under any circumstances...'" Throughout the novel, Thomasin goes along with her fate, and is rewarded with happiness at the end of the story through her second marriage. However, not all heathpeople are as in sync with nature as Thomasin. Christian Cantle's character shows views opposing fatalism. This is a very superstitious man who is afraid of most everything. Basically, his fears take him out-of-line with fate, yet it is also his fears that put him back on-track.

This is illustrated during the November 5 bonfire. When darkness comes, Christian is the only person who suggests that all the heathfolk head home right away and that, "Fifth-of Novembers ought [not] to be kept up by night except in towns. It should be by day in outstep, ill-accounted places like this!" This suggestion is spurned by the universal human fear of the dark and unknown. However, what he is suggesting would break rituals, which are the way for the heathfolk to cope in their fatalistic society. However, the other heathfolk tell him that is a foolish idea. Christian's low self-esteem gives him fear of speaking out against them, and he returns to his fated course. Another time, Christian's extreme superstitious nature leads to rebellion as well.

When he wins a raffle on the way to delivering guineas

to Clym and Thomasin, Christian thinks that this is a sign that he is lucky. Although he has no wife or girlfriend, his prize of a gown-piece elates him. This leads to his game with Wildeve in which he lost all of the guineas that were supposed to be delivered directly to Thomasin and Clym. His superstitious nature allowed him to get involved in something so risky, but, despite his flaws and mistakes, Christian is basically at-peace with nature, and feels very much at home on the heath.

In contrast with Clym's ability to accommodate his life to survive the heath, his mother, Mrs. Yeobright, cannot fulfill her ananke, as she goes against her fate, and, consequently, dies. This occurs when Mrs. Yeobright's fatal flaw is revealed; she has a bad habit of meddling into her children's affairs. When this is combined with her ananke, which is to bare the burden of Thomasin and Clym, it leads to disaster.

She, like most other heath people, disapprove of Eustacia Vye, and when she finds out that Clym is interested in her, is unhappy. One day, when she and Clym are walking on the heath, they separate; Clym heads to Mistover Knap to see Eustacia, while Mrs. Yeobright's destination is for the Quiet Woman Inn. Mistover Knap is representative as a place for outsiders, and Mrs. Yeobright is burdened because she knows that Clym is on the wrong path.

This separation to different places on the heath is also symbolic of the start of a spiritual separation between Mrs. Yeobright and Clym that will never fully be resolved. After this, Mrs. Yeobright's meddling becomes an issue when she interferes between Thomasin and Wildeve's marriage by plotting to give Thomasin money unbeknownst to Wildeve.

This use of money, which is an unnatural substance, goes against physis, and causes sinister happenings to occur. The money causes a slew of misunderstandings and coincidences which lead to Mrs. Yeobright's journey to Clym's house. The "closed door incident" is too much of a burden for Mrs. Yeobright, and she is at the point of being unable to continue to fulfill her ananke.

Her dying words are, "I have a burden which is more than I can bare." This leads to the establishment of Clym's ananke, which is to bare the burden of his mother's death. This is quite ironic because his mother's ananke was to bare the burden of him; in a way, they have reversed roles.

Although Mrs. Yeobright could not fulfill her ananke because of her fatal flaw of meddling, because Clym holds fatalistic views and can easily adapt to new obstacles in life, he is able to continue to flourish on the heath. Contrary to Clym, Eustacia Vye held rebelled against fatalistic views.

Her dream is leave the heath, which she feels she doesn't belong in. Ironically, her ananke is to stay on the heath. This discrepancy between fate and Eustacia's rebellion of, or misconceived notions about, her fate, are shown immediately with her introduction.

When she is first incorporated into the story, she is standing on top of a high hill. Hardy decides to introduce Eustacia as being higher than nature, almost superhuman, a goddess. She is observed to be so high in the air that, "nothing that could be mapped anywhere else on the celestial globe."

It being twilight, the way the sun reflects onto the hill, Eustacia's observer cannot distinguish where the hill ends and Eustacia begins. Hardy says that Eustacia gave the hills a "perfect, delicate, and necessary finish." Eustacia is truly meant to be a part of nature.

But, as incredible as she looks as a part of nature, she moves, and the effect on the hill is palpable: "...the discontinuance of immobility in any quarter suggested confusion... The figure perceptibly... shifted a step or two... [resulting in] displacement..."

Eustacia's movements were awkward, and disturbed the beauty of nature that she should have beautified. Her awkwardness in this scene is symbolic of her rebellion against nature and her fate. It also shows the irony of how this superhuman character who should be the goddess of nature, decides to rebel against her subjects.

This introductory scene sums up Eustacia's fatal flaw and foreshadows her conflict with the heath. Besides being a goddess of nature, there is an allusion to the "Queen of Love", symbolic of Eustacia. There is something about Eustacia that makes men fall in love with her. As she rebels against being the goddess of nature, she also abuses her privileges of being the Queen of Love. The combination of her rebellion and abuse leads Eustacia to whatever she wants, illustrated through Wildeve, Clym, and Charley. It was destined that Wildeve would marry Thomasin. However, Eustacia could not accept this, because she wanted to prove she could be with Wildeve if she so wanted.

On the night of his wedding, Eustacia sets a bonfire as a signal to him to meet her. Being the Queen of Love, naturally Wildeve cannot turn down this summoning. Besides interfering with fate, (Thomasin and Wildeve's), she uses the bonfire, a symbol of the innocence of the heathpeople, and turns it into a sign of corruption. Even after Wildeve and Thomasin's marriage, she stays in contact with Wildeve, and, when she gets depressed over the fact that Clym will not, or cannot, leave the heath, Eustacia falls back on Wildeve to get her out. Eustacia should never have been in contact with Wildeve after his proposal to Thomasin, because he and Thomasin are destined to be together. This refusal to accept fate leads to sneaking around, Mrs. Yeobright's death, Thomasin's suspicions, Clym's anger, and, ultimately, Eustacia's death.

Just as Wildeve cannot resist helping Eustacia when she needs a favour, Charley, a young heathman, has the same problem. He is infatuated by Eustacia and will do anything for her. While Charley only holds a small part in the book, his entire role consists of helping Eustacia. When Eustacia wants to dress as a mummer to get into the Yeobright Christmas party to see Clym, Charley is more than willing to help her for the price of fifteen minutes of holding Eustacia's hand. When his fifteen minutes are up, Charley is regretful that he used all fifteen minutes and can barely let go of Eustacia's hand.

Although Eustacia could care less about Charley, this admiration adds to her conceit that she can have any man she wants, including Clym. Later in the book, Charley sees Eustacia gazing at the guns in her grandfather's house, contemplating suicide. At this point Eustacia has hit rock bottom, and, protectively, Charley locks up the guns in the stable.

It is Charley's love of Eustacia, and his heathfolk innocence, which keeps her alive; he doesn't just physically prevent her potential suicide, but shows her that people still care about her.

Although still depressed, Eustacia's small rejuvenation allows her go on, but leads her to plot with Wildeve to go to Budmouth. Once again Eustacia is trying to leave the heath. When this materializes, and she is about to leave for Budmouth, she dies, because the heath cannot allow even a goddess to go against fate and break her ananke. In regards to Clym, Eustacia's flaws included over-confidence and an abuse of her position as the Queen of Love.

When Eustacia finds out that Clym is returning to the heath, she immediately knows that she will be with him. It is at this point that she hastily tells Wildeve that she will not marry him. This frees her for Clym, who she thinks will bring her to Paris, a life that she dreams of constantly. Eustacia does not have any doubts that Clym will not think twice before fulfilling her wishes, even before they have met. When they finally encounter each other, Eustacia and Clym's fascinations are mutual.

However, they are so infatuated with each other that neither of them listens to each other's wishes, and there is unspoken hostility; Clym plans to stay on the heath and set up a school for the heathpeople, whereas Eustacia thinks that Clym is going to be her knight, and sweep her away to Paris. Eustacia is so conceited and used to everyone doing whatever she wants she believes that Clym will eventually abide by her wishes, even if they conflict with his own.

But this is not what happens, as Clym is no ordinary person. Clym's ananke becomes clear when Mrs. Yeobright dies, and he knows he must stay on the heath to bare the burden of his mother's death. He is not as quick to yield to another's wishes without considering his ananke, which cannot be fulfilled if he journeys abroad.

Even so, Eustacia still has hopes of Paris until Clym goes blind. At this time, she realizes that they will never leave the heath, and that their marriage isn't working out. When Eustacia hears Clym singing while working as a furze-cutter, she cannot take it anymore. Eustacia becomes crazed, and leaves Clym. Once again her conceit overwhelms her, as she feels she is better than having a furze-cutter for a husband, and feels that Clym should feel the same way.

Eustacia could have lived as the goddess of nature and the Queen of Love and accepted the life that was given to her on the heath if she would have abided by her fate. But, her narcissism and pride, hybris, made Eustacia think that she was better than the people of the heath, and she viewed her surroundings with condescension.

Eustacia was an extraordinary person; she was supposed to help the heath, not belittle it. When she tried to escape with Wildeve, her ananke was clearly being broken, and the result was death. Eustacia fought against the inevitable, which was one argument that even she was not above. However, Eustacia lead a life of torment as an outsider, because she held different beliefs and dreams than the average heathperson.

Yet, in her death, Eustacia was happy and peaceful. The description of Eustacia's dead body car.ries a reference to light, "...her complexion... seemed more than whiteness; it was almost light." Her expression is described as "pleasant", and following descriptions carry references to nature, with the words "country" and "forest". These all hold positive connotations, and I believe that with her death, she was ironically happy, peaceful, and finally in-sync with nature. She was at last free of the dejectedness of the heath.

In a story based on the greatness of nature and preaching the goodness of a simple life, Thomas Hardy's fatalistic views can be summed up with the appropriately primitive theory of survival of the fittest. Those on the heath that followed fate and could adapt to their surroundings, (Clym, Thomasin, Christian, and the heathfolk), survived.

On the reverse side, those on the heath who could not deal with traditional life, (Mrs. Yeobright, Wildeve, and Eustacia), perished, leaving room for new and potentially better citizens to occupy their places.

Through Clym and Eustacia's actions and interactions with other characters in the book, Hardy shows that he favors this view and tries to emphasize that individuals should not rebel against fate, because, as the word implies, it is inevitable.

The heath will be forever; mankind is only transitory. Instead of unhappy rebellion, man should aim for the most of what life offers in one's lifetime, and a happy, fulfilling existence will follow.

Chapter 11

Arthur Hopkins on "The Return of the Native"

The growth of illustration in periodicals is... part of the pattern of popular fiction, although to what extent it increased readership is a moot point. Certainly it rapidly increased after the great era of wood engraving associated with the forties and fifties....... publishers found they could provide pictorial accompaniment to text more cheaply as mass production cut costs. Where in the forties and fifties a publisher might see roughly £120 of the £400 spent on a 30,000 run of a monthly serial going for illustrations, by the sixties his costs were cut by one-third.

In Illustration and the Novels of Thomas Hardy, Arlene M. Jackson notes that in the 1860s and 1870s "The illustrations for Belgravia and other magazines... often cost £2-3 per square inch for drawing and engraving". Given the relative costs of illustration versus text, it is perhaps not surprising that in its table of contents Belgravia gave prominence to its "List of Illustrations": "The magazine was proud to announce to its audience that artists such as Fred Barnard, Arthur Hopkins, and R. Caldecott were among its contributors".

Such illustrators of the realistic school helped the reader suspend disbelief and focussed on dramatic moments in the text, avoiding morally 'unsafe' scenes and issues. Thus, the mimetic illustrations tended to make even so daring a story as The Return of the Native, with its obvious parallels to Flaubert's Madame Bovary, acceptable to the broad readership that Hardy had to address if he were to remain a professional writer of prose and turn his back forever on architecture. Having had his manuscript of The Return of the Native rejected by the prestigious Cornhill, which had carried the pastoral Far From the Madding Crowd in 1874 and which from its inception in 1860 had published such prominent writers Thackeray and Trollope, the even more illustrious Blackwood's and even its rival, Temple Bar, Hardy (wishing to avoid Tinsley's Magazine, which in 1872 had published A Pair of Blue Eyes) now tried Belgravia, A Magazine of Fashion and Amusement. Dalziel notes the incongruity of a story about characters described by contemporary reviewers as of "low social position" appearing in a magazine whose pretentious title was intended to attract lower-middle-class readers wishing to move vicariously in fashionable, upper-class society....

Although by 1870 the British reading public by Terry's estimate numbered perhaps 200,000, Hardy had had little success in marketing his early novels until he had serialised Far From the Madding Crowd, which like many other Hardy stories bears striking resemblance in some respects (including bigamy, illegitimacy, and fraud) to the sensation novels of M. E. Braddon and James Payne. However, by 1888 Mudie's Catalogue listed eleven titles of Thomas Hardy, a number of works equal to those of George Meredith‹a respectable showing, though well behind R. Ballantyne's 39 titles. One may well wonder to what extent Hardy's being, as he once remarked to Cornhill editor Leslie Stephen, "a good hand at a serial" helped boost his popularity. Certainly being published in Belgravia, which also brought out in serial such works of Collins as The Haunted Hotel, must have led to his popular acceptance as an entertaining as opposed to a merely instructive writer.

And an important part of that appeal to a mass readership must have been the illustrations aççompanying the dozen or more serial instalments of novels running in Belgravia. As Meisel observes in Realizations, these monthly illustrations must have "helped immensely to bridge the intervals..., and found a use, during the accumulation of monthly parts..., as a handy aide-mémoire". The image is far more lasting, in fact, than the momentary impressions of scene and character derived from the initial reading, and may connote more than the text itself denoted. "The collaboration of picture and text in the art of the novel is thus ultimately an attribute of style [i. e., the artist's interpretation of the text], operating as a presence and influence in the language as well as in the narrative organization".

These pictorial influences, however, have been weighed by only a handful of Hardy's modern critics, who have experienced his novels in volume rather than magazine format. Even when a modern attempts to experience Hardy as his first nineteenth-century readers would have done, reading the chapters in their original serial groupings and pausing to reflect and anticipate as the magazine reader would have done, without the illustrations that initial reading cannot be recreated. The difference between a part-reading in volume and an authentic serial reading is that the illustrations, published usually as frontispieces or to face a particular page, condition the reader's response to the text, causing him to compare 'word- picture' to plate.

In fact, out of the twelve illustrations for The Return of the Native, eleven are intended to depict specific moments, as the quotations which serve as the picture-titles suggest. Although they set the scene, providing both background details and strong notions about the appearance and behaviours of certain characters, the serial illustrations do not necessarily curtail the imaginative experience. Rather, they fix certain scenes in the mind as benchmarks of the story's action, telegraphing to the reader what one sensitive reader has felt are memorable in the coming instalment.

Then, too, an initial illustration tends to provide the reader with a "realization"..; that is, the reader, having scene the picture, awaits its arrival in the lines of the text, so that the passage illustrated provides a moment of stasis, of reflection, and possibly even of comparison between the artist's and reader's conceptions the scene. The reader must then mediate between the two images. The graphic artist therefore was not merely complementing the work of the novelist, but was acting as co-presenter and interpreter. The collaborative project of an illustrated, serialised story required personal harmony and aesthetic agreement between the two.

Whereas much is known about the relationships between certain nineteenth-century collaborative pairs‹for example, between Dickens and his illustrators from The Pilgrim Edition of Dickens' collected correspondence‹little is known about the connections between Hardy and his serial illustrators, owing to the limited number of Hardy's letters that have survived. However, the record of each artist's work affords certain clues about the relationship, as in the Christmas mumming scene, which Arthur Hopkins illustrated operating on certain cues that Hardy had provided. In the absence of information that would reveal the extent of collaboration between an illustrator and a novelist, one is forced to examine the relationships between the text and the accompanying pictures, just as the Victorian readers of such magazines as The Belgravia and The Graphic would.

At the time of his brief collaboration with Hardy, Hopkins (1848-1930) was living at Notting Hill. In 1875 he had exhibited his first painting, "The Mowers," at The Royal Academy; there followed "The Call to Supper" (1876), "The Quay," and "The Plough" (1877). "Though still a relative newcomer at the time when Chatto and Windus first commissioned work from him in 1877, he had already established a reputation through his contributions to such leading periodicals as the Cornhill, Good Words, the Graphic, and the Illustrated London News".

An admirer of John Everett Millais, Hopkins possessed both the dramatic flair predilection for depicting scenes from country life that the illustrations for Hardy's novel would require. Jackson asserts that "he was not personally selected by Hardy but received the commission by virtue of his position as staff illustrator for Belgravia ". Since Hopkins has only one plate in volume 34 of Belgravia prior to the start of the Hardy novel, he was likely working on projects for other publications earlier in 1877. It is possible that the work he showed in 1878, "The Apple Loft," is related to his April, 1878, illustration for

The Return of The Native, in which he depicts a melancholy Thomasin in just such a location. Hardy wrote Hopkins that he thought that illustration particularly good.

The letters from Thomas Hardy to Hopkins in his capacity as Belgravia 's illustrator reveal that the artist was not familiar with the entire text of The Return of the Native, but was having to work with one installment at a time. Hardy thus felt it necessary to explain to the artist the main threads of the plot and the relationships between the principal characters, and to provide sketches of a mummer's clothing and staff, which the artist subsequently employed to revise the May illustration, to which Hardy's second letter reacts. "I am glad to receive a letter from you," Hardy wrote Hopkins on February 8th, "for it is more satisfactory when artist and author are in correspondence". Consequently, even if Hopkins was hardly playing Phiz to Hardy's Boz, the two were in a collaborative relationship, although undoubtedly one arranged not by themselves, but by the co-editors of Belgravia.

HARDY'S NOVELS OFTEN HAVE ILLUSTRATIONS IN PERIODICAL BUT NOT BOOK FORM

Smith, Elder did not use the serial plates for the triple-decker edition of The Trumpet-Major (26 October 1880). The omission of serial illustrations was usual, but by no means absolute. While the three-volume edition of The Return of the Native in 1878 did not include any of Arthur Hopkins' Belgravia plates, the Smith, Elder edition of The Hand of Ethelberta (two volumes, 1876) used both Du Maurier's Cornhill vignettes and his full-page plates.

Although Smith, Elder (the publishers of The Cornhil) utilized all twelve of Helen Patterson Allingham's full-page plates from their magazine for three-volume edition of Far from the Madding Crowd (1874), they reproduced none of her vignettes. On the other hand, Du Maurier's Laodicean plates from Harper's (1880-1), Reinhart's Romantic Adventures of a Milkmaid plates from The Graphic (1883), Paget's Well-Beloved plates from The Illustrated London News (1892), Hatherell's Jude the Obscure plates for Harper's (1894-5), and most notably Herkomer and associates' plates for Tess of the D'Urbervilles in The Graphic (1891) did not appear in the subsequent volume editions of those serialised novels. In the instance of The Graphic plates, the large-format illustrations did not lend themselves to the medium of the conventional volume.

Such an explanation, however, is not feasible for the plates of either The Return of the Native or The Trumpet-Major since Belgravia and Good Words were small format literary monthlies whose plates could easily have been adapted to suit volume publication. Norman Page suggests that "the illustrating of serialized fiction was a publishing convention rather than a deliberate choice made by the novelist". If Hardy published in a non-illustrated journal such as The Atlantic Monthly, there were naturally be no illustrations prepared for the serial.

Illustrator George Du Maurier offers a further explanation for the general lack of illustrations in the volumes of Hardy's Wessex Novels: the more affluent (and, therefore, presumably better educated) reader of books "visualises what he reads (at the moment of reading) with the mind's eye... in a manner so satisfactory to himself that he wants the help of no picture; indeed, to him a picture would be a hindrance". The preponderance of the reading public, including the majority of serial readers, argues Du Maurier, "do not possess this gift, and it is for their greater happiness that the illustrator exists and plies his trade."

Yet another theory as to why illustrations for Hardy's novels in periodicals did not always find their way into the first volume edition is advanced by Arlene Jackson, who asserts that the double or triple-column format of Victorian literary magazines made possible a more precise positioning of plates than book layout permitted.

While greater care could be given to book illustrations, there were certain aesthetic advantages in magazine illustration. One of the disadvantages of book illustration was the separation of the engraving from the text when it was printed on a separate page, particularly when it was printed on a different and better grade of paper than that used for the text. Often a blank page or a sheet of facing tissue separated the book illustration from the text. Sometimes the format called for the book to be turned sideways in order to view the illustration.

In the magazines, and especially newspapers such as The Illustrated London News, the engraving often appeared on the same page as the text, and was thus well integrated with the story it accompanied. Thus, the illustrated Victorian periodical achieved a narrative-pictorial synthesis that book publishers found it difficult to emulate, the exception being the Christmas Books of Charles Dickens, small, expensive propositions that featured illustrations dropped with great accuracy into the accompanying (and complementary) letter-press.

Thus, rural and working class readers in Great Britain (and presumably immigrant English-as-Second-Language readers in America) found that the illustrated magazine supported their reading more than did conventional books, cost far less than bound volumes, and offered better value in that, in addition to a serial instalment, the magazine would feature a plethora of other articles and illustrations, often of the "educational" or "improving" type such as John Wood's on natural history.

The principal consumer of published books (particularly novels) in the United Kingdom were fee-based commercial circulating libraries such as Mudie's Select Lending Library (1842-1937); in 1880, this firm actually chose to purchase bound copies of Good Words in order to stock its regional centres with copies of The Trumpet-Major instead of buying the Smith, Elder triple-decker‹ironically, the very book format favoured by libraries such as Lane's Minerva, Booth's, and Mudie's, which bought at substantial discount from publishers. Apparently Walter Besant, concerned that his All in a Garden Fair (1883) was about to meet the same fate from Mudie's as The Trumpet-Major, had telegraphed Hardy to clarify what had happened to his book three years earlier.

Hardy replied:

I have been trying to recollect since more particularly

about the Trumpet Major‹but I can only recall the fact that I was disappointed in the number Mudie subscribed for‹considering the general success of the book‹and it is probable that I now know for the first time the true reason‹that they were waiting for the magazine‹but did not say so..... Now that nearly all the magazines are pubd at 6d it will be very awkward for us‹Country subscribers to the libraries are often supplied with a serial story cut from the magazine‹and bound up.

Little wonder, then, that of the initial run of a thousand copies printed by Smith, Elder on 26 October, 1880, by "the beginning of 1883 there remained unsold 250 unbound quires and 53 cloth-bound sets of the novel".

Chapter 12

Literary Analysis on "Return of the Native"

"Never was harmony more perfect than that between the chaos of her mind and the chaos of the world withoutBetween the drippings of the rain from her umbrella to her mantle, from her mantle, to the heather, from the heather to the earth, very similar sounds could be heard coming from her lips; and the tearfulness of the outer scene was repeated upon her face. The wings of her soul were broken by the cruel obstructiveness of all about her". What words of analysis and criticism can a reader offer to a novel filled with lines such as these? Thomas Hardy's masterpiece, "The Return of the Native," is a testament to the possibilities and pulchritude of the English language as well as to the complexities of beauty, happiness, and the human nature and its inevitable path to tragedy.

As Hardy paints a backdrop for his tale and begins to develop a society of incredibly intricate characters, he twists in several subtle and symbolic themes into an already profound novel. Most notably, he introduces the novel's setting, the temperamental heath, as a key character. Hardy effectively personifies both the literal and social environments of his story as the Heath in this brilliant novel that thrives on symbolic ambiguity and contradicting perceptions. "The Return of the Native" is composed of a small group of characters, each violently unique and ferociously passionate in their own way. Accordingly, each of them approach their environment individually and possess a distinctive relationship with the Heath. Egdon Heath is the first character introduced in the novel, honored with a four page description of its beauty, mystery and sympathy for the human condition. It is described as alluring; though not in a definable way.

Its beauty, Hardy says, directly reflects the similarly uncertain beauty of man: it is "neither ghastly, hateful nor ugly, neither commonplace, unmeaning nor tame, but, like man, slighted and enduring; and withal singularly colossal and mysterious in its swarthy monotony".

Its nature is unpredictable and a matter of perception, as is that of the humankind. The Heath represents a standard of beauty and significance that appeal to the more mature of human emotions. In this, Hardy facilitates an understanding and hospitality in the Heath for the tragedy he later endows on it.

This capacity for tragedy and human emotion compels each inhabitant to be ingrained with a fierce, inescapable relationship with the Heath: a happy prospect for some and a bleak one for others. For Eustacia, the Heath embodies Hell itself. Superficially, she sees at as an open-air prison whose furze and thorny bars segregate her from the romantic world of wonder that she longs for. As Hardy adds detail to her character, however, it becomes clear that it is not so much that the Heath represents a tortured Eustacia's prison, but rather that it represents everything a very selfish Eustacia is not.

Its brooding consistency, its unconventional beauty, its power and its ambiguity frighten Eustacia and her preconceived ideals, causing her to feel suffocated in an environment where she has more freedom to be romantic than on any street of Paris. Yet it is this woman who falls so passionately in love with Clym Yeobright, a young man whose relationship with the Heath that bore him falls at the extreme opposite end of the spectrum from Eustacia.

For Clym, the Heath is everything Paris is not the same as it is for Eustacia, but in Clym's eyes this is the Heath's greatest advantage, not its most dreary shortcoming. However, even though Clym is able to see the beauty and promise of the Heath, his infatuation with it is as devastating as Eustacia's intense hatred for it.

The temporary affliction of blindness is a scathingly obvious metaphor on Hardy's part to symbolize Clym's single focused, blind ambition - equally dangerous and powerful as Eustacia's romanticized selfishness, though not as evident.

Both lovers are obsessed with the Heath, in essence one with its ugliness and the other with its beauty. In the beginning, it is this very contradiction that attracts the two, but as the dust settles around the final pages of the story, it is clear that it is the very contradiction that pushed them apart. In the end, the individualized selfishness of Clym and Eustacia reach their zenith; hers in her suicide and his in his inescapable guilt.

The Heath predicted this outcome, however: it fostered it from the beginning, it shaped their personalities in their youth, it breathed into them its teasing ambition and designed their tragic flaws to mirror its own. The Heath, or any such symbolic environment is deceivingly influential in its natural beauty and subtle, underestimated power. "The most thorough going ascetic," Hardy explains, "could feel that he had a natural right to wander on Egdon: he was keeping within the line of legitimate indulgence when he laid himself open to influences such as these".

The environment of Thomas Hardy's tragic novel plays as integral a role as any human character. The physical environment of the Heath has a direct influence on the psychologies and motives of the all the books characters, most importantly Clym and Eustacia, and its moods and consistencies reflect the social atmosphere Hardy tries to depict: vague, foggy, and above all unreliable.

The reflection serves as a double metaphor, however: what is reflected in the physical beauties and eccentricities of Egdon Heath is found in the social atmosphere of the people cradled in it, but also in the complexities of human nature itself. It is a soft mockery of man's pompous belief that he is civilized, when in reality he is as wild, rugged and unforgiving as the Heath, and subject also to the whims and wills of the shadowed landscape that he has unconsciously adopted as his own, willingly or not.

Today, Victorianism is thought of as another word for sexual repression. Yet the Victorian Age (1839 – 1901) was also a period of profound social commentary and social developments. The literature of the time addressed such significant issues as the growth of English democracy, the education of the masses, and the impact of industrialization on the working class.

One constant of the Victorian Era was that it was a time of an increased sense of social responsibility. In her early days on the throne, Victoria was viewed as liberal in her beliefs.

A marked change came in 1840, when she married Albert, her mother's nephew and prince of Saxe-Colburg Gotha. Albert was conservative, moralistic, and prudish; Victoria adopted similar attitudes. After his death in 1861 she reigned for another forty years and never remarried. Her personality influenced all of society and set the tone for the age. In a way it provided a moral compass that provided a sense of constancy in a turbulent time. Politically, the era was characterized by a prolonged economic boom. England reigned as a prosperous and dominant world superpower. In 1853, England, the Ottoman Empire, the Kingdom of Sardinia, and France fought a military conflict against Russia, in what was known as the Crimean War.

It was fought to keep Russia from widening their influence in the Ottoman Empire and the Middle East. The conflict ended with the Treaty of Paris, signed on March 30, 1856. The novelist most commonly associated with the Victorian Age is Charles Dickens (1812 – 1870), whose books were modest about sexual relations; yet, they are aggressive in portraying the wretched social conditions of urban life.

Thomas Hardy is also associated with the era, even though his works were considered controversial and even prurient according to Victorian standards. Hardy's sexual openness in portraying Eustacia's and Wildeve's lust for each other even when they are married to others was viewed as shocking. It certainly violated the sensibilities of the time, and earned Hardy a legion of detractors who looked on his works as a form of pornography.

COMPARE AND CONTRAST

1840s Milk production in dairy farming is all done by hand.

1878 The first commercial milking machines are produced in Auburn, New York.

Today Dairy farming is automated. Cows are kept in small enclosures that allow no room to move and seldom come into contact with humans.

1840s The typewriter is a new invention. Patented in 1843, it uses the concept of the moving carriage to make letters strike evenly.

1878 The typewriter is greatly improved when the Remington Arms Company added a shift key that would allow the same document to include lower — and upper — case characters.

Today Typewriters are practically obsolete. Word processing makes any desktop system capable of professional-quality graphics.

1840s The first rail lines are just beginning to connect major urban areas, with passenger train travel starting in the 1830s. The only transportation available to inhabitants of Egdon Heath is primitive, such as horse-drawn carriages.

1878 Railways are common across the English countryside. They link cities and allow travel to even isolated areas.

Today With automobiles providing convenient personal transportation, travel to any point in England is quick and easy.

1840s Human behaviour is a matter for speculation by philosophers and fiction writers.

1878 The first laboratory for experimental psychology is opened by Wilhelm Max Wundt, making a science out of the study of the mind.

Today The latest developments in psychology have been in the area of treating depressions and violent behaviour with mood-altering drugs.

CRITICAL OVERVIEW ON THE RETURN OF THE NATIVE

Before it was even published as a novel, The Return of the Native had already been rejected by Leslie Stephen, the editor of the prestigious Cornhill Magazine. Stephen objected to the hint of ex-tramarital sex and found it inappropriate for a family magazine. The serial ran in Belgravia, which, according to Desmond Hawkins, Hardy found to be an inferior publication. The initial critical response to the novel was mixed. A review in Athenaeum deemed it "distinctly inferior to anything of his we have yet read."

The reviewer also took issue with the language used by the characters, which seemed "pitched throughout in too high a key to suit the talkers." That same month critic W. E. Henley reviewed the book in The Academy. He found the work highly artificial but was reluctant to say so, because Hardy himself seemed sincere. On a positive note, he praised the opening descriptions of the heath and of Eustacia to be among the best things written in the English language — but that was not enough to make up for the weaknesses. Henley summarized all that was good and bad about Hardy's work in one seemingly endless sentence:

that he rarely makes you laugh and never makes you cry, and that his books are valuable and interesting rather as the outcome of a certain mind than as pictures of society or studies in human nature; that his tragedy is arbitrary and accidental rather than heroic and inevitable; and that, rare artist as he is, there is something wanting in his personality, and he is not quite a great man.

More than a decade later, Francis Adams pointed out the same strengths and weaknesses. Of Hardy's characterization of the dialogue of country maids, he wrote, "Nothing more ridiculous than this has been done by any writer of anything approaching ability in our time, and it is as false in characterization as it is absurd in conception." He went on to praise Hardy's artistic gift for making characters' environments reflect in their personalities, "a single harmonious growth of spiritual and natural circumstances."

Negative critical responses did not seem to trouble Hardy as much as the artistic constraints of having to please Victorian sensibilities. In 1894, the first book-length analyses of Hardy's fiction were published: Lionel Johnson's The Art of Thomas Hardy and Annie Macdonell's Thomas Hardy. Hardy mentioned them in a letter to a friend that year: "are too laudatory. They are not in bad taste as a whole, if one concedes that they had to be written, which I do not." It is generally accepted that he wrote no novels after 1895 because of the changes that he had to make to every piece in order to tone down any suggestion of sexual passion.

In the decade after his death, Hardy's reputation declined. His fiction was too outdated to hold much interest — it was half a century since Return of the Native, and in the meantime modernism had redefined literary tastes. T. S. Eliot asserted that Hardy was "indifferent even to the prescripts of good writing: he wrote sometimes overpoweringly well, but always very carelessly; at times his style touches sublimity without ever having passed through the stage of being good." His literary reputation soon revived, though, when critics started to take a new look at his work after the celebration of the hundredth anniversary of his birth in 1940. Since then, his six major novels — Far From the Madding Crowd, Return of the Native, The Mayor of Casterbridge, The Woodlanders, Tess of the D'Urbervilles, and Jude the Obscure — have held significant places in the ranks of English-language literature.

Chapter 13

Criticism of Thomas Hardy's Writing

DAVID KELLY

Kelly is an instructor of Creative Writing and Literature at Oakton Community College in Illinois. In the following essay, he examines how the timelessness of Egdon Heath actually helps support the plot's reliance on chance. Upon delving into any number of essays focused on Thomas Hardy's The Return of the Native, one is almost certain to come across a few important issues. The first issue is the character of the setting, Egdon Heath, which Hardy establishes in that long, lovely description in the first chapter and then comes back to throughout the book.

More than most novels, even the bulk of Victorian romances, this book uses the setting as a character, a living presence, and not just as a buffer to linger over in between scenes. It seldom fails to impress. Critics who do not think much of Hardy's attributes as a novelist will usually point out, to soften the tone of their criticism, how he brings Egdon Heath to life — it's their way of paying homage to the man whose literary reputation is firmly established. Similarly, critics often point out his greatest weakness as a fiction writer: that he often stretched credibility too far by expecting his readers to believe that awkward twists in the plot happened because of coincidence.

These two outstanding aspects of The Return of the Native, though often mentioned just in passing and almost always separately, are in fact supports bracing one another — wedges of the same frame that Hardy used to present a unified world-view. The timelessness of the heath, and the unlikely confluence of the events that go on there, blend to create a unique place where nature itself is unnatural. Stories, of course, have to happen somewhere; moreover, the stories that are the most artistically sound use their settings to manifest what is happening to the characters.

Some novels, especially if they are set in the present and under familiar circumstances, can take their settings for granted, offering up names of towns and streets and occasional descriptions of the surroundings. When the location will probably be unfamiliar — most notably in science fiction or fantasy or historical fiction — the writer is obliged to paint a fuller landscape. What is notable about The Return of the Native is that Hardy could have effectively set the scene with far less detail than he did in fact use. It is a desolate area; the people there live as their ancestors did; the railroad has not arrived yet. That covers all that needs to be covered.

Instead, he opens the book with a haunting description that extends from sky to ground, from dark to light, and from the present to the past. Other novels occur in settings that have evolved in ways corresponding to the laws of history, but the rules of physics don't apply to Egdon Heath. In his study of Hardy's career, Richard Carpenter cites John Patterson as identifying the heath as Limbo or the Cimmeron of Homer — places that are balanced between this world and Hades — not miserable but certainly not places of life. Hardy writes that the heath has the ability to "retard the dawn, sadden noon, anticipate the frowning of storms scarcely generated, and intensify the opacity of a moonless midnight to a cause and dread."

The character of this place is so crucial to telling this story that it is expanded across six pages, which is an incredible amount of space for a novelist to spend on a description of anything. Also telling is the fact that it is situated first in the book, establishing its importance before any specific human characters are introduced. Carpenter describes this setting as more than an image: it is a convenient narrative tool, allowing Hardy's characters to summon one another across miles with signal fires and also to bump into each other unexpectedly as they wander the twisted paths through the furze. "By confining nearly all of his action to its terrain," he writes, Hardy "achieves a unity of place which markedly aids in the creation of dramatic effects."

It is a handy set-ting for events that have to be brought together in order to make the story work, but it is in no way a superbly successful one. If Egdon Heath were flawless in drawing readers into the novel's magical spell, the reader would be left feeling completely satisfied about the reality and inevitability of what he or she is told goes on there. Instead, the reader is left conscious of the hand of the author as coincidences abound, apparently there only for his storytelling convenience.

Stories always depend on coincidental events. Hardy appears to not have recognized the boundary that separates "did not anticipate" from "could not anticipate" — and that line, wide as the Mississippi River, separates tragedy from potboiler. A turn of events like Clym Yeobright's semi-blindness, for example, seems to materialize pretty quickly in the story, but it follows naturally from Clym's sudden dedication to be a great educator, which follows from his impulsive high-minded character, and is therefore grounded in the story.

Diggory Venn always shows up unexpectedly and fortuitously, so the reader can accept him as either a supernatural presence or an extremely prepared guardian. Eustacia and Wildeve are drawn together by a similar restlessness, so it is no wonder that their internal clocks would direct them both to the East Egdon "gipsying" at the same time. The adder that bites Mrs. Yeobright is the natural result of life on the heath. Eustacia is devious enough to loiter outside of the chapel when Wildeve is marrying, so there is no stretch of reality in her being the wedding's witness.

Even the event that starts the whole novel into motion — the canceled marriage between Thomasin and Wildeve —

seems only to be a matter of coincidence to the people in the book. Readers recognize this as one of those psychological non-accidents, reflecting the fact that one of these two subconsciously wanted the ceremony abandoned — although it is unclear whether the hesitant party is Thomasin, who changed towns suddenly at the last moment, or Wildeve, who forgot to change the license. These coincidences can all be explained, and they even afford readers some fun in recognizing that life in the novel can be as unruly and unpredictable as it is in the world.

Other coincidences are harder to swallow. Readers who can get past the idea that Mrs. Yeobright and Wildeve and Johnny Nunsuch all arrive at the cottage at the same time still have to accept the fact that Clym would happen to choose that particular night, after months, to visit his estranged mother's house. Wildeve's fortune arrives out of nowhere, just in time for Eustacia to notice him again. The strangest of all, perhaps, is Fairway showing up late the night Eustacia is leaving, almost as an afterthought, with Clym's letter: it is hard enough to believe that he would happen to write when she happens to be leaving, but having a very minor character show up and say he had forgotten the letter until the drama is mounting shows a truly half-hearted effort on the part of the writer to simulate reality.

All readers of conscience are left to wonder how much the heath's wonderful, unique character can be allowed to account for the gaps in the story's credibility. To some extent, a lot: the otherworldliness that is so richly established allows Egdon Heath to excuse itself from any standards of behaviour that are generally expected. If the laws of evolution are suspended there, then the laws of chance must be so too, since the one leads to the other. The same glitch that has left the heath unaltered for a thousand years also makes it possible for money to rain down unexpectedly from a previously unknown source, or for Diggory Venn to show up whenever his appearance would help the story.

In fact, Hardy not only flaunts the fact that chance rules, but he actually uses the readers' diminished expectations as part of the story's fabric. The characters who have any sense of the outside world become impatient with the slow, staid pace at Egdon Heath and they try taking fate into their own hands, creating tragedy. These characters include Eustacia and Clym, who has lived in Paris, the capital of the civilized world. Wildeve, an educated man, is able to sense a world beyond the heath, but he lacks the fortitude to do anything about it. When he inherits a lot of money later in the novel, he makes plans to break free of the heath and traverse the globe, but this hope is what leads to the tragedy at the book's end. Wildeve and Eustacia find out that the law of the heath is not outside of nature, that it is their nature.

Trying to change is what causes trouble in an environment where change is the one thing that cannot happen; and, because their energies cannot produce the results that were intended, the force expended careens off into the void and then bounces back in ways not expected. Readers who accept the fact that time has passed the heath by do not have to strain too hard to see that the same mysterious force that stops time is not universal—that the real-world passions of Eustacia and Yeobright and Wildeve will bring loose energy into the place and create chaos.

The question at the centre of all of this is whether Thomas Hardy is the force that made the heath, or if the novel's unique elements can be accounted for naturally. One thing that is certain is that Hardy felt that the Egdon Heath he presented was a description, not a creation. Photographs and the testimony of other writers who came after him seem to bear out this idea, that the place before the arrival of technology was just as it had been for thousands of years. In old pictures, it looks just as desolate as the moon would look if it grew weeds.

However, the old photos were shot with the theme of desolation in mind, thanks to Hardy: he observed the land and then added the idea that it willed itself to not change. Today, that area in the south of England is plenty inhabited, as cultivated as any other, proving, if such is necessary, that it had no magic aura that sealed it. Thomas Hardy, like any good novelist, saw a unique situation and took advantage of that opportunity to create his own mythology.

Much as I try, I cannot find causes for the strikingly bold "coincidences" I have mentioned, but I do feel that they belong in the novel. The same property that made Egdon Heath unique also allows characters in the book to stroll up with letters sent long ago, or to all decide at once to go to the same place. Like early physicists, the readers' job might be to identify the unseen currents and principles that make actions lead to unexpected results in this one field; or, like early theologians, the reader might just have to accept the fact that all that occurs is related. The degree to which Hardy's surprises are or are not believable goes beyond the events themselves and depends on how much one believes in the author and his world.

THEMES

Time

The role of time and the effect of its passage are major themes in the novel. As the story spans eighteen months, the landscape of the heath remains unchanged — that consistency is reflected in the people who live on the heath for generation after generation. They are creatures of tradition, following the same wedding rituals, the same harvest rituals, the same holiday traditions and the same folk remedies (such as the traditional cure for an adder's bite) that has been handed down to them. Sometimes traditional beliefs lead to hostility, like the fear of Eustacia Vye being a witch.

The characters who encounter difficulty are the ones who are not content to live in rhythm with country life. Most notably, Eustacia is impatient with life on the heath, wishing for the "bustle" of Paris. Wildeve is also bored with life on the heath. When he inherits a large sum of money, he plans to tour the world. Clym is the most divided character in the novel; Eustacia assumes that he is too worldly to settle down in the country, but he is able to appreciate the beauty of the land's timelessness.

[W]hen he looked from the heights on his way he could

not help indulging in a barbarous satisfaction at observing that, in some of the attempts at reclamation from waste, tillage, after holding on for a year or two, had receded again in despair, the ferns and furze-tufts stubbornly reasserting themselves.

NATURE

Hardy introduces his readers to the landscape of Egdon Heath before introducing any characters. This emphasizes the important role that the natural landscape will play in the story. His description of the natural setting can be taken as symbolic of the people who live there—"neither ghastly, hateful, nor ugly: neither commonplace, unmeaning nor tame; but, like man, slighted and enduring." It can also be taken as a simple acknowledgment that people come to resemble the place where they live.

For instance, the extreme heat of the August day when Mrs. Yeobright is turned away from Clym's cottage may be perceived as symbolic of her turmoil. Hardy addresses this issue directly when he has Eustacia wander out into a violent storm on the night of her greatest mental anguish: "Never was harmony more perfect than that between the chaos of her mind and the chaos of the world without." If the people of Egdon Heath seem carefree, it is because they are comfortable in their surroundings.

The character who appears to be most in tune with nature's mysteries is Diggory Venn. He does not look like a human because of the red dye that has seeped into his skin and hair, and he does not operate by the rules of human interaction, instead appearing and disappearing mysteriously at night. It is not surprising that in the end he becomes a dairy farmer — making his living with domesticated animals, in harmony with nature but not completely subject to its whims.

CONSCIENCE

The characters in The Return of the Native are motivated by their consciences more than any other driving force. Their attempts to avoid social confrontation are not guided by concern about what others will think, but by what harm they will do to others. This is evident in the opening chapters, with Thomasin's return after her aborted attempt to be married; although eloping is considered shameful, Thomasin and Wildeve are unconcerned about that social stigma, which is quickly forgotten anyway.

On the other hand, Wildeve is unwilling to go through with his wedding to Thomasin when he feels that he might end up regretting it and longing for Eustacia. When they do marry, it is not to satisfy the social requirement, but because of Wildeve's failed romantic life. Diggory Venn is driven to assure Thomasin's happiness, passing up opportunities that could benefit him in order to protect her. Telling her about Wildeve's involvement with Eustacia might make her forget Wildeve — thereby clearing the way for him — but Venn cannot hurt her. So he keeps silent.

Late in the novel, when Eustacia realizes that Wildeve has become the rich, worldly husband that she always wanted, she does not run away with him because she cannot hurt Clym. At her house, he says that he could not abandon his wife either, but later, when Eustacia is leaving town, he is willing to run away with her, still making sure that Thomasin will receive half of his inheritance.

POINT OF VIEW

This novel is told from the third-person point of view, which means that the narrator is a disembodied voice, referring to each character as "he" or "she." However, the narrative is not omniscient. This means that the narrator looks at the story unfolding from different points of view, but when it settles on any particular viewpoint it stays consistent, if only for a short amount of time. When new information is introduced into the story, that information is initially understood only in terms of the narrator's point of view at the time.

For instance, when Wildeve first appears, readers are not told who he is; his character is revealed by what he says. Clym is a mystery for Eustacia to fantasize about long before his thoughts are related. In fact, even when they do talk outside of the Christmas party, the narrative shifts from her perspective to his then back to hers. Giving readers access to just one person's experience at a time is called "limited omniscience."

By limiting the flow of information to the reader, Hardy is able to create a sense of mystery in the story. This is accomplished because the motivations and intentions of the characters are not always immediately clear. When Hardy wants to convey theories and opinions, he frequently presents a scene in which several of the local characters are gathered together and talking while doing something else.

This occurs in the bonfire scene in the chapter called "The Custom of the Country" and in the later chapter where people gather and discuss the best way to deal with a snakebite. A contrast to this is the scene of hauling the bucket out of the well: general knowledge of the subject of bucket retrieval is conveyed directly from the narrator to the reader here, rather than through the conversation of the locals.

STRUCTURE

This book was written for magazine serialization, and this is reflected in its structure. Actions occur within specific episodes, and future developments in the story are foreshadowed. Chapters end with lines that are meant to raise curiosity, a technique that is effective to keep readers of novels turning the pages. Moreover, it was meant to inspire excitement so the reader would buy the next month's installment.

A good example of this technique is when Thomasin returns unmarried from Angelbury. The chapter ends with her aunt asking, "Now Thomasin what's the meaning of this disgraceful performance?" Readers know that the explanation will follow, but it does not follow right away. Viewers of television — where shows are regularly scheduled in weekly installments — are very familiar with this technique.

Critics have also contended that this book is structured like a Shakespearean drama. Most of Shakespeare's plays were organized in five acts, with a climactic conclusion in the last act. Although The Return of the Native is presented in six books, most critics agree that its artistic structure only requires five — the sixth was added to please general audiences that wanted to see everything turn out all right in the end. A clue to the book's debt to Shakespeare is the reference to King Lear, one of Shakespeare's greatest tragedies, in the introduction.

SYMBOLISM

The names of Thomas Hardy's characters are almost always symbolic of their functions within his novels, and the names in The Return of the Native are no exception. "Wildeve" suggests someone on the verge, or eve, of wildness, while his first name, Damon, is commonplace enough to suggest that he will never break out of the mold. Eustacia is derived from the word "eustacy," which means a change in the level of the sea all around the world, indicating the immense changes that she is set to bring into the lives of the people on the heath and beyond.

It also rings of the prefix "eu-," which has an Latin meaning of "good" and an Old Norse meaning "to want," and from "ecstasy." Her last name, "Vye," indicates the character's combative stance toward the world. Clym's last name, "Yeobright," combines the word "yeoman" which indicates a servant or underling with the indication of his natural intelligence, or brightness. There are minor characters here also given names that are common words that appear in dictionaries, such as "Nunsuch" (normally spelled "nonesuch"), "Christian," and "Fairway."

SETTING

The sweeping topographical and historical description of Egdon Heath that opens this book is considered to be one of the finest extended descriptions in all of English literature. The importance of this setting to the events of the novel cannot be overemphasized. It is the land's flatness and barrenness that has made it useless for development, which means that the civilized world has passed it by. The residents of the heath are isolated and possess their own distinct culture, separate from the rest of the world.

Eustacia is feared by the ordinary people and alluring to Wildeve and Clym for the same reason, because she keeps herself separate from the ordinary people; she is treated as if she has supernatural powers, as if she can transcend the land's hard demands.

Clym is treated as an almost mystical personage because he has been to Paris, even though there is no indication that in Paris he was treated as anything more than a jeweler's clerk. The only way for people of the heath to gain wealth is to inherit it from far away, as Wildeve does, or to earn it in other places, as Diggory Venn does.

Chapter 14

Critical Analysis of "Tess of D 'Ubervilles"

Through life people may fault, or get on the wrong side of the tracks. Yet hopefully they keep faith and then willingly they may recoup and redeem themselves by recovering. Many believe that, - Tess in, Tess of the d'Urbervilles was a great example of this. In Hardy's Victorian age novel, Tess of the d'Urbervilles, he illustrates casual wrong, the will to recover, the growth of love, and death.

Almost everybody has done something casually wrong and not think much of it, many call this indifferent nature. Tess is no stranger to casual wrong. Throughout her life indifferent nature has occurred. Her parents were not the greatest of parents. She had a tough life, she was poor. When she met Alec d'Urberville, she was considerate and kind, but later on Alec took advantage of her and seduced her in a forest called the Chase,

"He knelt and bent lower, till her breath warmed his face, and in a moment his cheek was in contact with hers. She was sleeping soundly, and upon her eyelashes there lingered tears."

She then later fell in love with Angel, and married him. Angel found out about Tess' past experience with Alec, and he could not forgive her, even though it was all Alec's doing. Thus it is clear that casual wrong follows her and yet the wrong is not made by her. Tess' true strength is her determination to overcome her misfortunes. When the Durbeyfields' horse, Prince died, Tess took control of the situation of the horse's death and the beehive delivery.

She takes care of the kids and she had done well in school, even though Tess seems to go nowhere. Also when she leaves her job of taking care of the flock at the d'Urberville household, because of her experience with Alec, it showed she tried to take control of the situation. Even when Alec was following her home on his carriage asking her why she left,

'Her lip lifted slightly, though there was little scorn, as a rule, in her large and impulsive nature. "I have said I will not take anything more from you, and I will not-I cannot! I should be your creature to go on doing that, and I won't"'

Indeed it is shown that Tess has a very strong will to recover.

There was a growth of love shown by Alec, Angel and Tess.

Alec had a love for Tess in which he forced her to love him, but Tess refused until eventually she had no choice.

'"....,you agree willingly to let me do it again, and no handkerchief."

She sighed. "Very well, sir!" she said.'

When Tess first met Angel, they both had a growing love for each other, but it all stopped when they got married and Angel found out about Tess having sex with Alec. Angel, then did not want to have anything to do with her, but Tess still loved Angel. While Angel was in Brazil, he learned what a fool he was to just leave. Tess, so he came back to England. Tess then killed Alec in order for Angel to feel better about the old situation, but it was not a good plan, because now they are wanted. The growth of their love seemed to go to far in this case.

Although Death is a natural part of life, it is not a pleasant one. When the Durbeyfields' horse died, it seemed to foreshadow worse things to come. Tess' own death and Alec's who was murdered by Tess, "....She listened. The dead silence within was broken only by a regular beat. Drip, drip, drip." Consequently the murder of Alec, by Tess, will lead to her own death.

In Hardy's Victorian age novel, Tess of the d'Urbervilles, he illustrates casual wrong, the will to recover, the growth of love, and death. It seems nothing went right for poor Tess in her life. She was confused, and had a lot of expectations on her, from her mother, and she put a lot on herself. She tried her hardest, but her life ended up as a tragedy.

HARDY ON RELIGION

In Tess of the d'Urbervilles, we gain insight into Hardy's view on religion as he uses his characters to make observations that may have been quite disconcerting to his Victorian readers. This is not to say that Hardy abandoned his views on religion, instead, he "became an agnostic, [and] he remained emotionally involved with the Church." Hardy's greatest dispute was with the dogma or beliefs of the church.

Hardy had once wanted to become a minister but abandoned that idea when he could no longer afford to attend the university. Robert Schweik, a Hardy critic, relates that Hardy became interested in religion on a personal level—that the subject of infant baptism particularly affected him. Hardy could see no harm in baptizing an infant if doing so makes the family of the child feel better about their child's salvation. This position is made clear in the scenes with Tess and Sorrow.

The scene is played out in Chapter 14 when Tess baptizes Sorrow. She learns that her own ceremony is the same as if it were performed in church; however, on the subject of a proper Christian burial, the local vicar replies, "Ah—that's another matter." In the true sense of charity, Hardy argues, Tess should have been allowed to bury Sorrow in a proper manner, not be relegated to the part of the cemetery that has unbaptized infants, drunks, and the damned.

The burial is carried out under the cover of darkness, not during the daylight hours, to protect Tess and to shield her from the scorn of churchgoers. Hardy's point is that Sorrow's burial should have been treated as any other burial. The position of the church is too harsh, Hardy seems to argue, when Sorrow is christened in the proper manner, but is not given a proper Christian burial.

Also, the positioning of pagan and Christian rituals makes for an interesting look at the dichotomy that exists in the smaller rural areas. Some rituals, now obscured by the passage of time, were assimilated into Christian ceremony. The May Dance, for instance, in Chapter 1, celebrated the end of the winter and the beginning of summer. Druids and other pagans of the area would have celebrated that date with a ceremony of sorts.

Also, Tess, before she is literally sacrificed for the good of society, journeys to Stonehenge, the temple of monoliths used for sun worship and possibly human sacrifice. Tess says to Angel about the pantheon, "And you used to say at Talbothays that I was a heathen. So now I am at home." Also, Hardy recollects the earlier ancient Greek tragedies by invoking the name of Aeschylus, the principal writer of Greek tragic drama, to close his work, not biblical or modern sagas, as we would have imagined a nineteenth-century writer to do.

Hardy quite possibly sees religion abandoning the people, with dogmas that do not mesh with a modern society. In Tess, with few exceptions, Hardy's portrayal of the "traditionally" religious people is not particularly complimentary. Take the casual remarks by Angel's brothers, Felix ("all Church") and Cuthbert ("all College"). They are quite involved in themselves, changing their beliefs and values to match the times. Both brothers are clerics without compassion, possibly in the same mold as the Vicar in Marlott.

If religion is as shallow as Hardy predicts, then the sign painter and his art are the worst form of shallowness. The sign painter who wanders the countryside uses the simplest texts he can find to put on his religious signs. When Tess asks if he believes in the text about "sin not your own seeking," he replies, "I cannot split hairs on the burning query." Essentially, he is not educated enough to think of a reasonable answer, and his perspective on religion is limited.

Hardy saw this in the common folk he knew and was loathe to think that their religious beliefs were so shallow that they did not understand the deeper meanings of the texts they had read. Also, the sign painter saves the hottest sign messages for rural districts, where the ordinary folk would be frightened and cowed into submission. These seem to be "religious views on a poker chip"—philosophical entreaties to urge folks to turn to the Bible for aid. But these signs seem to miss the deeper meanings of the scriptures, which Tess seems to understand, not just the superficial meanings espoused by others. Likewise, Alec is the worst kind of convert, a sinner who renounces his former ways but becomes a sinner again at the slightest hint of temptation. The signs put up by the sign painter and Alec's conversion all point to a faith that is fleeting at best.

However, not all clergy are poor representations of religion, nor all believers false. Tess, for example, has an uncomplicated religion, a simpler and deeper understanding than her education would allow. She is as powerful as any clergyman when she baptizes Sorrow, but realistic when she realizes that she must pay for her sins when confronted by the police.

Similarly, Angel's father, Reverend Clare is a good man, with good intentions, and a good message. He is part of the evangelical movement who practices what he preaches. He is described as Paulist or Pauliad, from Paul of Tarsus, who believed that salvation came through grace and belief, which came through emotional responses rather than intellectual ones. Thus we see Hardy from two separate perspectives, one who uses biblical allusion with the knowledge of a believer, but the skepticism of an outsider.

HARDY'S COMPARISONS

Hardy uses comparison throughout the novel to reveal character and theme. The most obvious comparison is between Angel and Alec. The juxtaposition of Angel, who represents the ideal love of Tess, is contrasted with Alec, who represents the sexual possession of Tess. Since neither character is a perfect personification of good or evil, Hardy has both men exhibit both passion and coldness when they interact with Tess. Angel is passionate about Tess and his love for her, while he coolly dismisses her after learning of her torrid past. Alec is at first cool in his treatment of Tess as a possession, a symptom of his class, and then he decides later that he cannot live without her.

Hardy's Tess is filled with these side-by-side comparisons. Peter J. Casagrande, in his book Tess of the d'Urbervilles: Unorthodox Beauty, coins a new word "beaugly," a combination of the words "beautiful" and "ugly." He argues that the novel is chock-full of these comparisons: poor/rich, good/evil, Angel/brothers; Tess/her siblings; high class/low class, and past/present. Even the title of Casagrande's work, "Unorthodox Beauty," suggests a beauty that is does not conform to the standards by which other novels before or since Tess have been judged.

Hardy himself points the out the rationale for his philosophy: "The business of the poet and novelist is to show the sorriness underlying the grandest things, and the grandeur underlying the sorriest things." Another Hardy critic, Linda Shires, makes the observation that, Hardy's treatment of his characters is "blatantly non-stereotypical." Now we have a novel that challenges stereotypes and sets the tone for several other Hardy works.

The poor versus rich comparison should not escape modern readers. Alec's seemingly endless wealth contrasts with the Durbeyfield's abject poverty. Hardy uses this juxtaposition to demonstrate the difference between the "haves" and the "have nots." However, even Hardy makes the point that at sometime in the distant past, just as Alec and his kind take advantage of Tess and her kind, the ancient d'Urbervilles had their way with the poor of their time: "Doubtless some of Tess d'Urbervilles mailed ancestors rollicking home from a fray had dealt the same measure even more ruthlessly towards peasant girls of their time." But Hardy does not forgive the sins of the past or present saying, "To visit the sins of the fathers upon the children may be a morality good enough for divinities, it is scorned by average human nature; and it therefore does not mend the matter." While not forgiving Alec for his misdeeds, Hardy does make some attempt to understand Alec's actions as a part of his class.

Also, Hardy attempts to comprehend good and evil. The poor down in Marlott have adapted a fatalistic attitude best represented by the saying, "It was to be." Tess questions the contrast between the forces that have dealt her a less than fair hand—"I shouldn't mind learning why—why the sun do shine on the just and unjust alike." Tess' query is one that has perplexed men since the dawn of time: why is there good and evil in the world? Hardy invokes the ancient Greek views on good and evil, along with the Torah and the Old Testament and New Testament of the Bible, as well as Milton's view found in Paradise Lost in an attempt to understand what motivates men to perpetrate either good or bad.

Another contrast is found in the families themselves, the Durbeyfields and the Clares. The Durbeyfields, even though impoverished, have a closeness that binds them. Tess' weakness is her siblings and their well being. In fact, Alec uses his wile to tempt her, much like the character of Satan uses temptation in the Bible and in Milton's Paradise Lost. Hardy describes Tess' siblings as "six helpless creatures, who had never been asked if they wished for life on any terms, much less if they wished for it on such hard conditions as were involved in being of the shiftless house of Durbeyfield."

Angel and his brothers, on the other hand, do not share the closeness that Tess' siblings share. Angel's brothers would find it difficult to aid each other, let alone others who might be in dire circumstances. Hardy comments "they [the needy] were to be tolerated rather than reckoned with and respected."

Hardy also contrasts the lifestyle of the farms where Tess works: Talbothays and Flintcomb-Ash. Hardy describes the Talbothays region in breathtaking terms of green valleys and abundant life. "The river itself, which nourished the grass and cows of these renowned dairies, flowed not like the streams in Blackmoor ... The Froom waters were clear as the pure River of Life shown to the Evangelist ...." Flintcomb-Ash, on the other hand, is described as "sublime in its dreariness." Marian, Tess' friend from Talbothays, calls the farm a "starve-acre place," not like the lush dairy at Talbothays. Hardy also sets up a contrast between the men who run each farm. Flintcomb has Farmer Groby, a mean-spirited man who demands that his workers work even harder. Mr. Crick from Talbothays uses humour and aplomb to motivate his workers.

These contrasts serve to reveal the nature of the people, places, and situations that Tess encounters. They also enable Hardy to make subtle and not-so-subtle observations about how people, both good and bad, interact act with and affect one another, for good or ill.

HARDY'S USE OF SETTING

Usually, we can look at the setting of a novel as a small portion of a work. With Tess, however, nature is a close second only to the main characters. Therefore, the reader is obligated to examine Hardy's use of setting and environment in Tess. Tess of the d'Urbervilles takes place in Wessex, a region encompassing the southern English county of Dorset and neighboring counties Hampshire, Wiltshire, Somerset, and Devon. The setting consists of more than the location, however, particularly in this novel.

Nature, as a part of the setting, is an essential element in understanding the novel. In addition, the countryside and the folk who inhabit the area provide more than a mere backdrop upon which Hardy tells his tale. They are, in fact, unnamed characters in the novel.

In Tess of the d'Urbervilles, the characters and setting mirror each other. Tess moves from a world that begins in the beautiful regions around Marlott. She goes to The Slopes to "claim kin" and the environment is lovely and formal, but also contrived (consider the new house where she expected to find an old one). The setting at Talbothays, where Tess experiences her greatest happiness, is lush, green, and fertile. Flintcomb-Ash, on the other hand, is a barren region, reflecting the harshness of the work and the desolation of Tess' life. The story ends in the equally mysterious Stonehenge region.

With his Wessex novels (Tess, The Mayor of Casterbridge, Far From the Maddening Crowd, and Jude the Obscure), Hardy documented a way of life, a pattern of speech, and a pattern of thought that serves as a historical account of life in southern England at the end of the 1800s. As Simon Gatrell notes in Kramer's The Cambridge Companion to Thomas Hardy, "He had begun to understand that he was the historian of a Wessex now passed, the recorder of a series of unique micro-environments, ways of life and speech, which together had formed a cultural whole." This element makes Hardy's notation about Wessex life timeless. Also, we see a type of existence that dated back several hundred years, possibly back to ancient times. Thus, Tess, even though it is set within a specific timeframe, has an ethereal quality that seems to transcend time.

The two main farms, Talbothays and Flintcomb-Ash, represent the best and worst of farm life. The farm is the only world that Tess knows. She never travels more than 50 miles from her place of birth. The whole of the work is rurally set, and with the level of detail, we can see Hardy's intimate knowledge of the inner workings of a nineteenth-century farm. Little evidence of machinery invades the novel and the main form of transportation is either the horse or the horse cart. Draft animals are necessary for survival and prosperity; we see evidence of Prince's death and the effect his passing has on the Durbeyfields. A new horse is very important to the existence of the family.

The entire series of chapters that follow Prince's death, with Tess going to The Slopes, is based on the economic need for a horse. Only twice do we see "modern" machines in the novel, the train delivering the Talbothays milk to London and the threshing machine used at Flintcomb-Ash. Otherwise, modern farming equipment is not a key component of farming techniques practiced in Wessex.

However, the machine at Flintcomb-Ash is like a monster that must be fed and maintained. We see evidence of this in Chapter 47; "the engine which was to act as the primum mobile of this world" and "it was the engine-man." Thus, the machine is an omnipotent presence, demanding to be tended to at all times. The workers have lost their identity and their ability to communicate when the machine is working at full tilt. Contrast this machine, which seems difficult to control, with the pastoral workings of the dairy at Talbothays.

This is not to say that the dairy is without modern machinery; it has modern butter churns, powered by hand and horsepower, but nothing like the steam threshing machine. A further comparison is the setting of the two farms. Talbothays is portrayed as a beautiful place, in a rich agricultural region of southern England—"the valley in which milk and butter grew to rankness, and were produced more profusely, if less delicately, than at her home—the verdant plain so well watered by the river Var or Froom." We cannot help but be charmed by the life of the dairy, with milking, churning butter, and making cheeses. Furthermore, only positive things happen to Tess while she is there.

Flintcomb-Ash, on the other hand, with part of the name being "ash," is mired in mud, rocks, poor conditions, and near starvation. Marian, formerly of Talbothays, has come to Flintcomb for work and calls the new farm "a starve-acre place. Corn and swedes [rutabagas] are all they grow." Alec reappears at the farm to begin his renewed "courtship" of Tess. Farmer Groby's treatment of his hired hands is not as sympathetic as Dairyman Crick's as he tells Tess, "But we'll see which is master here."

Taken as a whole, the villages of Marlott, Emminster, and Trantridge are small towns easily managed by visitors and townsfolk alike. The vast countryside of the novel, the rich farmland or the poorer farm areas, outline an important part of nineteenth-century English agriculture, one where the newly founded Industrial Revolution has yet to take hold. It is upon this framework that Hardy writes one of his best novels.

Through life people may fault, or get on the wrong side of the tracks. Yet hopefully they keep faith and then willingly they may recoup and redeem themselves by recovering. Many believe that, Tess in, Tess of the d'Urbervilles was a great example of this. In Hardy's Victorian age novel, Tess of the d'Urbervilles, he illustrates casual wrong, the will to recover, the growth of love, and death.

Almost everybody has done something casually wrong and not think much of it, many call this indifferent nature. Tess is no stranger to casual wrong. Throughout her life indifferent nature has occurred. Her parents were not the greatest of parents. She had a tough life, she was poor. When she met

Alec d'Urberville, she was considerate and kind, but later on Alec took advantage of her and seduced her in a forest called the Chase, "He knelt and bent lower, till her breath warmed his face, and in a moment his cheek was in contact with hers. She was sleeping soundly, and upon her eyelashes there lingered tears."

She then later fell in love with Angel, and married him. Angel found out about Tess' past experience with Alec, and he could not forgive her, even though it was all Alec's doing. Thus it is clear that casual wrong follows her and yet the wrong is not made by her.

Tess' true strength is her determination to overcome her misfortunes. When the Durbeyfields' horse, Prince died, Tess took control of the situation of the horse's death and the beehive delivery.

She takes care of the kids and she had done well in school, even though Tess seems to go nowhere. Also when she leaves her job of taking care of the flock at the d'Urberville household, because of her experience with Alec, it showed she tried to take control of the situation. Even when Alec was following her home on his carriage asking her why she left,

'Her lip lifted slightly, though there was little scorn, as a rule, in her large and impulsive nature. "I have said I will not take anything more from you, and I will not-I cannot! I should be your creature to go on doing that, and I won't"'

Indeed it is shown that Tess has a very strong will to recover.

There was a growth of love shown by Alec, Angel and Tess.

Alec had a love for Tess in which he forced her to love him, but Tess refused until eventually she had no choice.

'"....,you agree willingly to let me do it again, and no handkerchief."

She sighed. "Very well, sir!" she said.'

When Tess first met Angel, they both had a growing love for each other, but it all stopped when they got married and Angel found out about Tess having sex with Alec. Angel, then did not want to have anything to do with her, but Tess still loved Angel. While Angel was in Brazil, he learned what a fool he was to just leave

Tess, so he came back to England. Tess then killed Alec in order for Angel to feel better about the old situation, but it was not a good plan, because now they are wanted. The growth of their love seemed to go to far in this case.

Although Death is a natural part of life, it is not a pleasant one. When the Durbeyfields' horse died, it seemed to foreshadow worse things to come. Tess' own death and Alec's who was murdered by Tess, "....She listened. The dead silence within was broken only by a regular beat. Drip, drip, drip." Consequently the murder of Alec, by Tess, will lead to her own death.

In Hardy's Victorian age novel, Tess of the d'Urbervilles, he illustrates casual wrong, the will to recover, the growth of love, and death. It seems nothing went right for poor Tess in her life. She was confused, and had a lot of expectations on her, from her mother, and she put a lot on herself. She tried her hardest, but her life ended up as a tragedy.

Chapter 15

Tragic Heroism in Tess of the D'Urbervilles and Othello

In tragedy the reader often sympathizes and empathizes with the protagonist who attains "wisdom through suffering." Tess Durbeyfield, in Thomas Hardy's Tess of the D'Urbervilles and Othello, in William Shakespeare's Othello are protagonists who elicit the sympathy of the reader as they suffer, act, and triumph over their antagonists, who are embodied by the characters of Alec D'Urberville, Tess' wealthy defiler, and Iago, Othello's amoral lieutenant.

In both works the protagonists succumb to the pernicious influences of revenge, which are instigated by their antagonists and result in the deaths of the protagonists. Such tragedy in the protagonists' stories allows the reader to experience catharsis and realize the tragic heroism of Tess Durbeyfield and Othello.

Tess Durbeyfield, an innocent dairymaid with "innocent instinct towards self-delight," displays her character in her persistent devotion toward Angel Clare, her husband. Her suffering is evident in her defilement by Alec D'Urberville, a wealthy aristocrat, and in her separation from her husband. In the "First Phase" Tess is physically taken advantage of by D'Urberville who recognizes her innocence and vulnerability. Later, in "Phase the Third," she then falls deeply in love with Angel Clare, an affluent agriculturist. Tess soon alienates Angel by revealing her earlier encounter with D'Urberville.

Othello is an outsider and soldier who "loved not wisely but too well." His noble character is evident in his overwhelming fidelity towards his wife, Desdemona: "My life upon her faith," and the reader is quickly cognizant of the strong relationship between Othello and his wife. However, he is manipulated by Iago, his amoral lieutenant, and Othello's reality about his wife becomes twisted by Iago, who cleverly uses rhetoric to persuade him that his wife is disloyal. Iago informs the reader of Othello's transformation: "This may do something.

The Moor already changes with my poison." Eventually, Othello is driven to murder his wife as a result of Iago's deception: "Get me some poison, Iago, this night. I'll not expostulate with her, lest her body and beauty unprovide my mind again. This night, Iago!"

At the conclusion of each work the protagonist reaches a realization of her/his actions and accepts the responsibility for the consequences. In the novel, Tess realizes how D'Urberville abuses her and the importance of Angel Clare, her husband, and therefore murders D'Urberville and begs Clare to accept her into his life again: "I could not bear the loss of you any longer- you don't know how entirely I was unable to bear your not loving me!"

Tess accepts the consequences for her actions and accepts her execution: "it was as is should be. Angel, I am almost glad- yes glad." In the play, Othello experiences a consciousness in Act V, scene ii: "Are there no stones in heaven / But what serves for the thunder? Precious villain!" He then accepts the consequences for his actions and commits suicide: "I kissed thee ere I killed thee. No way but this, killing myself, to die upon a kiss."

Tess Durbeyfield, in Thomas Hardy's Tess of the D'Urbervilles, and Othello, in William Shakespeare's Othello, are tragic heroes because they suffer, face great losses, and triumph in their attainment of wisdom. As they languish, act, and defeat their antagonists, they elicit the sympathy of the reader. The protagonists' acceptance of their actions (death) allow them to symbolically triumph. Their stories and consequential tragedies allow the reader to experience catharsis, as they identify with their suffering.

A DOLL'S HOUSE AND TESS OF THE D'URBERVILLES

During the late nineteenth century, women were beginning to break out from the usual molds. Two authors from that time period wrote two separate but very similar pieces of literature. Henrik Ibsen wrote the play A Doll's House, and Thomas Hardy wrote Tess of the D'Urbervilles. Ibsen and Hardy both use the male characters to contrast with their female counterparts to illustrate how women are stronger by following their hearts instead of their minds.

Ibsen uses Torvald, to depict a world where men choose to follow their minds in place of their hearts. Ibsen has Torvald believe that he is truly in love with his wife Nora. Torvald believes he will "risk my life's blood, and everything, for your sake."The author sets the reader up to believe that Torvald is a chivalrous guy who would give life and limb to defend his true love, as the author believes that any real man would. Later in the play, a circumstance arises where he is given the opportunity to defend his wife.

He does a 180 degree turn around and explains to his wife that "no man would sacrifice his honour for the one he loves."The author shows the stupidity of Torvald with his misconception of honor. In actuality when a man sacrifices himself for the one he loves it brings him honor. Torvald is viewed as a true hypocrite. Torvald also believes the most important thing is to "save the... appearance."

He follows his mind, only interested in what is best for society. Ibsen illustrates him as a truly weak human. In contrast to Ibsen, Hardy takes an intellectually free thinker, Angel, who shows a very close minded perspective on events instead of opening himself to his true inner feelings. When Angel's bride reveals to him that she has committed the sin of pre-marital sex as did Angel, he begins to reveal to the reader his ignorance. In her sin, "forgiveness does not apply." Angel's double standard shows the reader that sexism even existed in the free thinkers of the time period like Angel. He believed that his wife's sin was not "a question of respectability, but one of principle."Hardy mocks Angel because he ironically believes himself free from the church, but in actuality his mind is a prisoner to their principles.

Angel "overlooked what [Tess] was, and forgot the defective can be more than the entire."Angel forgets that he still loves Tess because he has become a slave to his thoughts and ideas. Hardy suggests that when man follows his mind, it leads him astray, but when following his heart he will never miss the path to happiness and fulfillment. Both Ibsen and Hardy portray a time period where men follow their minds and society, their heart is solely for the pumping of blood, and their word is only as good as far as you can throw it.

NARRATIVE TECHNIQUE IN TESS OF THE D'URBERVILLES

"All works of fiction tell a story but what sets them apart is the particular way in which the story is told". Discuss the narrative technique of Hardy in Tess of the D'Urbervilles and what this method enables hardy to achieve. The narrative technique of an author in any novel is crucial to the readers understanding of the narrative. The way in which a novel is written influences the way in which the reader interprets the events which occur throughout the novel and allows the author to convey the feeling of time, place, and people in the society in which the author is attempting to impart to his or her readers.

In Tess of the D'Urbervilles, author Thomas Hardy uses a variety of narrative techniques in order to convey his own impressions of the society in which both he and his character Tess lived. Hardy's use of a third person omniscient narrator who is all knowing adds to the vulnerability of Tess by the reader's knowledge of what other characters say and do, whilst simultaneously detaching himself from the tragedy of Tess.

The use of extensive description of setting by Hardy allows the reader to interpret the action, reactions, and moods of the characters in relation to the specific atmosphere in which they exist at the time and the influence which such a setting has on the character's feelings and emotions. Hardy's use of religious and mythological allusions and metaphysical symbols allow the reader to reflect on the religious and sociocultural environments in which the narrative is set so as to allow the reader to better understand and interpret the actions and emotions of the characters due to the reader's knowledge of their environmental influences.

An effective narrative technique used by Hardy is the provision of a more direct means of communication between his characters and the reader. This is achieved through the use of dialogue, letter writing, and songs and poetry. Dialogue between characters allows Hardy to present his characters to his readers in a more direct way. It permits Hardy to allow his readers to interpret the characters in a way which is less influenced by his own narration and by which the readers are able to judge for themselves the characters by how they speak and communicate with others as well as the content of their converse.

Letter writing and songs and poetry allow the reader to be directly informed of the actions and their rationale as well as the feelings of a specific character by which the reader is able to interpret these being influenced by the specific character rather than Hardy himself, and also allows the reader an insight into the social and cultural backgrounds of the society as reasoning for the characters behaviour and emotions.

The way we read, interpret, and reflect on a novel is greatly influenced by the author and his or her use of narrative techniques in order to appropriately convey the characters and their society. An omniscient narrator is one who knows all and sees all. It allows the reader and indirect insight into the actions and emotions of specific characters.

The omniscience of the narrator allows the reader to not be influenced by the character in the interpretations of the character's behaviour and feelings and also encourages the reader to sympathise with Tess in her tragic and unfortunate predicament. Using such a narrative technique, Hardy allows himself to be somewhat detached from his characters, often appearing as though he himself does not sympathise with the tragedy that is Tess.

The effect of the novel not being narrated by Tess is that

we as the reader are given a perception of the lives of other characters which Tess herself is unaware of. It allows us to interpret for ourselves the predicament which characters other than Tess are placed in through our own eyes with the influence of Hardy and not through Tess. However, this style of narration prevents the reader from having a direct line into the thoughts and feelings of Tess and other characters, and does not allow for the character to directly communicate with their readers in a way which would inform the readers of the workings of the character's mind, what they do, and why they do it. However Hardy manages to overcome this difficulty through the use of other narrative techniques such as dialogue and letter writing.

Setting in this case refers to the specific surrounding environment and it's atmosphere in which a character exists at a specific point in time. The particular setting in which a character exists reflects the character's moods, actions, reactions, and their rationale for these, whilst the setting also influences how a character behaves.

Hardy's comprehensive description of these settings also conveys to the reader the insignificance of individual characters in relation to the social atmosphere in which they live as a whole. Upon the commencement of chapter two, Hardy describes the county of Marlott and the surrounding Vale of Blackmoor in terms of its rural beauty and cultural atmosphere whereby a May Day dance is being held.

This description of setting reflects the peaceful atmosphere of the county at that time, much like that of Tess and her family, creating suspense for the events to come. Prior to Alec's violation of Tess, Hardy describes the setting of Chaseborough as "a decayed market town" (Chapter 10) where Alec, Tess, and their companions have chosen to spend their evening drinking.

An atmosphere of chaos and disorder has thus been set with Tess's intoxicated and unruly companions turning into "satyrs clasping nymphs" (Chapter 10). This creation of a embroiled and uncomfortable environment for Tess alerts the reader to advancing events. Hardy makes note of the fog in the woods which is regarded as a metaphorical representation of entrapment. It is during this tumult that Alec takes advantage of the sleeping Tess.

In the second phase of the novel, Tess is seen making her way back to Marlott at which point she is overtaken by Alec. Tess refuses converse with him and leaves him to go down the "crooked lane" (chapter 12). It is here where we realise that Hardy's created topography of Wessex represents the moral condition of the characters. Two distinct setting placed in stark contrast to each other are Tess's journey to The Slopes where Alec lives and Tess's journey to Talbothay's dairy.

Upon departing for The Slopes, Tess is reluctant and indisposed to her impending situation. She does not enjoy the journey in the least, feeling that her excursion will result in unwanted consequences. However travelling to Talbothays Tess's ride is swift and pleasant.

Tess feels a sense of purpose in beginning a fresh new chapter of her life, and considers the journey more of a "pilgrimage" (chapter 16). Upon arriving at the dairy, Tess observes that this a place of good spirits where "she appeared to feel that she really had laid a new foundation for her future" (chapter 16). Hardy juxtaposes the residences of both Alec and Angel, contrasting Alec's estate on The Slopes and Angel's elevated dwelling.

This contrast in setting reflects Tess's respective relationships between herself and both Alec and Angel. In the midst of the blossoming relationship between Tess and Angel at the dairy, Hardy describes the setting as "oozing fatness and warm ferments... the hiss of fertilisation... The ready bosoms existing there were impregnated by their surroundings". (chapter 23). This description of setting reflects the relationship between Tess and Angel and the atmosphere in which their relationship matures. However this was not to last. Following the demise of Tess and Angel's marriage, Tess arrives at Flincomb Ash.

Such a name conveys the impression of a stark and desolate setting which reflects Tess's on misery and suffering. The land in harsh and barren, possibly representing the love of lack thereof between Tess and Angel. The work is onerous and toilsome, contrasting considerably with Tess's joyful labour at Talbothay's.

Tess's depression reaches it's climax here in the barren wasteland and "the joyless monotony of things" (chapter 46). it is amidst this desolate and destitute environment where Alec surfaces again to declare his love for Tess. Tess refuses his pleas, still hoping for the return of her beloved Angel. When Angel finally does return, it is amidst the luxurious seaside resort at Sandbourne whereby Tess is described as being expensively dressed and living in affluence.

This setting conveys the impression of both an inappropriate environment for Tess, representing her union with Alec, but also a prosperous environment representing her reunion with Angel. Hardy's effective use of dynamic setting is used in order to allow Hardy to convey the moods and feelings of his characters which are reflected by the setting in which the specific characters exist at that time.

Hardy's characters are greatly influenced by the religious and social environments in which they live. Religious and mythological allusions enable Hardy to convey these aspects of his society to his readers. In the opening of the novel, the first character the readers are introduced to is Parson Tringham. No physical description is given and his dialogue is limited, creating an alluding and mysterious figure. The parson represents the religiosity of Hardy's society and communicates to the readers that this is a religious society, whilst also setting the scene for Tess's introduction to the readers and for the events to come.

At the commencement of the second phase of the novel "maiden no more", Tess is seen burdened with a heavy basket and a large bundle. This can be regarded as the metaphysical symbol of oppression and hardship. Some time later as Tess and Angel depart from the dairy after their wedding ceremony, a cock is heard crowing. Such is an omen of bad luck, and according to biblical references, the cock crowing three times as it had done intensifies the omen even more. This religious allusion represents the religious implications and consequences for Tess's decision not to inform Angel of her past, whilst also creating suspense for the reader as to the events to come.

An effective narrative technique used by Hardy is dialogue between characters. How a character speaks and what they say allow a greater insight into the nature of their individuality. It permits the reader to judge the characters on the basis of their own communication with other characters rather than on Hardy's own interpretation of their converse. Dialogue also informs the reader of a specific character's thoughts and feelings as well as their intentions and rationale for previous actions. Upon the commencement of the novel, the reader is introduced to John Durbeyfield.

His dialogue with the unknown parson indicates to the reader that this is an uneducated man who is a member of the lower classes. His dialect may give an indication of his county of origin but also conveys to the readers that he is possibly intoxicated, which we later find out he is, and also slightly pompous without reason.

Thus Hardy's use of dialogue here sets the scene for Tess's introduction to the reader. Also used by Hardy in order to create a more intimate relationship between the characters and his readers is the use of letter writing and songs. Having set their wedding date for New Years Eve, Tess and Angel relish their time together, however upon trying on her wedding dress, Tess cannot help but remember one of her mother's songs:

"That would never become a wife
That had once done amiss" (chapter 32)

This song allows Tess to return to her childhood in her adulthood, and also allows her to convey a typical value of the society in which she lived, a women who had committed an indiscretion in her early years shall never be married. This song also imparts to the reader Tess's fears and doubts, and the extent to which her guilty conscience is imploring her to inform Angel of her past. During the climax of Tess's depression whereby she is in a state of "utter stagnation" (chapter 41), Tess receives a letter from her former dairymaid friend Marian, asking Tess to join her at Flincomb Ash. Once having arrived at Flincomb Ash, and Tess having subjected Alec to an "insulting slap" (chapter 48), Tess resolves to write to Angel, imploring him to "save me from what threatens me!" (chapter 48). Having returned home to her ill mother, only to be informed of her father's death, Tess now resolves to write to Angel yet again, this time in a bitter letter abusing Angel for his mistreatment of her. Having received no reply from Angel, Marian and Izz write to Angel beseeching him to return to Tess. The use of letter writing enables Hardy to create a more intimate relationship between his characters and the readers, allowing the readers to understand the character's behaviour and their rationale.

Hardy's use of an omniscient narrator, descriptive setting, allusion and metaphysical symbols, and letter writing and songs in Tess of the D'Urbervilles enables Hardy to influence the way his readers understand an interpret the events of the novel. These narrative techniques are highly effective in establishing a relationship between the characters and the reader and also in conveying to the readers the various aspects of Hardy's society.

An understanding of these religious, social, and cultural aspects allows the reader to rationalise the actions and emotions of the characters in relation to the society in which these character's live. It is crucial for the readers to comprehend the background and aspects of Hardy's society in order that they be able to realistically explicate the plot of the novel in relation to the environment in which the characters exist.

Chapter 16

The Novels of Thomas Hardy

We have it on his [Hardy's] own assurance that the Wessex of the novels and poems is practically identical with the Wessex of history, and includes the counties of Berkshire, Wilts[hire], Somerset, Hampshire, Dorset, and Devon — either wholly or in part. Hardy set his "Novels of Character and Environment," as he did most of his other novels, poems and short stories, around the market town of Dorchester ('Casterbridge'), near his boyhood home at Bockhampton, on the edge of 'Egdon' Heath. Although both Anthony Trollope (1815-82) and George Eliot (1819-80) had used similar settings in their novels, Hardy's rural backdrop is neither romantic nor idealized. From the publication of his first novels Hardy's critics accused him of being overly pessimistic about humanity's place in the scheme of things.

In 1901, Hardy expressed the notion that "non-rationality seems...to be the [guiding] principle of the Universe." In all his fiction, chance is the incarnation of the blind forces controlling human destiny," as Lord David Cecil remarks in Hardy the Novelist. Ironically the blind forces of 'Hap' seem to favour certain characters while they relentlessly pursue those who deserve better, such as Tess, as well as those whose ends we might regard as proof of Nemesis or Poetic Justice (Sergeant Troy in Far from the Madding Crowd, Lucetta in The Mayor of Casterbridge, and Alec in Tess of the d'Urbervilles).

An entry in Hardy's notebook dated April 1878 gives us a clue to the guiding principle behind his fiction:

A Plot, or Tragedy, should arise from the gradual closing

in of a situation that comes of ordinary human passions, prejudices, and ambitions, by reason of the characters taking no trouble to ward off the disastrous events produced by the said passions, prejudices, and ambitions.

In Women and Sexuality in the Novels of Thomas Hardy, Rosemarie Morgan provides an interesting footnote to Hardy's handling of Nemesis in Tess:

Hardy's 'sadistic tale' does, of course, mete out punishment in equal measure: the fallen woman's true love is brought home from his 'Brazil' 'a mere yellow skeleton' condemned to live out his days with a 'spiritualized Tess' whom he may love but may not marry.And her seducer suffers death by her own hand, which plunges into his body a killing blade‹divine retribution surely.

These tremendous emotions experienced by Hardy's powerful and elemental characters are in contrast to the placid, accepting natures of the lesser mortals whom we meet in the taverns of Casterbridge, around bonfires, and harvesting in the fields. Critics generally feel that Hardy intends these rustics to be taken as "the symbol of the great majority of humdrum mortals," a chorus in the original Greek sense that "gives the reader a standard of normality by which he can gauge the... heights and depths to which the main characters rise and fall." Social gatherings such as the opening bonfire in The Return of the Native (1878) and the planning of the Skimmington in The Mayor of Casterbridge, for example, suggest the choric scenes of Greek tragedy and more particularly of the commoners of Shakespearean drama.

Like the great tragedies of fifth-century Athens and Elizabethan England, Hardy's Novels of Character and Environment convey a strong sense of fatalism, a view that in life human actions have been predetermined, either by the very nature of things, or by God, or by Fate. Hardy dramatized his conception of destiny in human affairs as the Imminent Will in his poetry, especially in his poetic drama of the Napoleonic wars, The Dynasts. By his emphasis on chance and circumstance in the plots of his stories Hardy consistently suggests that human will is not free but fettered. In both Tess of the D'Urbervilles and Under the Greenwood Tree, for example, he employs chance coincidence as more than a mere device of plotting.

Dick Dewey in Under the Greenwood Tree is called away to a friend's funeral on the same day that his beloved, Fancy Day, is to début as the church organist, and Angel returns to Tess from Brazil and near-death after she has established a commonlaw marriage with Alec. In The Mayor of Casterbridge (1886), Hardy seems to apply the concept of 'Fortune's False Wheel' (which Chaucer discusses at length in "The Monk's Tale" and to which Shakespeare alludes many times in King Lear) to the rise and fall of Michael Henchard: starting as a poor hay-trusser with a drinking problem, he renounces alcohol and works his way up to become the town's leading corn factor and mayor, only to undergo a startling series of reversals and end life an outcast.

Although Far from the Madding Crowd has some of the qualities of Shakespearean comedy, most of the Novels of Character and Environment (also known as "The Wessex Novels") such as The Return of the Native are tragic in their conception. The conclusion of the former, however, is not entirely happy, while the latter's ending with the marriage of the enigmatic Diggory Venn and the pathetic Thomasin was the consequence of Hardy's modifying his original plan to satisfy the readers of his serial version.

This feeling of the constant attrition, and final obliteration, of the human shape and all human structures, permeates Hardy's work. Interviewed about Stonehenge he commented that "it is a matter of wonder that the erection has stood so long," adding however that "time nibbles year after year" at the structure In contrast to 'grand' ruins both inanimate and human, a minor and more normative character such as publican of the Three Mariners, Mrs. Stannidge, has a more even life; yet is the jovial inn-keeper really more fortunate for not having been tested by experience? Hardy like Milton could "not praise a fugitive and cloistered virtue."

In The Return of the Native, Hardy clarified the happy "blessings" of mediocrity:

A well-proportioned mind is one which shows no particular bias; one of which we may safely say that it will never cause its owner to be confined as a madman... [or] to be applauded as a prophet....

Like Joseph Conrad, Thomas Hardy attempted in his fiction to comment on the macrocosm of the human race through an intense study of a microcosm well known to him, the rural society of nineteenth-century 'Wessex', where, from time to time, dramas of a grandeur and unity truly Sophoclean are enacted in the real, by virtue of the concentrated passion and closely-knit inter-dependence of the lives therein.

Despite an obvious fascination for those capable of powerful emotions and tragic fates, Hardy nevertheless expresses sympathy for the lower orders, then rapidly departing their ancestral cottages in search of a better standard of living in the "urban roar" (to quote Hardy's lyric "Where the Picnic Was") of England's industrial cities. Hardy attempts to record such customs as the mumming (inThe Return of the Native) and the skimmington (in The Mayor of Casterbridge), and such superstitions as the fetishistic wax doll (in RoN), for these folk-ways were being swiftly destroyed, along with the old folk-lore and orally-transmitted ballads and tales, by education, migration, and printed books and papers.

Complementing his minor roles as folklorist and anthropologist, Hardy was very much the social critic. In his fiction, not only natural forces (such as the adverse weather that assists in ruining Michael Henchard in The Mayor of Casterbridge) but also human society seem bent on crushing the sensitive and imaginative individual. Society inflicts its gratuitous suffering through exercising outworn conventions and superficial values, as well as through the new age's emphasis on efficiency.

The "passionless permanence" of Egdon Heath in The Return of the Native and the Roman antiquities of The Mayor of Casterbridge contrast with futile and pitifully brief human existence. In the novels of Thomas Hardy, time moves rhythmically, in seasons and ages, rather than mechanically, according to watch and even calendar.

As a realist, Hardy felt that art should describe and comment upon actual situations, such as the heavy lot of the rural labourers and the bleak lives of oppressed women. Though the Victorian reading public tolerated his depiction of the problems of modernity, it was less receptive to his religious scepticism and criticism of the divorce laws. His public and critics were especially offended by his frankness about relations between the sexes, particularly in his depicting the seduction of a village girl in Tess, and the sexual entrapment and child murders of Jude.

The passages which so incensed the late Victorians the average twentieth-century reader is apt to miss because Hardy dealt with delicate matters obliquely. The modern reader encounters the prostitutes of Casterbridge's Mixen Lane without recognizing them, and concludes somewhat after the 'Chase' scene in Tess that it was then and there that the rape occurred. In Hardy's novels female principals differ from one another far less than do his male principals. The temperamental capriciousness of such characters as Fancy Day, Eustacia Vye, and Bathsheba Everdene arises from an immediate and instinctive obedience to emotional impulse without sufficient corrective control of reason.

Hardy's women rarely engage in such intellectual occupations as looking ahead. Of all of Hardy's women, surely it is Tess who has won the greatest respect for her strength of character and struggle to be treated as an individual. As W. R. Herman notes, Tess rejects both the past and the future that threaten to "engulf" her in favour of "the eternal now", but these inexorable forces close in on her nonetheless at Stonehenge, symbol of the ever-present past. Hardy's attitudes towards women were complex because of his own experiences.

Certainly the latter stages of his own marriage to Emma Lavinia Gifford must have contributed much to his somewhat equivocal attitudes. On the one hand, Hardy praises female endurance, strength, passion, and sensitivity; on the other, he depicts women as meek, vain, plotting creatures of mercurial moods. As a young man, Hardy was easily infatuated, and easily wounded by rejection. Often he describes his bright and beautiful heroines, many drawn from such real-life figures as school-mistress Tryphena Sparks, at length: the blush of their cheeks, the arch of their eyebrows, their likeness to particular birds or flowers. Even modern female readers accept the truth of Hardy's female protagonists because, despite his implication that woman is the weaker sex, as Hardy remarked, "No woman can begrudge flattery."

Rarely do his minor female characters have either inner strength or spiritual power or physical beauty. He treats them with a fond irony, as with Bathsheba's maid Liddy in Far from the Madding Crowd, with her "womanly dignity of a diminutive order." Although the old furmity vendor of MoC, androgynous or an "anti-woman" as she has been dubbed, appears on only a few occasions, Hardy treats her with the same respect and faithfulness of description that characterize his treatment of "Wide-Oh" in the same novel. Perhaps, as in The Well-Beloved, Hardy's chief female characters are based on the artist's personal conception of the feminine ideal.

The quiet, shy, strong-minded, moral, and responsible Elizabeth-Jane of The Mayor of Casterbridge endures the trials of poverty, but is able to learn from bitter experience, even providing herself with an education in the classics, just as young Thomas Hardy, the former Dorchester architect's apprentice, had done.

The independently-minded Bathsheba of Far from the Madding Crowd is, in contrast to Elizabeth-Jane, a non-conformist because she tries to run her own farm and manage men; yet Hardy has her act with a spontaneity of feeling and feel at times inferior to men. However, the novelist reveals his sensitivity towards the situation of women in his society by showing Bathsheba's all-too-modern conflict between the desire for marriage and that for individuality and independence.

In all of Hardy's great novels there are frustrating, imprisoning marriages that may reflect his own first marriage. Though these relationships may seem almost 'sexless' to the modern reader, they are nevertheless quite believable. The "stale familiarity" that characterizes the relationship between young Susan and Michael Henchard as they trudge towards Weydon- Priors in the opening pages of The Mayor of Casterbridge is a nimbus that hangs over the unions of Eustacia and Clym inThe Return of the Native, Lucetta and Farfrae in The Mayor of Casterbridge, Bathsheba and Troy in Far from the Madding Crowd, and, of course, Jude and Arabella in Jude.

The novelist, united in holy acrimony for all but three of the thirty-eight years of his first marriage, clearly saw the need and argued eloquently for reasonable and human divorce laws. Unsuitable matches in his novels inevitably lead to suffering for both partners. Early in the same year which saw the death of Emma Hardy, the novelist expressed the opinion in Hearst's Magazine (1912) that "the English marriage laws are... the gratuitous cause of at least half the misery of the community." There is a strong element of wish- fulfilment in Hardy's sparing Donald Farfrae in The Mayor of Casterbridge a protracted marriage to the egotistical and small-minded Lucetta.

Hardy put so much of himself into his fiction that it is hardly surprising he gave it up for poetry after the hostile reception of his last and greatest novels, Tess and Jude. It was his cynical pessimism and social realism rather than his sympathy with his largely female protagonists that led him into difficulties. Hardy's heroes, like Clym and Jude and Henchard, are able to struggle actively with their destiny, form plans for opposing it, try to hew out a recognized place in the world. The women in his novels have no such outlet, and this makes their situation more tragic.

They are limited to a very few, easily recognizable social roles, and they are always subject to sexual domination and destruction from men:

Alluding to Samuel Taylor Coleridge's The Rime of the Ancient Mariner, Hardy felt that "A story must be exceptional enough to justify its telling. We tale-tellers are all Ancient Mariners, and none of us is warranted in stopping Wedding Guests (in other words, the hurrying public) unless he has something more unusual to relate than the ordinary experience of every average man and woman." From Hardy's first ventures into fiction he had attempted "the adjustment of things unusual to things external and universal."

Carl J. Webber notes the following characteristics of Hardy's fiction evident in what was probably a re-working of his first effort:

- Its stage is chiefly set in rural Wessex.
- It is topographically specific, to a degree unparalleled in English literature.
- It deals with Dorset farmers, and shows sympathetic insight into the life of this class.
- It does not avoid an impression of artificiality whenever "polite society" is involved.
- The dialogue is often unreal, and there is occasional stiffness of language, with involved sentences, awkward inversions, split infinitives, etc.
- In marked contrast with these rhetorical defects, there is frequent felicity of phrase, particularly in descriptive passages, and the author's alert senses, all of them, often leave their mark.
- Nature interests him for her own sake, and his treatment of her is often poetic.
- There are many literary allusions and quotations, and references to painters, musicians, and architects [in imitation of George Eliot].
- The use of coincidents and accidents is overdone; and plausibility is often stretched to the extreme.
- There is a secret marriage.
- There is a pervading note of gloom, only momentarily relieved.
- It all comes to a tragic end (sudden death).

All these elements, discernible in 1886.

Although the frequent iteration of sensational event, surprise, dramatic suspense, irony of circumstance, and reversal of fortune strain the probability of his novels, as he was well aware, Hardy took comfort in the realization that probability of character is far more important than probability of incident. "This accords with Hardy's last definition of tragedy: 'The best tragedy — highest tragedy, in short‹is that of the Worthy encompassed by the Inevitable'. In "Thomas Hardy's Tragic Hero," Ted R. Spivey argues against Ernest Baker's contention that Hardy's heroes are never quite tragic in the Aristotelian sense because they suffer not from a clearly-defined hamartia (an undermining flaw or fatal error in judgement) but from "paralysis of the will." Spivey contends that Hardy "was a writer of tragedies, a tragic poet, if you will, who did his work in prose" rather than in the traditional tragic medium, verse drama.

In his great novels — The Return of the Native, Jude the Obscure, Tess of the D'Urbervilles, and The Mayor of Casterbridge — Hardy saw man beaten down by forces within and without himself and sought to record man's eternal struggle with fate. This is also what the Greeks and Shakespeare do. Conceding that Hardy's heroes lack the universality, the rich intellects and imaginations of Shakespeare's heroes, Spivey nevertheless sees in Tess and Jude "souls capable of great feeling, souls capable of exultation" and "nobility of passion". He concludes that "Tragedy for Hardy is the defeat of the romantic hero's desire to reach a higher spiritual state.

The drives of Hardy's characters to achieve states of love and ecstasy are powerful enough to make his chief characters among the most passionate in English literature". His tragic heroes and heroines cry out defiantly against their fate, but accept their doom with an insight into and an awareness of the forces of evil which have effected their downfall; by the very strength of their passions Hardy's protagonists command our sympathies, "and we experience a feeling that someone of great worth has been lost when we see them destroyed". Although we do not meet them on the stage, Hardy's heroes and heroines are specifically "tragic" in the Aristotelian sense because they elicit from the reader the requisite (and somewhat contradictory) responses of pity and fear.

Phantoms, or the Child in Time

Use the crypt as a more symptomatic structure (to read readings)?

Shall I sing, dance around around around,

When phantoms call the tune!
Hardy, 'Song to an old Burden'
And where is truth? On tombs? for such to thee
Has been my heart – and thy dead memory
Has lain from childhood, many a changeful year,
Unchangingly preserved and buried there.
Shelley, 'Fragment: The Sepulchure of Memory'

Thomas Hardy's poetry, like his life, is full of secrets: occasions not specified, biographical identifications which cannot readily be made, lacunae left to us as the residue of those bonfires at Max Gate from 1918 on, in which he and then his second wife Florence destroyed early diaries, letters, drafts, stirring the ashes of the fire to ensure that no fragment remained to contradict the picture given in his disguised autobiography.

Or perhaps we are dealing with ancestral secrets never committed to paper, dying with the memories of his tight-lipped and childless siblings. That secrecy, or its possibility, is thematized regularly in the poetry; a late poem, 'The Single Witness', even has a protagonist willing to kill to preserve a family secret, and Hardy's final poems in the mode of the envoi contain repeated references to what he will take with him to the grave.

The movement between apparent confession and withdrawal of context is typical of Hardy's poetry, and is close in structure to his description of the freedoms offered by lyric – the declaration in the Life that 'Generally, speaking, there is more autobiography in a hundred lines of Mr. Hardy's poetry than in all the novels' coexisting with repeated warnings in his prefaces that his poems are 'fancies' not to be confused with 'fact', so that biographical inferences are both licensed and obstructed. The result is a sense that the author is at once present and absent, both the source of affect in the poetry and, ostensibly, simply a ventriloquizer of 'seemings'.

There is, accordingly, a necessary obscurity, a gap in meaning which is constantly presented to the reader of Hardy's poetry, and which is structural rather than simply involving a poverty of information. Some of his poems are so deeply obscure that they appear to be about nothing, signalling an absence which nonetheless generates poetry and subsequent interpretation.

A good example is the inaptly named 'An Experience', a poem which self-consciously describes anything but the nature of the experience which is supposedly its subject; which defines it almost entirely in terms of negatives – it was not 'In anything that was said, / In anything that was done' – and concludes with a declaration that it was something that the speaker 'Was never to forget', still with no obvious objective correlative for the reader.

This chapter offers an account of the notion of the secret in Hardy from a number of perspectives: theoretical, interpretive, and (in a limited sense) biographical. In order to provide a framework for my analysis, I will begin with the work of psychoanalysts Nicholas Abraham and Maria Torok.

From the 1960s, Abraham and Torok began to offer a reinterpretation of Freudian practice focused less on childhood sexuality, repression and conversion than on the way in which the expanding self encounters and deals with traumatic events and losses, either in terms of the subject's own experience or that of others. The terms introjection and incorporation are central to their work, the former designating a 'healthy' encounter with the world, broadening the ego; the latter involving a trauma which is simply absorbed into the self or body as a foreign presence.

Focusing on the mechanism of incorporation, they produce a psychic topography which includes the crypt – the site of a 'preservative repression'; of an incorporation which, in contrast to the dynamic repression of neurosis, cannot (in theory – this is a contentious proposition) be accessed indirectly or expressed via such mechanisms as projection and denial; which is cloaked in a silence which disrupts the possibility of linguistic expression itself. Typically, the crypt is associated with mourning, with the incorporation of a lost object.

A related, and arguably more useful concept is that of trans-generational haunting, articulated via the notion of the 'phantom'. As Torok defines it, the 'phantom' is a formation in the dynamic unconscious that is found there not because of the subject's own repression but on account of a direct empathy with the unconscious or the rejected psychic matter of a parental object. Consequently, the phantom is not at all the product of the subject's self-creation by means of the interplay between repressions and interjections. The phantom is alien to the subject who harbors it. Moreover, the diverse manifestations of the phantom, which we call haunting, are not directly related to instinctual life and are not to be confused with the return of the repressed.

These are 'family secrets', relating to parents or other love-objects, or to those in previous generations, and passed down as an area of the psyche which is interdicted. The phantom typically appears not in displaced symptoms, but in imaginings which seem to come from outside the self, which are 'gratuitous' (as in phobias or obsessive behaviour) or 'ventriloquised'. Psychology here moves closer to one of its suppressed origins in spiritualism; in the nineteenth-century psychologizing of the uncanny. As Nicholas Rand comments, Abraham and Torok are 'primarily concerned with converting obstructions into guides to understanding... ways in which signification can be conjectured despite its apparent absence'.

It is also important to note that Abraham and Torok first encounter the phantom as an effect in the analyst, that is as something already transferred to another person who listens and interprets.To study the phantom, then, may also be to study its effect a as a symptomatic structure in others – potentially on anyone who forms an affectual link with the analysand. It is to read with an attention to slippages involving the incorporation of another: the 'I' of the patient's story, Torok suggests, often conceals another, in a movement like that of the author's into a displaced first-person, an 'I' which is disavowed, ghostly, and which signals a removal of affect in the self – since the affect is another's.

Cryptonomy as practiced by Abraham and Torok can seem, to the reader outside a tradition in which analytic practice might provide its own justifications, a rather arbitrary search for linguistic clues.Neither does one wish to retrospectively psychoanalyze Hardy. But the strength of their work is that it allows us to conceptualize material which is unspoken and unspeakable, and to conceive that material as part of a broader family history, with all the economic and even political vicissitudes that involves. As Esther Rankin comments, 'reconstituting an unspoken trauma does not imply inventing a false, fantasized past history for a character but rather understanding that that the text calls upon the reader to expand its apparent parameters to include invisible scenarios'.

She adds, however, that 'although predating the events of the text, these unelaborated dramas have no reality outside the outside the limits of the text. Such limits, however, have to be construed as extending beyond their readily available borders. The drive beyond the text, with a fictionality both disavowed and partially admitted within this psychoanalytic tradition, is complicated, as suggested above, by the possibility of incorporation on the part of the reader, involving a carrying of the phantom into yet another psyche – a story of Hardy's readers told in one part of this chapter.

'Family Portraits': Haunting Pain: There are a number of features of Hardy's poetry which suggest less an analysis in the terms offered by Abraham and Torok than a convergence of terminology: a fascination with intergenerational haunting and areas of psychic resistance, with phantoms and secrets. Hardy offers a startlingly self-conscious version of the crypt in his late poem 'Family Portraits'.[The last of the great phantasmagoric series including 'The Pedigree' and 'The Chosen', with its description of three 'picture-drawn' people stepping from the frame it provides another version of the love-triangle which Hardy had recently explored in The Famous Tragedy of the Queen of Cornwall. The three give their names – though to the poem's speaker ('Full well though I knew') rather than to the readers, then,

They set about acting some drama, obscure,
The woman and he,
With puppet-like movements of mute strange allure;

Yea, set about acting some drama, obscure,
Till I saw 'twas their own lifetime's tragic amour,
Whose course begot me;
Yea – a mystery, ancestral, long hid from my reach
In the perished years past,
That had mounted to dark doings each against each
In those ancestor's days, and long hid from my reach;
Which their restless enghostings, it seemed, were to teach
Me in full, at this last.
But fear fell upon me like frost, of some hurt
If they entered anew
On the orbits they smartly had swept when expert
In the law-lacking passions of life, – of some hurt
To their souls – and thus mine – which I fain would avert
So, in sweat cold as dew,
'Why wake up all this?' I cried out. 'Now, so late!
Let old ghosts be laid!'
And they stiffened, drew back to their frames and numb state,
Gibbering: 'Thus are your own ways to shape, know too late!'
Then I grieved that I'd not had the courage to wait
And see the play played.
I have grieved ever since: to have balked future pain,
My blood's tendance foreknown,
Had been triumph. Nights long stretched awake I have lain
Perplexed in endeavours to balk future pain
By uncovering the drift of their drama. In vain
Though therein lay my own.

The 'mystery' here is encoded both as organic inheritance ('blood's tendance') and as an original 'drama'; both as hurting the speaker via a direct transference ('some hurt / To their souls – and thus mine') and as producing a mirroring repetition in his actions. Causation is uncertain; indeed, in the earlier version of the poem the stanza beginning 'Why wake up all this' precedes the third stanza above, refering to the 'orbits' of the actors, and the later phrase 'which I fain would avert' replaces an earlier 'but I found them inert', shifting the question of causality radically from the past to the present of the speaker.

Moreover while in the 1924 version the poet is reactive, asking 'Could it have hurt [to have watched?]', in the 1928 version he is fearful and preemptive, as if slowly admitting that the blame was in fact his, and that the hurt is bound up with a willed failure to watch and see the truth.

This is close to the mechanism of disavowal or repudiation as described by Freud and Lacan: the narrator seems both to already know the story ('full well though I knew') and to refuse to know it ('Why wake up all this?'). He seems to see that the story has tragically predicted his life ('therein lay my own'), but also suggests that the mystery remains intact, unopened, as does the question of the future.

The unstated and deeply compulsive material of this 'drama' is bounded, then, by what is, formally, a refusal to remember. The poem exists in the space of what Abraham and Torok call incorporation, expressed in the ventriloquism, puppet-drama, and phobic avoidance which they see as characteristic of the phantom, the 'mute' and 'numb' state of both the actors and speaker suggesting – but never fully expressing – trauma.

The phantom is incorporated as a rigid and frozen foreign object in the psyche, the marker-stone of a secret (becoming-stone is a state traced in Hardy's reading and his poetry, from his marking of lines in Byron's 'The Prisoner of Chillon', 'Among the stones I stood a stone / And was scarce conscious of what I wist', to the late poem 'A Wish for Unconsciousness': 'If I could but abide / As a tablet on a wall').

Something strikes the speaker dumb, stiffening and freezing, obscuring the story or origins; in both 'The Pedigree' and 'Family Portraits' the word 'drift' punningly suggests a cloud-hidden primal scene, a drift which we cannot quite get.For Abraham and Torok the material of the crypt or phantom cannot be represented directly, but can appear as an 'undecipherable fetish'. The interdicted 'silent word' is, they comment, can appear as such an image as Hardy's poem presents: their phrase is 'love disguised and dressed up in a "painting"'.

I am not suggesting that 'Family Portraits' can be directly

applied to Hardy's life (what is there to apply?), but rather that it offers an account of what it is like to read Hardy, or to have to read into Hardy's poetry.

We are presented with various repeated traumatic scenes which invite interpretation, which offer to solve the mystery, but also face a form of psychic censorship which exiles reading to a deferred and subjunctive mood (the 'had been triumph' which signals an unachieved meaning). Meaning is both present and absent, both figured and declared to reside in an undeclarable literalness. This is a structure we find throughout Hardy's verse, nicely defined by the two mirrored quatrains of 'The Wound':

I climbed to the crest,
And, fog-festooned,
The sun lay west
Like a crimson wound:
Like that wound of mine
Of which none knew,
For I'd given no sign
That it pierced me through.

Here the 'sign' is both everywhere and nowhere to be seen; the 'wound' is first bodily and deployed (to signal redness) in a simile in which its visibility is the point; but then becomes a vehicle in a strangely unrelated simile in which the invisibility of the a psychic wound is signalled. It is gestured at in the demonstrative pronoun ('that wound'), but only specified in a doubly displaced form: a sunset like a wound, a (physical) wound like 'that' (psychic) wound. Trauma is both revealed and hidden in this language.

Many of Hardy's poems are encoded in this way, so that, to take an example almost at random, anyone who has read deeply in Hardy can immediately recognize in his cryptic poem 'Where Three Roads Joined' a vocabulary of terms shared with other poems – life laughing onwards; a scene of blankness; muteness in its witnesses; a 'spectre-beridden' place; the void of a 'plumbless well' down which hopes and happiness roll; a dwelling on memory and loss – so that the poem is perfectly readable; even though the details of what it refers to are absent, the reader understands the structure of that absence.

At this point, however, I want to move away from the metapsychology of the phantom (though the subject will remain implicit) to a more specific set of concerns raised by 'Family Portraits', relating to the issues of wounding and pain, and ultimately the notion – not fully articulated in this poem, but circulating throughout Hardy's work – of childhood trauma. For all that 'Family Portrait' describes the impossibility of fully representing its own subject-matter, it is possible to follow threads and clues which extend into Hardy's other texts.

One such clue is the repeated phrase in the final stanza, 'balk future pain' – a phrase Hardy added as he re-wrote the poem, replacing 'heal my own pain'. Pain is an interesting issue, not only because of the metaphorical link to the idea of psychic wounding or trauma which we have already seen in 'The Wound', but more generally because in the nineteenth century physical pain become an increasingly problematic issue for progressive and Darwinian traditions.

In what follows, we will move rather circuitously from a general consideration of the topic back to the issue of childhood pain.

With the waning of religious interpretations of pain (pain as punishment, as Fall), and the possibility of its elimination in many situations as a result of advances in medicine and humanitarian action, a debate on its meaning ensued; a debate which broadened to take in issues such as vivisection, the subject of a Royal Commission in 1875-6 (cruelty to animals is of course a recurrent concern in Hardy's writings). Darwin was a witness in the hearings of the Royal Commission.

His interest in the treatment of animals, as one commentator notes, 'effected a powerful conjunction between the assault on pain and the accomplishment of [his] life-work'. But from the evolutionary point of view, the model in which pain was simply the stimulus for action, as in putting the hand in a fire, seemed to fail to account for persistent forms of pain (particularly those with no apparent trauma).

In The Expression of Emotion in Man and the Animals,

Darwin includes pain in his discussion of the stronger emotions, borrowing Herbert Spencer's economic argument that pain produces an 'overflow of nerve-force' which 'must expend itself in some direction', taking over successive systems of muscles, beginning with those closest to the seat of pain and continuing with the most-used (facial muscles, speech).

This argument explains the expression of pain in terms of discharge. But Darwin has trouble uniting this view with that of the utility of pain, and indeed the reference to 'nerve-force' suggests the way in which the intensity of pain in humans is a special consideration. For T. H. Huxley, that intensity of human pain was an effect of evolutionary advances which places consciousness increasingly in tension with the rest of nature.

Its excessive nature, the sense that in evolutionary terms its intensity hardly seems necessary (even if it can sometimes be interpreted as a signal of bodily disruption or danger), meant that it seemed like a reminder of a kind of thought which inheres in the body – the complement, Elaine Scarry has recently argued, of imaginative activity which projects the self outwards into other objects.Thinking on the evolutionary redundancy of pain was to culminate in the 1930s in Gerald Stanley Heard's Pain, Sex and Time.

His book begins with a simple question: is human evolution continuing, and are there untapped human potentials we have not exploited? His answer is a qualified 'yes': the potential is there, but such energies are at the moment wasted. The proof is in the pain: for Heard – as for the early Freud of the Project for a Scientific Psycholoy – pain is waste psychic energy which has not been tapped (thus, the mind can exclude pain if it is concentrating hard on other things). The aim of existence is 'to be conscious in a way which uses up the energy which was leaking and discharging in pain'.

Hardy attacked philosophical attempts to explain away pain in a 1886 note on Hegel, noting that the argument that 'real pain is compatible with formal pleasure – that the ideal is all, etc.' does not offer much consolation to those in pain. Schopenhauer, in his powerful essay on 'The Vanity and Suffering of Life' had attacked the Hegelian subordination of individual pain to human destiny in a similar way. For Schopenhauer pain is a 'positive' force in the neutral sense that its presence outweighs all other factors, while well-being is only strongly defined when it is succeeded by other states: 'We feel pain, but not painlessness; we feel care, not the absence of care; fear, but not security... for only pain and want can be felt positively, and therefore announce themselves; well-being, on the other hand, is merely negative.

Pain binds the individual intensely to a particular moment (in contrast to the Hegelial dialectic, which lifts us towards transcendence), representing the predicament of consciousness in the world, a state of 'debt'.

Hardy was also undoubtedly influenced by John Stuart Mill's famous indictment of the indifference and malevolence of Nature in the first of the Three Essays on Religion; it is echoed in his response to a 1902 review of Maeterlinck's Apology for Nature:

Pain has been, and pain is: no new sort of morals in Nature can remove pain from the past and make it pleasure for those who are its infallible estimators, the bearers thereof. And no injustice, however slight, can be atoned for by her future generosity, however ample, so long as we consider Nature to be, or to stand for, unlimited power.

The same harsh doctrine is expounded in a letter attacking Henri Bergson in 1915. Writing to Caleb Saleeby, who had sent him a copy of Creative Evolution, Hardy denounces Bergson's mixture of Vitalism and materialism: the most fatal objection to his view of creation plus propulsion seems to me to lie in the existence of pain.

If nature were creative she would have created painlessness, or be in process of creating it – pain being the first thing we instinctively fly from. If on the other hand we cannot introduce into life what is not already there, and are bound to mere recombination of old materials, the persistence of pain is intelligible.

Pain, here, is the mark of 'mechanism', of animal responses which cannot be eradicated by an act of will, and ultimately, of a view of the world which sees it determined by germplasm rather than élan vital. In both the passages above it is the residue of the past which is linked to pain – an observation which makes 'balk[ing] future pain' an impossibility.

Having denounced Bergson for his Dualism, Hardy continues, in a passage examined in the previous chapter: 'You must not think me a hard-hearted rationalist for all this. Half my time (particularly when I write verse) I believe – in the modern use of the word–not only in things that Bergson does, but in spectres, mysterious voices, intuitions, omens, dreams, haunted places, etc., etc.'. Belief in some provisional 'modern sense' would ultimately involve a refusal to confront the difficulty of positions which cannot be reconciled.

If we put these passages together, then it is apparent that pain and the spectral are close together in Hardy's mind – not as cognate, since pain must be believed in whereas spectres are simply assented to, and any notion of the life-force as having an immaterial existence is ruled out. Rather, pain and the spectral are connected in that both represent evolutionary traces of an earlier existence; they act as the human residue of a past which must, strictly, be interpreted in material terms, but which nevertheless represents an ineradicable haunting. Pain is ghostly, a haunting persistence of 'old materials'; or of the material itself in its historicity.

Correspondingly, any rationalist attempts to eradicate pain are dubious – as in the comic episode in Hardy's The Hand of Ethelberta in which the heroine attempts to decide her course of action using Mill's Utilitarianism, reading there that 'The ultimate end... is an existence exempt as possible from pain, and as rich as possible in enjoyments, both in point of quantity and quality'. Interestingly, Mill adds that the standard here is 'not the agent's own happiness but that of all concerned', and Ethelberta notes carefully that 'all concerned' normally refers to a small family circle – initiating her self-sacrifice in the name of her siblings.

The self may be sacrificed to the family, just as in Hardy's genealogical poems the 'line' may render the individual subject ghostly. Tess O'Toole notes (and she is thinking of Tess of the

D'Urbervilles) the way in which for Hardy 'the genetic product appears not as an example of rejuvenation but as a crypt inhabited by the relics of those long dead', producing 'the genetic legatee as a kind of ghost or specter'– a ghost inhabiting the site of an ancient passion.

If pain is a register of the spectralized past, the formula 'to balk future pain' which began this discussion is also interesting for the word balk. The noun balk is, the OED suggests, descended from a root meaning 'bar'; its oldest and later dialect meanings refer to ridges or unploughed areas separating different plots. Some of the meanings of the verb are connected, though 'to balk' also has the meaning of shunning a place, hesitating (as in a horse balking at a jump), as well as the common transitive meaning of frustrating or placing an obstacle before.

'Balk' thus has some of the complexity of Freud's antithetical words: it is to mark out ownership by creating a barrier, but also a refusal to cross a barrier. What is enclosed is this a space both shunned and guarded – the space of the phantom. Indeed, the word 'balk' is explicitly linked to a sexual secret in 'A Sunday Morning Tragedy', Hardy's controversial poem on abortion: the herb supplied by a shepherd is meant to 'balk ill-motherings' in ewes. Here balking is preventative abortion, the shunning of a life which will prove traumatic.

As in Schopenhauer, the issue of pain finds its ultimate focus in the question of being born: Schopenhauer cites Lessing's admiration of his son's understanding, when he refused to be born and 'had to be forcibly brought into [life] with the forceps, but was scarely there when he hurried away from it again'. Hardy's 'To an Unborn Pauper Child', with its stress on the triumph of pain over pleasure, reads like a verse commentary on this essay. The issue of the lost, aborted or mis-placed child leads us to a more developed cryptonomy in Hardy. First, however, a excursis into an interesting episode in critical history, and what we might call the cryptonomy of reception.

Randy's Hand, or the Lost Son

'Free among the dead, like unto them that are wounded,

and lie in the grave: who are out of remembrance, and are cut away from thy hand'.

Psalm 88, as marked by Hardy

Yet It may wake and understand
Ere Earth unshape, know all things, and
With knowledge use a painless hand,
A painless hand!

Chorus of the Pities, conclusion to Dynasts Part II

In the late 1960s the world of the Hardy Society was disturbed by the claims of Lois Deacon, an 'amateur' scholar from Dorchester, that she had uncovered the greatest mystery of Hardy's life: the existence of a child called 'Randy' (Randolph or Randall), fathered in an affair with his cousin Tryphena Sparks and raised by Tryphena's older sister Rebecca. 'Hardy's marriages were childless', as Deacon rather bathetically notes in the book which she co-authored with Terry Coleman, Providence and Mr Hardy (1966), 'but he was probably not altogether without issue'.

Her claims were based largely on an identification of a photograph of a boy in a family album, made by Tryphena's daughter, Eleanor Bromell, near death at the age of eighty-six. This, for Deacon, was supported by 'internal' evidence in the form of readings of a number of poems said to deal with the affair and illegitimacy ('To an Orphan Child', 'The Place on the Map' and others), as well as other details like initials in family albums, lacunae in Hardy's autobiography and omissions in the genealogy which he drew up. The aim of Providence and Mr. Hardy is to rescue Tryphena from her 'suppressed' status, and reveal Randy to the world.

Nothing if not an industrious reader, Deacon also 'discovered' further scandal in the tangled skein of Hardy family history. She suggested that Tryphena was not in fact the daughter of her aging parents (her mother Maria, Hardy's aunt, was an improbable 46 when she was born), but was in fact the illegitimate issue of her older sister Rebecca and Rebecca's employer.

And – a final twist – Deacon more cautiously suggested that Typhena and Hardy may have been more than just cousins, and adduces evidence that Rebecca was in fact the early illegitimate offspring of Hardy's mother Jemima (neé Hand), subsequently passed off as the child of her elder sister Maria, already married to James Sparks (such transferences were a common rural practice, and are described in Hardy's 'A Hurried Meeting').

This makes Tryphena Hardy's niece – a fact which Hardy was unaware of at the time of their romance, Deacon proposes, but which he subsequently learnt, and which works its way into the Shelleyan theme of near-incest in his late novels. 'Randy' would thus be the issue of a series of tangled illegitimacies and transferences across generations and between sisters.

Deacon's work has been the object of some derision amongst Hardy's subsequent biographers – perhaps understandably, since she can offer no real proof of Randy's existence (there are no written records relating either to his supposed birth in 1868 or death sometime before 1917), and instead engages in highly selective and speculative biographical readings of poems. One Hardy scholar, F. R. Southerington, did support her in 1968, and one or two reviewers thought the story likely enough. Hardy's most recent biographer, Martin Seymour-Smith, is more charitable in describing her book as 'a speculative novel of what, just possibly, might have been'.

But the important question here is perhaps less 'is the story true?' than 'what supports and generates such narratives'? Why is the story so persuasive as a 'speculative novel'? For Deacon is not the only example of a reader who concretizes phantoms in biography: if she obligingly supplies a child to deal with Hardy's childlessness, the sobre-minded biographer Michael Millgate suggests that Hardy might have been impotent – a suggestion vigorously contested by Seymour-Smith, but illustrative of more than simply biological speculation since it attempts once again to identify a defining area of 'deadness' in Hardy, a phantom presence. Deacon's symptomatic reading responds, that is, to a real trauma in Hardy, a trauma which is inevitably reproduced in the stories told by his readers. Deacon's comment in an earlier pamphlet suggests her own involvement in a drama of veiling and unveiling, a play of desire and identification: 'What most Hardy biographers have not perceived is that although Hardy frequently draws a discreet veil over the truth, he invariably leaves gaps and rents in the veil through which he later sheds a powerful and revealing light'. Through these gaps Tryphena emerges as 'the dark lady of the lyrics', the key to Hardy's poetry of non-specification.

One key to Randy – though one which might too easily represent a premature acceptance of a deconstructive line – involves seeing him as a linguistic ghost, a retracing of Hardy's texts and accounts of his life. As Southerington reports, Eleanor Bromell 'described [Randy] as "delicate", "frail", older than herself, fond of birds, reading poetry, and of drawing'; she also claims that she was an architect. All these were, of course, Hardy's own attributes, suggesting that one unstated case for 'Randy' – unstated because formal, and perhaps also because it suggests a slippage in Mrs Bromell's memory – seems to be a homology between father and proposed son, another intergenerational mapping.

A similar sense of assimilation is present in Deacon's stress on the singularily of Tryphena. If Hardy's biographers note that he may have had liaisons with many women in the period around 1868 (including Tryphena) and that he identified many women as the model of Tess, Deacon wishes to make Tryphena the great Ur-romance of his life, incorporating even Emma Hardy's body: 'Poor Emma Lavinia! She lent her very eyes and hair, her riding-habit and her Cornish home of St. Juniot's for the effective disguising of the dark-haired Dorset Tryphena in A Pair of Blue Eyes'.

Tryphena multiplies within his texts. When Tess is described as younger than she looks, Deacon notes that Tryphena had been similarly accused when she applied for the job of headmistress in Plymouth. But a footnote adds that a parallel phrase ('looked more womanly than she really was') is applied to Geraldine in An Indiscretion.

Here, the very conventionality of the phrase is evidence

of its application to a specific 'real' context. In a similar way, Hardy's texts multiply evidence in the world: a footnote remarks that 'it is curious that' a church in Brixton, only one and a quarter miles from where Tryphena taught, 'should be called St. Jude', and that a house in Topsham, 100 yards from where she lived, 'should be called "St. Jude's Cottage"'. The 'should' here signals a textual agency; 'a pattern emerges', Deacon and Coleman note, even as they weave it.

Such 'textual' readings co-exist with a desire to find a 'real' Randy, a body behind the text (Abraham and Torok comment that 'the analyst-judge also acts as a morphologist: they have to reconstruct the event from a few scattered bodily fragments'). For Deacon the reality of the body is supplied above all by the two photographs which she identifies as being Randy. But one interesting detail in the story of 'Randy' concerns a missing part of the body, what we could call a 'phantom' limb. Mrs Bromell made repeated reference to an injury to his right hand, attributed to two different causes (a cycling accident, a dog).

This is a detail both Deacon and Southerington fuss over without attempting to do more than link it indexically to the boy in the photograph – the latter eliciting opinions from a medical expert that the boy in the photograph might conceivably be missing fingers. It is as if in providing another detail of identity – there was a boy, his hand was hurt – it acts as a symbol of a larger absence.

But we might also see that loss as inscribed within the story itself: 'Hand' is Jemima Hardy's 'maiden' name – the name she had when, Deacon suggests, she bore the illegitimate Rebecca, Randy's alleged grandmother (an earlier name in what Hardy called his 'beclouded' maternal line, incidentally, was Childs or Childses. The wounded hand us thus a stigmata marking the ancestral mystery rather than 'proof' of it; it points to the wronged woman, and perhaps also the absent father, the man who makes his living by his pen.

Like Oedipus's swollen-footedness (oide--o-pous), a wound signals incest, a maiming and a secret naming (Oedipus is also etymologically oi-dipous, Simon Goldhill points out:

'alas, two-footed', as if he were himself the answer to his own riddle. Randy as riddle; Randy as handy; Randy as the name for desire; 'Randy' as only a stroke away from being an anagram for 'Hardy' – Deacon's story of incest and endogamy itself seems to generate tricks and embodied clues.

Here we might pick up a clue which Deacon misses, and continue with her supplementary story using a poem which features both a bastard child and a missing hand, 'Panthera'. Panthera is a veteran Centurion who still feels twinges in 'the hand he had lost, shorn by barbarian steel'. This is the 'phantom limb' which emerged as a focus in nineteenth-century neurological work, particularly in Weir Mitchell's writings on American Civil War victims – an entity which suggests the virtuality of the body, its being coordinated by an image of phantasmic unity, a body-image. The tale is told by an old soldier, who himself doubts the story Panthera told him years earlier, 'His mind at last being stressed by ails and age: 'Yet his good faith thereon I well could wage'.

The speaker had wished for offspring, even if illegitimate, to continue his line, and Panthera had warned him off it with an account of his own Palestinian love-child, fathered during an idyllic stopover in Nazareth over thirty years earlier, and only re-encountered at the point where the son is being crucified for sedition at Golgotha. Panthera recognizes the weeping mother, but does not care to 'close the silence of so wide a time'. The narrator casts doubt on the story, which Panthera seems to want to believe, despite acknowledging 'vagueness of identity' in this case.

This is the shockingly apocryphal Ur-tale of Christ, the child of mysterious origin (for volume publication Hardy was careful to supply a headnote detailing a number of sources for the legend, as if wishing to disclaim it as his 'issue'). The relationship to the canonical text is important here: the story is told by a would-be father who can only watch him at the point where the son is, like the limb, cut away from him and assigned an afterlife in an entirely separate text with a different story, which both covers and interdicts–balks – the apocryphal account. This might be read, in Deacon's manner, as simply an allegory of the story of Randy. But more obviously, it signals the questions of paternity and narrative which surround the issue of textual authority itself: who authors this account, the Centurion with the missing hand and the secret, or the later teller who doubts the story?

How does it relate to the text of the Gospels, ostensibly written by the hand of God? 'Panthera' is a poem on the mysteries of identity within an order which is double-coded: the centurion recognizes the 'ardent blood' of Christ as his own only through the mother and his memories of a sexual idyll, but she is nonetheless decked in the symbolic insignia of the Virgin (blue cloak) rather than simply being depicted naturalistically. The story supplies a naturalistic account of the paternity of Christ, but nonetheless depends for its force – and for an explanation of these events on Panthera – on the Christian world-view.

As in 'Family Secrets' we can attempt to press a little further, to riddle the language of the poem. It is 'cynic Time', the narrator tells us, which maims Panthera and breaks his spirit. 'Cynic' is a word Hardy uses in 'The Pedigree' to mark the twistings of a genealogy, its tendency to go awry: the 'cynic face' and 'cynic twist of the page' suggest the palsy known as a cynic spasm, a deformation of the self created in its antecedents, rather than cynicism in the philosophical sense. Panthera suggest that the lesson of the story is 'That when you talk of offspring as sheer joy / So trustingly, you blink contingencies', adding that 'He who goes fathering / Gives frightful hostages to hazardry!'

'Blink' is used in its older meaning of flinching from something, shutting one's eyes to it: that is, balking [at] future pain. We can also ask what the Centurion hopes of his child – and it is here that Hardy's pessimism intersects most forcibly with Christianity. If he, the 'ardent soldier', shares his 'ardent blood' with Christ, then he expects nothing of the future, no flame to be kindled. The root of the word 'ardent' is ardere, to burn, a root Hardy turns to in 'A Commonplace Day'. There he writes, almost tautologically, of 'that enkindling ardency from whose maturer glows. The world's amendment flows', before noting that it 'has missed its hope to be / Embodied on the earth'. Ardency or enkindling passion is, then, that hope for a meaning to history which is incarnated in Christ (in 'Panthera') but also frustrated, 'benumbed at birth' ('A Commonplace Day'); it is what dies with the day which 'is turning ghost', and which is figured forth in the embers of the fire which Hardy rakes.

Compare the following exchange recorded by Ernest Brennecke in his 1925 biography. Visiting Max Gate, he had suggested that Hardy was a 'ardent meliorist'. Hardy replied: 'I am not... And really, you must never call me "ardent" about anything. I am not. I am as indifferent as I find it possible to be. I wish you success, however. Good-day.' Here, 'ardency' is reduced to a suppressed trace; the word is cancelled. The disruption of Judeo-Christian history described in 'Panthera' is thus the reducing of a flame (perhaps even the Pentecostal flame) to ashes, reducing history to a succession of dead days, to a denatured geneology carried in Hardy's story of the lost child and the wounded hand.

Interestingly, the hypothetical existence of a 'hidden' story of Christ has been linked to Abraham and Torok's thinking by Nicholas Royle in a recent review article taking in the starting combination of translations of Derrida's Spectres of Marx and The Nag Hammadi Library of Coptic Gnostic texts.Royle argues that these early Gnostic texts 'phantomize' our reading of the Gospels, and playfully proposes his own phantom text, a non-existent and at best fragmentary story he describes as 'ashes in the wind'.

In this phantom text, Jesus speaks to Mary Magdalene after his crucifixion, explaining that he was not the one who was crucified; he had been replaced by a 'stranger' – initiating, for Royle, a dissolution of Christianity's haunted onto-theology into a theology of the lost other. This kind of experiment in deconstructive Christianity (including the figure of the 'real' Christ who survives the crucifixion, perplexed by his cult) was common enough in the late nineteenth century, and seems to find echoes in late twentieth-century theory.

Hardy's fiction contains a striking example of haunting

akin to that which we have seen in 'Panthera' and in the Deacon case – one of many examples of lost or displaced children in his prose, most famously the self-cancelling children of Jude the Obscure. In her description of the 'cancelled words' in Far from the Madding Crowd, Rosemarie Morgan describes the material which Hardy revised or removed under pressure from his cautious editor Leslie Stephen as the book was serialized in the Cornhill Magazine, Morgan tells a story of suppression and designification.

In the original drafts, Fanny dies with Troy's illegitimate and stillborn baby in her arms, and Bathsheba, now secretly married to Troy, sadly and compassionately inspects mother and baby in their coffin. Leslie Stephen was keen to omit the baby, but Hardy left it in – only, however, as a trace, present as the two words on Fanny's coffin which Gabriel Oak erases, 'and child'.

The 'massive cancellations' Hardy did agree to make, Morgan shows, 'have the effect of rendering the stillborn infant entirely invisible' – even, seemingly, to Bathsheba; and further revisions (and one spectacular reversal) shift Bathsheba from a position of empathy with Fanny to something closer to rivalry.The result is to produce a version of Bathsheba who is herself truncated and haunted by the phantom of the child, reduced to a barely-comprehendible passivity and pitifulness. Her motivations have, in the Cornhill, to be understood without the child whose trace is nevertheless there (and which was only very partially restored when Hardy revised the book again for volume publication).

Two of Morgan's comments are of further interest here: first, that Bathsheba was 'in his original conception of things, as vivid, as immediate, and as palpably real as his own flesh and blood', but is here reduced to being an 'echo' of that reality; and second, that Hardy spoke of censorship as 'paralysing'. Here we have a model for transgression, censorship, and the effect of that censorship on the subject, enacted both in the novel and in Hardy's encounter with social constraint. 'Cancelled words' signal the presence of the crypt (Morgan's title is taken from the volume of verse the secretive heroine publishes in The Hand of Ethelberta – their publication under a pseudonym again concealing origins). The crypt in turn opens into the space of reading – the space of Deacon's reading, but that, too, of the reader of Far From the Madding Crowd, and of all our reading.

What Deacon's excavations and extrapolations suggest is both the intensity with which Hardy's texts do generate readings in terms of phantasmic structures, absences and blockages, and at the same time the hazards of such interpretation. Perhaps the most puzzling aspect of her case is that amidst the welter of 'evidence' which she extracts from various poems in elucidation Hardy's allegedly tangled genealogy, she never cites the two poems which most directly and self-consciously address the issue of the 'dark doings' of genealogy: 'The Pedigree' and 'Family Portraits'. Where poems like 'The Place on the Map' can be mined for displaced clues, these poems meditate on the space of the secret itself.

'A deed back in time'

Where else might we pursue Hardy's ghosts? His family's 'authentic' ghost story, recounted to William Archer, also concerns a lost child. His mother dreamed that a sick friend came to her in the night, just at the point that, some distance away, the friend was dying. The woman appeared with her young child in her arms, 'but the odd thing was that, while she was sinking, she continually expressed a wish that my mother should take charge of the child'.Like the child attributed to Jemima Hardy in Deacon's account, it is offered to another, but its final location is uncertain – no mention is made of its subsequent fate. Phantom presence, orphan, supplement; in the story it never moves beyond spectral status.

This family story gestures towards the general instablity of the child in Hardy's texts, an instability which Deacon's account presents in a manageable way, making Little Father Time and other 'lost' children versions of Randy. Hardy often marked poems about dead or bereft children in his reading.The list of possible disruptions of childhood in his own poetry is immense, including illegitimacy; regret at lost children ('The Dead Bastard'); children disowned by their fathers ('The

Supplanter'); a woman killed defending a child not her own ('By the Barrows'); a dead child being christened ('Royal Sponsors'); a woman 'giving' her husband to a woman with whom he has a child ('A Wife and Another') or wishing to die so that another woman can have her husband-to-be and child ('The Wedding Morning'); a woman seeking a more vigorous father for her child; and a poem whose speaker wishes that a child whose mother has died might reincarnate her ('To a Motherless Child').

Children may haunt: 'The Bird-Catcher's Boy' describes a child who leaves a 'cruel' home and only returns as a ghost when the sea gives up his body. There are a number of poems including abortions ('the child – that should have been, / But was not, born alive' of 'The Ballad of Love's Skeleton'; 'A Sunday Morning Tragedy') and other poems recommending that children not be born ('To an Unborn Pauper Child'; 'The Unborn'; 'Epitaph on a Pessimist').

A cluster of these poems is situated in Time's Laughingstocks, the volume in which ballad-memory is most dominant, but also the first volume to appear after the death of Hardy's mother – a fact which might indeed suggest a posthumous release of memory, and even of interdicted material ('The Christening', for example, is a tale of a bastard child dated 1904, the year of Jemima's death; 'Panthera' is in the same volume, and other examples include 'A Trampwoman's Tragedy'; 'Unrealized' with its children whose mother is dead; and one of Deacon's favourites, 'The Dawn after the Dance', with its hinted illegitimacy).

It is interesting to meditate on Hardy's dry report in the Life that 'By reason of her parent's bereavement and consequent poverty under the burden of a young family, Jemima saw during girlhood and young womanhood some very stressful experiences of which she could never speak in her maturer years without pain, though she appears to have mollified her troubles by reading every book she could lay hands on'– a clue, perhaps, to the way in which his own investment in the literary imagination of childhood pain might indeed have centred on his mother.

One repeated topic is that of child fathered by the rival, with violent results: the 'cuckoo-child' placed in another's house (described in 'At a Pause in a Country Dance', 'A Conversation at Dawn', 'In the Restaurant' and many other poems; even Little Father Time). In 'A Flirt's Tragedy' a man hires a gigolo to seduce the woman who spurned him, then kills the gigolo after she becomes pregnant, raising the child as his only to have him flee his 'false father... [who] murdered my true!'

Arguably the most important such poems, offering a key to Hardy's metapoetics, are those in which the issue is the plotting of such a story rather than its actuality. In 'A Trampwoman's Tragedy' a woman pretends that her child is not her lover's, at which point he kills the imagined rival. In such poems, it is the story itself which generates violent acts. 'Her Death and After' also meditates on the status of the story of infidelity.

The protagonist is called to the deathbed of a woman he loves who married another; she suspects her unloving husband will not care for their lame newborn child:

Such my unease
That, could I insert a deed back in Time,
I'd make her yours, to secure her care;
And the scandal bear,
And the penalty for the crime.

The lover haunts her grave, and when he is challenged by the dead woman's husband (who has remarried and does, as predicted, neglect his first child) he concocts the story suggested by the dying wish, telling the husband that the child was indeed his; it is handed over to him to raise. This is the story of a fiction which activates a buried truth.

A 'deed' in the sense of a legal intention becomes a deed in the sense of an action validating that intention (as in typology), but there is a residue of guilt attached because the process involves the overwriting of history ('but compunctions loomed; for I'd harmed the dead / By what I said / For the good of the living one'). The 'deed back in time' is not a guilty secret, but rather the secret of a guilt: there is no original act of sin. This is perhaps the most cogent comment on the lost child in Hardy: as a device, it concerns itself with the failure of love to find its 'proper' locus; or a love which only finds expression outside its official channels, via an act of imaginative surrogacy which is, here, predicated on mourning.

This sense both of the need to recapture the past and of the violence of that process is also, as we will see, a feature of Hardy's relation to history generally. We can add a final, late, example of this notion of the encrypted (fictional) child. 'Aristodemus the Messenian', published in Winter Words, seems the grotesque product of a seriously decayed imagination, to the point where it is almost unreadable (understandably, it has received almost no critical discussion).

When King Aristodemus (circa 735 BC) decides that he must sacrifice his virgin daughter to save his people in battle, her lover attempts to prevent the act by claiming that she is pregnant, invalidating the sacrifice – the fictionalizing but recuperative gambit of 'Her Death and After'. The king refutes the story by ripping his daughter's womb open with his sword, an anatomical investigation and violation in which a vortex of issues – paternity, rape, birth, murder – devolve on the question of a sexual secret; a secret whose essence inheres, in fact, in being a fiction which generates rupture and uncertainty. What is in the womb? the poem asks, and the answer might be 'Nothing, just a story'. Could we say that this is the final displacement of the structured absence which constitutes Hardy's crypt?

It is not, I would suggest, easy to press further in discussing Hardy's family secrets; the point is less the need for a definitive account of 'what happened' – a need which in 'Aristodemus the Messenian' is shown to itself be violent – than an acknowledgement of the existence of a topic which is repeatedly raised and evaded, claimed and disclaimed, balked about and balked at; which is resolved into the story of another, or into silence. Some poems might suggest abortion or infanticide as one trauma; other poems the fostering of children. Both topics refer to the displacement of the child from its rightful position in the family, for reasons which are to do with the 'law' of morality, death, economics, or desire itself. For this reason, we might see Hardy as offering both a general account of the vulnerability of the child in rural society and an account of the effect of that vulnerability as it is transmitted through the family; the terror and displacement of childhood as both existential plight and psychic legacy. We might also see that plight as a historical residue, as in a passage from Mahaffy's Social Life in Greece (1874) which Hardy summarized: 'Not to be forgotten in our admiration for Greek culture – conflict between rich and poor: when the demos was victorious the children of the vanquished were trampled to death by oxen: when the rich got the upper hand they burnt in pitch all whom they got into their power'.

How is this related to the complex shift in attitudes which, recent historians of childhood have suggested, characterized the nineteenth-century? The early part of the century saw the continuation of earlier regimes in which the child was harshly disciplined, imprisoned, transported (up to 1870), or made to work at an early age. In the West Country, Hugh Cunningham reports, the children of the poor were bound out as rural apprentices as early as 8 years old.[At the same time, in the mid-century (the period in which Hardy was growing up), there emerged a heightened sense of the child as abused by these practices – as a being radically separate from adults, who should be freed from work, protected, educated and nutured.

This 'story of outrage' (as Cunningham calls it) was reflected in a variety of philanthropic institutions and legislation: the Ten Hours Act (1847), the Gangs Act (1867), the Agricultural Children's Act (1873); in the work of Barnardo and Booth in London in the 1860s; in the establishment of the National Society for the Prevention of Cruelty to Children in 1884.Scandals like the baby-farming and infanticide cases of the 1870s and Stead's exposure of child prostitution in 'The Maiden Tribute of Modern Babylon' (1885) focused attention on specific abuses.

There is also, some historians of sexuality have suggested, a progressive eroticization of abuse, and one might say a fictionalization of the subject. The most extreme claim here is that of the C. J. Somerville, one of a number of revisionist historians attempting to modify earlier studies by Ariès, Stone and others which had stressed the harshness of childhood up to the twentieth century. Somerville argues that stories of abuse by Dickens and others 'do not seem to have much to do with the actual suffering of contemporary children... Child characters were dying in record numbers in fiction even as actual child morality was declining.'

His conclusion that these figures represent 'the author's self-pity' is unnecessarily crude – one might, for example, argue that a decline in mortality is a necessary precondition of certain investments in children; and the figures suggest that it was only in the twentieth-century that child mortality figures fell sharply. But Hardy himself shows himself conscious of the child-victim as device in his work – in particular Little Father Time, who appears in Jude the Obscure as a figure for the foreclosure of hope, for a folding of the child back into death of the kind depicted in Elizabeth Barrett Browning's radical 'The Cry of the Children' and Robert Browning's 'The Pied Piper of Hamelin'. Little Father Time could, by an extravagant but not inconceivable leap, be a version of the child who hangs himself with cord and nail in 'Rope', one of the famous prose-poems which Baudelaire published under the heading The Spleen of Paris in Figaro in 1864. Baudelaire's child is full of 'precocious sadness' (compare Hardy's 'Age masquerading as Juvenility'), and with 'an immoderate taste for sugar and liqueurs'.

He is adopted by a painter who has used him as a model; when he is threatened with return to his indifferent parents, he kills himself (the story was based on that of a child who hung himself in Manet's studio). Baudelaire describes the death in terms which are both tender and sadistic; both 'the cheeky companion of my life' whom he mourns and 'the little monster had used a very thin cord which had bitten deeply into the neck and I now had to use a pair of small scissors to find the thread between the two rolls of swollen flesh'.

The story climaxes in the child's mother seeing the nail and cord, and asking for it after the painter is about to hurl it out the window; it is only later that he realizes that she plans to sell sections of it, since a rope from a hanging is considered a lucky charm. This commoditization has, however, already been prefigured in the painter's own activities, which both sexualize the child and associate him with fantasies of death. In painting him, the narrator reports, 'I made him carry the vagabond's violin, the Crown of Thorns and the Nails of the Passion, and the Torch of Eros.'

A similar undoing of the Victorian figure of the dying child as de-eroticized angel (Dickens's Little Nell, Stowe's Eva) is central to the story of Hardy's children, who flee from their violent parents ('The Flirt's Tragedy', 'The Bird-Catcher's Boy'), often dying in the process. The beaten or whipped child is, as James Kincaid points out, a fixture of Hardy's novels, even if a problematic one in terms of the kinds of identifications which the reader might make and the kinds of pleasures associated with it.

Kincaid ultimately sees the child as a figure for 'an erotics of loss'; like the Tamagawa pet, it is the toy that dies. It is 'this emptiness called a child'; it 'could be erased, was in fact in the process of being erased even as we packed the meaning in'.[More radically, U. C. Knopfelmacher points out the way in which Hardy's poetry can suggest a child-like return to a lost maternal body; a return involving the reversal of a harsh 'masculine' poetics which might impose discipline.Both these narratives, that of abuse and that of healing regression, confront the problem of pain, of what we have come to call 'trauma' – which is also, since Freud, the problem of consciousness and its obscured origins.

What happens to childhood pain? Into the twentieth century it was relatively common practice, in France at least, to operate on newborn babies without anesthetic, because they were thought to have, like animals, undeveloped nervous systems and little consciousness.Hardy was certainly aware of some of these issues: he was on friendly terms with Sir James Crichton-Browne, the leading Victorian child psychiatrist, who stressed the vulnerability of children and the necessity to avoid over-taxing their nervous systems (his emphasis on their susceptibility to mental disease points towards Little Father Time).

Hardy's work constantly returns to the issue of childhood pain and its persistence. His 'Lines' – really an epilogue – written for a performance on behalf Lady Jeune's Holiday Fund for City Children in 1890 are perhaps just the kind of awkward occasional verse that one skips over in the Collected Poems:

> *Most tragical of shapes from Pole to Line,*
> *O wondering child, unwitting Time's design,*
> *Why should Man add to Nature's quandary,*
> *And worsen ill by thus immuring thee?*
> *– That races do despite unto their own,*
> *That Might supernal do indeed condone*
> *Wrongs individual for the general ease,*
> *Instance the proof in victims such as these.*

The poem then wonders whether disadvantaged children would rather not have been born. These lines suggest a response both to the eugenic discourse of 'races' and Utilitarian calculus of 'general ease' and 'individual wrongs'. With Darwin the relations of resemblance between child and parent are re-coded, with issues of inheritance, variation and, in particular, the development of latent 'faculties' becoming part of a broader social calculus rather than simply an issue of patriarchal succession.

This concern is expressed in Herbert Spencer's essay on 'The Rights of Children' in Social Statics, in which he asserts that children have the same rights as adults, draws parallels with the emancipation of women, and attacks the 'coercive system' which employs force on children rather than developing self-control.

Spencer stresses the duty of the parent to create an environment in which the child's faculties might develop, rather than imposing a disciplinary framework. Hardy similarly focuses on the issue of environment, but registers the place of the individual consciousness within these larger social calculations. The 'wondering Child, unwitting Time's design' and the 'deed back in Time' are both formulae which register the plight of that maimed consciousness, and the paradoxical recovery of pain as part of what this poem (speaking of Lady Jeune's efforts) calls 'Some palliative for ill they cannot cure'.

This conclusion has all the pessimism of Freud's admission of the impossibility of ever resolving the traumas of childhood – though notably we have seen Hardy imply a more socialized account of childhood pain than Freud's patriarchical model. Hardy's account suggests disruptions which may be external to the family as much as internal.

Maria Torok has hinted at similar possibilities in her 1984 paper 'Unpublished by Freud to Fliess: Restoring an Oscillation'. Recalling Freud's abandonment of the thesis of actual trauma or abuse in childhood in favour of the notion of universal endopsychic fantasy, she discusses a 1897 letter to Fliess partly-suppressed, presumably in the interests of theoretical consistency, by the editors of The Origins of Psychoanalysis (1954), and only published entire in Jeffrey Masson's The Assault on Truth (1984). The letter describes in detail the sexual abuse of a patient and her mother, and concludes with Freud's proposal of 'A new motto; "What has been done to you, you poor child?"'

Was hat man, Dir, Du armes Kind getan? – the words are from the famous song of Goethe's illegitimate, abused and ultimately effaced child Mignon in Wilhelm Meister, set to music and rewritten throughout the nineteenth century. As Carolyn Steedman argues in her brilliant study of the Mignon legend, Strange Dislocations: Childhood and the Idea of Human Interiority, the story's framentary meanings which never achieve a total shape, representing the plight of the child itself as historical rebus, as a necessary obscurity. Torok notes that Freud's letter to Fliess contains its own comments on deletion. Freud writes:

Have you ever seen a foreign newspaper which has been censored by the Russians at the border? Words, whole clauses and sentences are blacked out so that what is left becomes unintelligible. A Russian censorship of this kind comes about in psychoses and produces the apparently meaningless deliria.

This, in Torok's commentary, is the mark of an uncertainty

within psychonalysis which is not simply local – was there abuse here? – but fundamental:

Circulating Freud's letters with fragments happening to pass 'Russian' censorship is enough to throw the reader and psychoanalysis into a kind of historical neurosis in which deletions impede us from attempting to read the fact of an oscillation as a symptom-symbol. Once this road is open, it will be easier to read the deletion itself, rendering it intelligible.

A similar question could be applied to the Hardy texts we have examined here: with their cancellations, burnings, and reticences, they are, as we have seen, systematically uncertain about the status of the child and of the trauma attached to the child; to childhood pain. The suppressed motto might be Hardy's, as applicable to the figure of Randy as to Lady Jeune's children, but suggesting a wounded self whose location is problematized by Hardy's own deletions and erasures.

Perhaps it is also the trace of the 'real' of history itself which is erased from Freud's text. One of Steedman's comments on Mignon is useful here: 'child-figures, and more generally the idea of childhood, came to be commonly used to express the depths of historicity within individuals, the history that was "linked to them, essentially"'.

The final phrase is a citation from the passage in which Foucault, in The Order of Things, describes 'The Age of History', the period in which, for Foucault, the self erupts from the continuum of the classical order, and history becomes, painfully, 'the mode of being of all that is given us in experience'. That sense of the intensity of human pain as out of step with a biological or even cosmic order which saw earlier, is one symptom of the pressure on the notion of origins, of originary trauma, within the new characterization of childhood which was growing up as Hardy did; as Steedman writes, 'a particular form of time came into being in the child's body'.

Giorgio Agamben has also argued that the infant is the place where 'the space of history' is opened; and where the discourse of the self-constituting subject erupts from the synchronicity of language. For Agamben, infants are liminal figures, representing the transition from death or non-being to life, and in this way they resemble, and may even come to be entangled with, ghosts rather than adults (since ghosts represent the transition from life to death, and from discourse to language).

The 'wondering child, unwitting Time's design' is, then, a trope for the historicity of the self: 'I had glanced down unborn time' is Hardy's figure for prophecy in 'I Said and Sang Her Excellence'. This is one conclusion: that Hardy's sense of the originary trauma of the self's historicity is what underwrites his sense of a haunting pain as written into the construction of the self.

But perhaps a more suitable point of closure is the healing offered by 'He Never Expected Much', Hardy's 'reflection' on his eighty-sixth birthday – surely one of the most astonishing poems in the English canon in its audacious claims for the continuity of the poetic self across eight decades, and in its redemptive minimalism. The poet addresses the World and says that it has 'kept faith' since childhood (note the conjuring of the year's brink as the mark of the self's entry into history: a topic taken up in the next chapter):

'Twas then you said, and since have said,
Times since have said,
In that mysterious voice you shed
From clouds and hills around:
'Many have loved me desperately,
Many with smooth serenity,
While some have shown contempt of me
Till they dropped underground.
'I do not promise overmuch,
Child; overmuch;
Just neutral-tinted haps and such',
You said to minds like mine.
Wise warning for your credit's sake!
Which I for one failed not to take,
And hence could stem such strain and ache
As each year might assign.

This appears less as a final confirmation of 'pessimism'

than as a fantasized utopian warning on the part of Time (or 'World', here), registering a healing contract which Hardy's poetry teaches us could never have happened; a constantly-renewed contract in which, impossibly, consciousness is always with the child and carried forward as intention, forever balking future pain.

A similar pastoral resolution is offered by another poem in Winter Words, 'The Boy's Dream', a poem which picks up on the tradition of Hardy's many bird-poems -- in particular 'The Blinded Bird', in which he had marveled that the bird could sing, 'Thy grievous pain forgot, / Eternal dark thy lot' (the Miltonic echo reinforcing the sense of the persistence of pain).

'The Boy's Dream' describes natural song as recompense for the lameness and deprivation of a 'provincial town-boy' who dreams of owning a green linnet. The poem begins with external circumstances, the courtyard he lives in, 'Where noontide shed no warmth or light', and the corresponding paleness of his face; it ends with his mood radiating outward as he dreams of birdsong: 'His face was beautified by the theme, / And wore the radiance of the morn.' An internalized nature, pastoral – the tropes of mourning return here as a final cure for the ineradicable memory of pain, closing the book on one of Hardy's enduring subjects.

Chapter 17

Hardy's Dead End Genders

I'm intrigued by the missing "the" in Daleski's title, before "Paradoxes of Love." It must be intentional. I've known Daleski for over twenty-five years-as a friend and colleague during my visiting semester at Hebrew University in Jerusalem (Spring 1972); as a fellow speaker at several recent Lawrence conferences; and as his host for a lecture at Brown. He seems to me always a careful writer, a forthright speaker, and one of the best close readers in the profession.

What does it mean, then-that missing "the"? It looks as if Daleski wants equal billing for those paradoxes, as if Hardy were so caught up in them as to be defined by them-or perhaps defeated. That seems to be the drift of Daleski's argument as the book begins and ends: "I... seek to show how a study of the major novels, taken in chronological order, reveals that he in fact drove himself to a dead end. His unremitting pursuit of his central subject [the failures of married love] finally exhausted it". Let's take his careful grammatical elision, then, as a sign of things to come.

The book has still other aims. In the Introduction, for instance, it shows Hardy's modernism, his proleptic affinities with Conrad, Joyce, Woolf, and Lawrence. Like Conrad, who wants only to make us "see" through a series of visual impressions, Hardy wants us to see "impression-pictures" like those "At the Society of British Artists" where "The impressionist school [was] strong". His characters focus accordingly upon each other through vivid visual impressions, and his narrators adopt them too: "To see in half or quarter views the whole picture... is the intuitive power that supplies the would-be writer with the scientific bases for his pursuit". Hardy's "scientific" desire to make visible things otherwise invisible, "so that the heart and inner meaning" is vividly revealed, takes him also in the direction of Joycean epiphanies, by which objects or dramatic moments body forth their "quidditas" or spiritual "whatness."

The famous scene in which Jude, from afar, "first sees Christminister," is Daleski's choice illustration of Hardy's epiphanic mode. And Daleski's application of that mode to characterization takes Hardy toward Virginia Woolf's moments of epiphanic being, of changing human character from consistent order to fractured views of "successively various persons" as circumstances dictate.

This fracturing moves Hardy also toward Lawrence's "allotropic states," toward his preoccupation with changing qualities of being rather than consistent characterizations, as in his own frequently selfdivided protagonists. Indeed, Lawrence would draw demonstrably on Hardy's precedents for symbolic actions and self-divided characters, particularly in Jude the Obscure, where Hardy advances most deeply toward exhausting the possibilities of sexual failure in or out of marriage.

As we have already noted, Daleski's central aim is to demonstrate that over-all exhaustion, to show Hardy as the pre-modern avatar of sexual failures, withdrawals,. catastrophic ends. In Far from the Madding Crowd and other early works he modifies that aim with Victorian solutions such as Bathsheba's companionate second marriage to Gabriel Oak. But the modern note is there in Bathsheba's "Diana complex," her attempt to be "sufficent to herself" an attempt she shares with half a dozen other women characters in Hardy's stories- and half a dozen males. It is that cross-gender sharing of Diana's aims that helps Daleski to get past the hazards of anti-feminism.

Perhaps also it explains his early delight in going beyond feminism and other recent movements (notably, deconstructionism) for a new look at Hardy's works. He explains that new look by the Diana complex, whether in male or female characters, as "a sense of self-sufficiency so strong that it inhibits a need or the ability to open the self to a sexual partner." But his use of Diana to expound the inhibitions of both sexes seems an oddly borrowed form of newness, indeed an almost feminist form; and in fact he previously presents his book as "a study in Hardy's treatment of gender in his major fiction," which seems to me a borrowed feminist approach-all the more so when he then "set[s] out to analyse the codes of both masculinity and femininity that are inscribed in [Hardy's] texts and [to] offer a revisionary account of his view of both male and female sexuality".

What is new here, for this former New Critical formalist who in a previous book was seeking "Unities" wherever he could find them, and who now seeks them through unifying "Paradoxes," like those New Critics used to knit together their analyses of modern poems? Well, like many of the rest of us, Daleski has learned much from his erstwhile opponents. In his text, if not in his title, he applies their terms-"gender," "codes," "deconstruction"-to his own post-feminist, post-deconstructionist aims.

Of course, he also claims credit for moving beyond still other feminist terms-"essentialism," "sexism"-to a fairer view of Hardy's women as something more than victims, and of Hardy himself as something more than "a crass determinist weighting the scales against them." But he neglects to say that his study owes as much in its procedures to these newly aging trends in criticism as it differs from them in its conclusions. Thus, whatever his unities and humanities, Daleski's Hardy reaches a dead end; he does not yield to public outcries against his sexual paradoxes, as other critics have long believed-no indeed, he exhausts them, he uses them up, and so reaches the ultimate deconstruction, the ultimate paradox: he stops writing novels.

Meanwhile, Daleski turns his new look on Hardy's heroines: they all possess free will, and since they always use it to make the wrong choices, they all prove to be accountable for their chosen fates! In Far from the Madding Crowd, for instance, Bathsheba is not altogether victimized by her rash marriage to Sergeant Troy; it is her own inhibiting or cool sexuality, rather, that throws him off as it contributes to his wanderlust. Admittedly, Hardy shows this cooling process obliquely rather than forthrightly; but he shows it nonetheless convincingly-as Daleski takes great pains to prove.

There may be some latent anti-feminism, of course, some blaming of the supposed "victim," in Daleski's relentless attempt to find such chosen coolness in Bathsheba and her sisters in half a dozen tales, "transcending all essentialism"; but his similar relentlessness with male versions of inhibiting choices (including Hardy's) gets him off the hook.

These gender similarities raise a puzzling question, nonetheless, as to the difference or differences between male and female sexual codes. There are two famous sensual heroines, for instance, in Hardy's tales: Tess and Arabella; but Tess is complicated by her adoration of Angel Clare, her ethereal persuasions; indeed she is all but denatured by them, and murders Alec D'Urberville, her sensual awakener, when he reverts from a shortlived religious conversion to sensual type. Arabella remains more consistent; but her passions quickly tire in marriage, and she leaves Jude in accord with Hardy's belief that, hot or cold, sexuality fails to sustain marriage. It seems safe to say, however, that most of his heroines are "cool": Bathsheba, the fickle Elfride in A Pair of Blue Eyes, the quickly cooling if romantically inflammable Eustacia Vye in Return of the Native, the oddly unmovable Grace Melbury in The Woodlanders, and the altogether maddening Sue Bridehead in Jude the Obscure.

The number of male Dianas in Hardy's fiction is just as large and just as varied; but with men Hardy is given to pairing his diffident heroes with sensual rivals for Diana's hand, as with Troy and Boldwood or Gabriel Oak in Far from the Madding Crowd, Alec D'Urberville and Angel Care in Tess, Clym Yeobright and Damon Wildeve in Return of the Native, or Edred Fitzpiers and Giles Winterbourne in The Woodlanders. Only in Jude the Obscure does he present a diffident male-Jude himself-with the opposing choice of sensual Arabella and ice-cool Sue. As Daleski points out,

Hardy himself was a diffident lover, drawn toward bolder sensual charmers like his father as types he wished to emulatethough he always casts them as arrogant libertines in his fictions. Similarly his most sensual heroine-Arabella-is also his grossest woman character.

Such patterns seem to me more Victorian than modern, as if Hardy were an unusually vocal and moral sexologist, hellbent on exposing the sexual failures of his age. Of course, his age refused to cooperate. More fastidious Victorians became even more vocal and clamored against Tess and Jude, and the exhausted Hardy let them have the final say.

So perhaps we must take him as modern, if only by default, in his moral and sexual vocalism, in his arrival at the dead end of his otherwise endless variations on failed marriages. He is in this respect a wastelander before his time, a T.S. Eliot without incipient faith, a Lawrence without positive sexual solutions for the ills of modern marriage, and he shares with such modern heirs the shock value of his sexual pronouncements.

There are moments, of course, when Hardy glimpses something of Lawrence's sense of sexual love as the great connecter, as when Troy tenderly kisses the dead Fanny and prefers her to Bathsheba; or when Hardy shows us glimpses of wholeness or completeness in Tess and Angel Clare as they appreciate each other's sexual selves-too late to save their own failed marriage. Certainly the vivacious Arabella at times exhibits a healthy rather than a vengeful grossness, as Lawrence saw.

These moments are in a way the book's triumphs, its anticipations of the better side of the sexual revolution to come, its tribute also to Hardy's rare appreciations of such central matters. "Only connect"-the Forsterian motto was on its way, as Lawrence and Daleski seem to have realized.

Meanwhile, we are fortunate to have such careful, subtle, detailed readings of the Hardy canon. Daleski's new look at that canon is always engaged, always close to the best criticism of its kind by other readers, always well worth our time and attention as it plausibly differs from them. My favourite moment in this regard is when he compliments Elaine Showalter for her fine reading of The Mayor of Casterbridge, then goes her one better by proving out Michael Henchard's latent homosexuality (which she had examined but then denied) through the erotic wrestling scene between Rupert Birkin and Gerald Crich in Women in Live, based on the similar wrestling in The Mayor of Casterbridge between Henchard and Donald Farfrae, and now used to confirm Henchard's deepest feelings. Such comparative ingenuities deserve a resounding Yes! if only because they explain much about Hardy's most complicated misogynist and, as most critics believe, his greatest character-or as Daleski might amend it, his greatest male Diana.

It is time that I acknowledged also that Daleski's current foray into gender criticism grows out of an early penchant for such matters, as in his dealings with "the forked flame" in Lawrence and its male and female reversals, or with the "divided heroines" mentioned in a more recent title, among them Tess Durbeyfield. Let us grant him, finally, the ingenious splendors hidden by his present awkward title and its secret feminist persuasions.

Chapter 18

Chronology

Titles of stories as they are best known are used throughout.

Some dates of composition are approximate.

1840 In the third year of Victoria's reign, Thomas Hardy is born on the 2nd of June in a large cottage bordering the heath at Higher Bockhampton, three miles outside Dorchester, Dorset. The eldest son of a violin-playing builder and an ambitious mother, Thomas Hardy received from the former parent a love of music, and from the latter a love of books.

1848 Hardy could read before he entered the new school at Lower Bockhampton.

1849 Hardy was transferred to a private school in Dorchester.

1856 Hardy articled with Dorchester architect John Hicks.

1862 Hardy moved to London to take up more advanced architectural work with Arthur Blomfield. At this time, he wrote many poems, but failed to get any published.

1865 March: "How I Built My House" [Hardy's first published work and first short story] appears in Chamber's Journal, 18 March.

1867 Returning to Dorset, depressed and disappointed by publishers' rejection of his early verse, Hardy assisted Hicks in church restorations.

1868 January: Hardy finished his first novel, The Poor Man and the Lady, and submitted to both

Macmillan and Chapman and Hall, but it was never published.

1870 7 Match. Hardy travelled to St. Juliot, northern Cornwall, to plan the restoration of the local parish church; here he met the rector's sister-in- law, Emma Lavinia Gifford

1871 March: Hardy published the sensation novel Desperate Remedies in three volumes with William Tinsley, but its sales were mediocre.

1872 June: Under the Greenwood Tree is published in two volumes by Tinsley, London. Instantly, critics compared it favourably to the work of George Eliot.

1872 Sept.: A Pair of Blue Eyes, illustrated by J. A. Pasquier, is published in Tinsley's Magazine in eleven parts, until July, 1873.

1874 Jan-Dec.: Far From the Madding Crowd is published in serial in the Cornhill Magazine in twelve numbers, illustrated by H. P. Allingham. February: Hardy agrees to have" Destiny and a Blue Cloak" published in the New York Times. F.B. Pinion describes this as" Hardy's first short story" in New Wessex edition of Thomas Hardy: Collected Short Stories (1988): p. 929. September: Hardy sends off finished draft of" Destiny and a Blue Cloak" to the New York Times; Thomas Hardy marries Emma Gifford on 17 September. October 4: "Destiny and a Blue Cloak" published in the New York Times.

1875 July: The Hand of Ethelberta is published in serial in the Cornhill Magazine in eleven numbers, illustrated by George Du Maurier.

1876 April: The Hand of Ethelberta is published in volume form; Hardy and his wife have moved to Yeovil. May: Last instalment of The Hand of Ethelberta.

1877 '"The Thieves Who Couldn't Help Sneezing" published in a children's annual. While living at

Sturminster Newton, Hardy writes The Return of the Native.

1878 January: The Return of the Native begins in serial in Belgravia (Jan.-Dec.), il. Arthur Hopkins. March 22: Hardy moves to Hardy and his wife move to Upper Tooting, near Wandsworth Common (London). April 6: "The Duchess of Hamptonshire" (as "The Impulsive Lady of Croome Castle") published on 6 and 13 April in Light (11 and 18 May in Harpers Weekly). July: An Indiscretion in the Life of an Heiress published in The New Quarterly Magazine, and the first of its five instalments appears in Harper's Weekly.

1879 April 19:"The Distracted Preacher" published in the New Quarterly Magazine and in five parts in Harper's Weekly(19 April-17 May). Hardy at work on The Trumpet Major.

1880 January: The Trumpet-Major begins in serial in Good Words (Jan.-Dec.), il. John Collier. April 15: "Fellow-Townsmen" published in the New Quarterly Magazine, pp. 335- 83 (17 April-15 May, in 5 parts in Harpers Weekly). October: Hardy is seriously ill for next six months. December: A Laodicean begins in serial in Harper's New Monthly Magazine (Dec., 1880-Dec., 1881) in 13 numbers, il. George Du Maurier.

1881 June: Hardy moves to Wimborne. December 5: "What the Shepherd Saw" published in the Illustrated London News, pp. 19, 22- 3. December 10: "The Honourable Laura" published as "Benighted Travellers" in Harper's Weekly, pp. 826-7, and 17 Dec., pp. 858-9; and on 17 December in Bolton Weekly Journal (Christmas Leaves).

1882 May: Two on a Tower begins in serial in Atlantic Monthly in eight monthly nos. July: "A Tradition of Eighteen Hundred and Four" sent off. November 25:" A Tradition of Eighteen Hundred and Four" published in Harper's Christmas (Dec.,

1882), pp. 26-7. December: last instalment of Two on a Tower in Atlantic Monthly.

1883 February:" The Romantic Adventures of a Milkmaid" sent off to the Graphic, beginning a nine-year relationship with this large-format weekly illustrated journal. March 1:" The Three Strangers" published in Longman's Magazine, pp. 569-88; in Harper's Weekly 3 March (pp. 134-5) and 10 (p. 151). June: the Hardys move to Dorchester, deciding to build a house there. June 25:" The Romantic Adventures of a Milkmaid" is published in the Graphic (Summer), pp. 4- 25, with four full-page illustrations by C. S. Reinhart; and in Harper's Weekly from 23 June to 4 August (with only three of Reinhart's illustrations). Hardy's essay "The Dorsetshire Labourer" is published in Longman's Magazine for July. By the end of the summer, Hardy has completed the children's adventure story Our Exploits at West Poley.

1884 Hardy is working on The Mayor of Casterbridge in this year. February 7: "The Duchess of Hamptonshire" is published as" The Impulsive Lady of Croome Castle" in Light (6 and 13 April): 7-8, 51-2; in Harper's Weekly (11 and 18 May): 370-1, and 394; as" Emmeline; or, Passion versus Principle" in the Independent (New York) 7 Feb., 1884 (pp. 215-35).

1885 February: "A Tryst at an Ancient Earthwork" written. March 15: "A Tryst at an Ancient Earthwork" published in The Detroit Post. April: The Mayor of Casterbridge finished. June 29: The Hardys move from ShireHall Place to Max Gate, a great house that he himself has designed and built on the outskirts of Dorchester. October 17 and 24: "A Mere Interlude" published in Bolton Weekly Journal.

1886 January 2: The Mayor of Casterbridge begins in weekly serial in The Graphic, illustrated by Robert

Barnes. May: Last instalment of MoC; first instalment of The Woodlanders in Macmillan's Magazine (12 parts). May 10: The Mayor of Casterbridge is published in two volumes by Smith, Elder. (London).

1887 February: Hardy finishes writing The Woodlanders; visits Italy. April: Last (12th) instalment of The Woodlanders in Macmillan's Magazine. August: "Alicia's Diary" written. September: "The Withered Arm" written. October 15: "Alicia's Diary" published in Manchester Weekly Times Supplement. December 31: "The Waiting Supper" published in Harper's Weekly, pp. 965-7.

1888 January 7:" The Waiting Supper" published in Harper's Weekly, pp. 17-19. January: "The Waiting Supper" published in Murray's Magazine, pp. 42-67, and February, pp. 199-218. "The Withered Arm" published in Blackwood's Edinburgh Magazine, pp. 30-48. May: Wessex Tales published by Macmillan. August: "A Tragedy of Two Ambitions" written. September:" The First Countess of Wessex" written. December: "A Tragedy of Two Ambitions" published in The Universal Review (537-60), with six illustrations by George Lambert.

1889 September: About half of Tess of the D'Urbervilles sent off. December: "The First Countess of Wessex" published in Harper's New Monthly 80 (20-43), il. A. Parsons and C. S. Reinhart.

1890 January: "The Lady Penelope" published in Longman's Magazine, pp. 279-287. May: A Group of Noble Dames sent off. July: Hardy revised A Group of Noble Dames and sent off. July, second half: Most of stories in Life's Little Ironies written. November-December 1: A Group of Noble Dames published in The Graphic, Christmas: No. 1: "Barbara of the House of Grebe," p. 4-5; Harper's Weekly 29 Nov. No. 2: "The Marchioness of

Stonehenge" (originally, "The Lady Caroline ") p. 9-12; Harper's Weekly 6 Dec., p. 959-62. No. 3: "Anna, Lady Baxby," p. 12-13; Harper's Weekly6 Dec., p. 962, 964. No. 4:" The Lady Icenway," p. 13; Harper's Weekly 13 Dec., p. 981, 984. No. 5:" Squire Petrick's Lady," p. 16; Harper's Weekly 13 Dec., p. 984. No. 6:" Lady Mottisfont," p. 16-20; Harper's Weekly 20 Dec., p. 994-5.

1891 March: "For Conscience' Sake" published in the Fortnightly Review 49: 370-382." The Doctor's Legend" in the New York Independent. March-June:" A Few Crusted Characters" published in Harper's New Monthly, illustrated by C. Green. april: "The Son's Veto" written. May: A Group of Noble Dames published by Osgood, McIlvaine June 27: "To Please His Wife" published in Black and White, 678-82, il. W. Hennessy. July 4: Tess of the D'Urbervilles begins its serial run in The Graphic, illustrated by Hubert Herkomer et al. November-December:" On the Western Circuit" published in The English Illustrated Magazine, il. W. Paget, and Harper's Weekly 28 Nov., il. W. T. Smedley. December 1: "The Son's Veto" published in The Illustrated London News: 20-21, 25. December 5: "What The Shepherd Saw" published in The Illustrated London News. December 26: Tess ends in weekly serial in The Graphic.

1892 July: Death of Hardy's father. October 1: The Well-Beloved begins in serial in The Illustrated London News December 17: Last instalment of The Well-Beloved (12 parts), il. Walter Paget.

1893 January: "The Fiddler of the Reels" sent off. March:" Master John Horseleigh, Knight" sent off. May: "The Fiddler of the Reels" published in Scribner's Magazine 13: 597-609, il. W. Hatherell. Hardy meets Florence Henniker. June 12: "Master John Horseleigh, Knight" published in The Illustrated London News, il. W. B. Wollen.

September: "An Imaginative Woman" finished; "A Tryst at an Ancient Earthwork" revised. October: Life's Little Ironies assembled. December: "A Tryst at an Ancient Earthwork" published in The English Illustrated Magazine (281-8), with four photographs by W. Pouncy. Hardy is working on Jude the Obscure

1894 February: Life's Little Ironies published by Osgood, McIlvaine. April: "An Imaginative Woman" published in The Pall Mall Magazine, 951-69, il. A. J. Goodman. December: Jude the Obscure begins in serial as The Simpletons, and then as Hearts Insurgent for remaining eleven parts, and in Harper's New Monthly Magazine (Dec., 1894-Nov., 1895), illustrated by William Hatherell.

1895 March: Hardy finishes writing Jude. November: Jude is published in book form.

1896 August: "A Committee-Man of 'The Terror'" sent off. November 22:" A Committee-Man of 'The Terror'" is published in The Illustrated London News, illustrated by H. Burgess. December 14: "The Duke's Reappearance" is published in Saturday Review: 14-16. Throughout the year, the critics' hostile reception to Jude dispirits Hardy. His growing financial independence leads Hardy to return to his first love, poetry.

1897 March: The Well-Beloved published in book form. July: "The Grave by the Handpost" finished. November 30: "The Grave by the Handpost" is published in St. James's Budget, illustrated by G. H. Patterson.

1898 December: Hardy publishes his first book of verse, Wessex Poems; many of the poems contained therein date well back to the 1860s.

1900 January: "A Changed Man" written; on April 21 and 28, it is published in The Sphere (419-421; 451-2), illustrated by A. S. Hartrick. December: "Enter a Dragoon" is published in Harper's Monthly (pp. 25-35), illustrated by A. Hayman.

1902 The Dynasts, in dramatic blank verse, is published in three parts, one of the longest poems in the English language.

1910 Hardy receives the Order of Merit.

1912 April: Hardy responds to the sinking of the Titanic with the elegy "The Convergence of the Twain (Lines on the Loss of the ''Titanic')." November: Life's Little Ironies published (Wessex edition; Preface dated "May, 1912"). Wessex Tales published (Wessex edition; Preface dated "May, 1912"). A Group of Noble Dames published (Wessex edition). The death of Emma Hardy sets off a wave of self-recrimination and regret in Hardy that prompts him to write (and re-write) many poems about their relationship, since termed "The Emma Poems."

1913 October: "A Changed Man" and Other Tales published by Macmillan. Poems of 1912-13 published.

1914 "A Changed Man" and Other Tales published (Wessex edition). Shortly after his marriage to young Florence Dugdale, the First World War breaks out.

1928 11 January: Hardy dies at Max Gate. His eighth and last book of verse appears posthumously. In addition to his short stories and novels 'of character and environment' he has left us 1093 poems, both lyric and narrative, and numerous essays.

1929 February: "Old Mrs. Chundle" published posthumously in The Ladies' Home Journal (Philadelphia) at the instigation of Florence Hardy. Hardy recollected having written the story between 1888-1890.

Chapter 19

A Literary Life of Thomas Hardy

Shame, no doubt, played its part in the painstaking defences the dying Hardy erected. But there was also a concern that too much reality might shadow the fiction, that prurient eyes might look too closely in the work for the man. And so they did. Admirers still seek out the combe where Bathsheba and Troy conducted their courtship. Who was the real Tess? Questions like these evade the truth they seek. The real life of a writer is the work, the vision honed from quite ordinary things.

Yet the biographies continue to search over and over the same ground, though it might be well to let it lie fallow. We are too near, though too distant, from Hardy to understand any more than is already understood. A High Victorian, he survived everyone, at work well into this century as a living bridge between two worlds of experience.

His fiction was a revolt against the Victorians. His poetry was a testament against the twentieth century. Hardy's feelings were contrary. His vision was deeply disturbed, for his protest was not against society, but against creation and providence. For all his kindliness, he was angry, and his anger was cosmic. Such a life is hard to understand unless we can make the imaginative transition.

This proves difficult. Hardy's crisis is not ours. We can see the revolt against sexual hypocrisy and the dominance of the machine. The first is a given of our times. The second accords some respect. But Hardy is not about a return to the country. He is about the workings of fate, of hubris and consequential tragedy. Hardy closed his Bible and saw a pagan world. His vision of nature is terrible, though his artistry is of great beauty.

Writing of Hardy (whom he disliked) Patrick Kavanagh wrote: 'Real roots lie in our capacity for love and its abandon.' Hardy for Kavanagh was a man looking down from a great height on a landscape he did not know. It is useful to recall that Hardy was an architect. He has grandeur without simplicity or humility. He isn't wilfully cruel, but he does seem loveless. How far this vision relates to his personal life is, I think, of secondary interest. Seeking direct connections is a false and philistine misreading. Writers do, if they are any good, use their imaginations.

Literary biography is thereby at a disadvantage. The shaping forces of childhood and education provide a fertile ground. The rest is increasingly enveloped in the mists of creativity and in the mythic sense a great writer is bound to generate. James Gibson is most useful on the early years. For the rest he treads well-worn paths. The history of Hardy's relation with Alexander Macmillan, his publisher, is recounted in full in Charles Morgan's The House of Macmillan which Mr Gibson quotes without additional material or fresh perspective.

On other matters Mr Gibson is unreliable. 'We shall probably never know what he thought of . . . D H Lawrence . . .' In fact, we know for certain Hardy never read Lawrence, and had only a vague notion of who he was. Of modernism in general, Hardy's dislike is recorded in Robert Graves's memorable passage in Goodbye to All That. Worse still is the author's confusion in believing it is Angel Clare who seduces Tess. It is Alec d'Urberville. The point is crucial to understanding the narrative. Clare's unfeeling hypocrisy compares badly with Alec's genuine wish to make amends for his brutal conduct, though in Victorian propriety it is Clare, the deceived husband, who behaves well.

The tragic irony of this is perhaps the quintessential situation in all Hardy's work. For Hardy morality was not a code but an existential response to the workings of fate. Therefore Tess shows herself by her stoic dignity to be as noble a soul as she is genteel by ancestry. Tess is the most tragic and most archetypal of all Hardy's heroines, as one who endures her situation without surrendering herself.

There are other ways of seeing women, but Hardy's is surely preferable to the patronising attitude of Dickens, though Dickens may be the greater artist. The modern preference is in Hardy's favour, but it can be Hardy without a full realisation of the tragedy. The Wessexery of Hardy is difficult to take. Possibly to offset the pessimism, he elaborated an artifice of twee regionalism, complete with maps of a renamed landscape. It is easy to respond to the work for its picturesque sepia quality. Gentle Tess, poor and proud, in bonnet and smock does not serve the true heroine and her situation. In brief, we really ought to pause before writing the life of one who wrote of life so deeply and so darkly that it may have disturbed him more than we can, or should, know.

LETTERS REVEAL HARDY SWITCHED TO POETRY OVER HARSH 'JUDE THE OBSCURE'

Thomas Hardy abandoned his career as a novelist because he was hurt by harsh reviews of Jude the Obscure, letters to be auctioned at Sotheby's have revealed. The prolific author and poet had always been sensitive to the opinions of critics. But letters from the collection of Frederick Adams, to be auctioned on 7 November, indicate what triggered Hardy to abandon writing novels and concentrate on poetry for the rest of his life.

An American journalist, Jeanette Gilder, was responsible for wounding Hardy the most, with her fierce comments about Jude's amorality. Later she requested an interview with Hardy in an attempt to set the record straight after her earlier hostility, but the author turned her down. With heavy irony, he responded: "My respect for my own writings and reputation is so very slight that I care little about what happens to either, so that the rectification of judgements ... and the way in which my books are interpreted, do not much interest me.

"Those readers who, like yourself, could not see that Jude ... makes for more morality than any other book I have written, are not likely to be made to do so by a newspaper article, even from your attractive pen."

Hardy admitted to his American publisher that he was "surprised" and "distressed" by the nature of one review. Even his friend, the novelist George Gissing, branded the book "Jude the Obscene".

Jude, a tragic working-class hero, is pitted against society and circumstances in the book. Hardy's agonised frankness about sexuality, divorce and adultery caused it to be seen as another "marriage-question" novel, and condemned in some quarters as coarse. The collection of three letters regarding Gilder, written in 1896, are expected to fetch up to pounds 6,000. They are part of more than 500 lots by Hardy in the largest collection remaining in private hands, and are estimated to raise pounds 500,000.

The sale at Sotheby's, expected to raise pounds 1.5m, also includes works by Virginia Woolf, complete with her revisions, expected to fetch up to pounds 40,000, and a comprehensive collection of works by the American poet-Robert Frost. Peter Selley, Sotheby's literature specialist, described the sale as unique.

POLANSKI'S READING OF HARDY'S TESS

William Costanzo commented in Literature/Film Quarterly in 1981 on Roman Polanski and his Tess film rendition of Thomas Hardy's novel Tess of the D'Urbervilles: Tess has crossed the Atlantic as a kind of emissary from Polanski. The romantic story of a victim of society, it comes unchaperoned to a land where the director is himself a fugitive from justice . After the brutal murder of Sharon Tate in 1969 ... after his flight from the United States and a prison sentence for illegal sexual intercourse with a minor, he has chosen as his subject the seduction of a young girl by an older man.

A Plot of Tragedy should arise from the gradual closing in of a situation. . . by reason of the characters taking no trouble to ward off the disastrous events.... (from Thomas Hardy's notebooks, quoted in Costanzo 72)

Was it something about women that he had known in his

own life or was it Hardy's tragic Tess in Tess of the D' Urben illes that Roman Polanski intended to film in Tess? According to Costanzo, Polanski wanted to return to "the universe of those authors who tell about certain things, the deepest of human sentiments . . . the ordinary tribulations in a rather cruel and rigid society". If it was Hardy's text that Polanski sought to replicate, if he sought to give moviegoers a literary classic, the film Tess may be interpreted as a re-reading. The hypothesis of this paper is that Polanski misread Hardy's novel by underestimating Tess's strengths and by overlooking Hardy's thesis concerning the catalytic role of family alcoholism in undermining her character.

According to Barthes and Scholes, a re-reading might be expected to invoke codes, or criteria outside the text, by which the text is to be interpreted. For example, Hardy's text might be interpreted vis-a-vis the code of Victorian culture in two ways-either supportive or critical of that culture with respect to cultural repression of women. Polanski, it seems, took the critical approach, arguing that the victimized Tess would not have been repressed but for the male forces against her. Such an approach is supported neither by consideration of Hardy's ideas about women nor by sound critical consideration of the novel. It is the contention here that Tess was a doomed character in the novel because of her family background rather than solely because of her gender and that her character is best understood by the "code" of family dysfunction, which only Hardy's narrative specifically highlights.

Although Hardy apparently intended to idealize women generally, his narrative comments show that he was more eager to explore the psychological origins of Tess, as he had done with such characterizations as those in Jude the Obscure and other works, while Polanski seems to have been content with romanticizing her victimization at the hands of men. While both "texts" of Tess reveal exploitative conduct by males in patriarchal Victorian culture, only Hardy's version offers any plausible theory for why Tess would resort to murder: Polanski's female is too vacuous to have the strength for such an act.

While both Hardy and Polanski intended, as much as possible from their male narrator positions, to be "on Tess's side," the film's casting of the frail Natasha Kinski emphasizes Polanski's extreme pity for Tess without recognizing the constituents of her personhood. To be sure, Hardy was also enamored of Tess, but he admired her and sought to describe the tragic deterministic circumstance of her plight rather than just her pitiable girlhood. But the real question is what "circumstance?" Only Hardy's biographer, Pinion, has noted the importance of family background to Tess's character: "Tess herself is a rather unusual character; her conscience makes her readily shoulder blame and guilt which more rightly belong to her feckless parents".

Hardy's narrative development of character is exacting, forced, overly "diegetic" (Scholes 144) in light of modern styles of characterization where characterization is more often "absent" (Docherty xi). Hardy's narrative tends toward the older, the mimetically duplicative, the one-dimensional type of characterization. Thus, Tess is "vulnerable," Alec is "predator," and Angel is "indifferent," whereas "real," modern characters are multi-faceted.2 Hardy's authorial craft develops the circumstances leading up to character traits that Polanski's film glosses over. Most Hardy critics focus on the impact of his narratives on character. Thus, J. Hillis Miller, called by Harold Bloom "our foremost Hardy scholar," calls Hardy's style one of "distance and desire". Miller says that Hardy's characters' minds are closed (deliberately), only dimly replicated, introspection disallowed, so that the observer can only infer longings and desires across the distance between characters.

If Miller's reading is correct, the "gaze" scenes in the film, such as in the beginning, after Alec first meets Tess and their eyes meet when he walks off, ought to bring out viewers' feelings of desire. In fact, the film only portrays blank stares which allow the observer to infer nothing about desire. According to Miller, it is Hardy, the novelist, and not Polanski, the movie-maker, who saw life in the "manner of a movie camera, with spatial and temporal detachment, cool self-possession," a "double vision" of author and character. Anderson (1990) and Kincaid (1991) likewise advert to the relative depth of Hardy's characterization that is lacking in Polanski's film. Hardy had a "feel" for the settings in Tess and for their place in history, their effect on character which Polanski did not. Although Polanski renders setting faithfully, indeed beautifully, he fails, without the help of Hardy's narrative or some cinematic innovation in lieu thereof, to tie setting to character.

Hardy's "doubly-visioned" characterization simply does not surface in the film. For instance, when young Tess is with her girl friends and her father shows up drunk, Hardy tells the reader that she feels embarrassed, defensive, and that her pride is hurt, even as her dialogue, the other half of the "double vision," says the opposite: "Look here, I won't walk another inch with you if you say any jokes about him". She doesn't like her father's behaviour but sticks up for him nevertheless, an attitude that is not conveyed in the film. She suffers the typical painful contradiction of feelings of all children of alcoholics, which such expert research on the alcoholic family as Alice Miller's For Your Own Good (1983) finds is so critical to the development of alcoholics' children, but the source of those feelings, her alcoholic family, is not apparent in the film. Her mother has lost all control over her as the result of the familial distortion produced by the father's drinking, but only Hardy offers the keen insight that mother, just like father, has a "problem":

All these young souls were passengers in the Durbeyfield ship-entirely dependent on the judgment of the two Durbeyfield adults for their pleasure, their necessities, their health, even their existence. . . six helpless creatures who had never been asked if they wished for life on any terms, much less if they wished for it on such hard conditions as were involved in being of the shiftless house of Durbeyfield.

That most of the elements important to Tess's character are absent from the film is a condition that even popular reviewers have noted. Thus, Pauline Kael, in the New Yorker, found such omissions as the "unbearable domestic tension," the narrative's "perfect fusion of the intuitive and the planned," and the "robust country girl" replaced by the blandness of Kinski. Writing in the New York Times, Vincent Canby was more personal: "Though the film is beautiful to behold, it has no more life than an exceptionally expensive, carefully made production for television's masterpiece theater . . . Polanski cannot be excused because . . . he wanted a Tess for his murdered wife, Sharon Tate, to act the part of."

Criticizing the film, Vedemaitis (1988) specifically attacks the lack of Hardy's character development as the film's most dissatisfying feature:

Whereas Hardy's Tess is proud, stubborn, intelligent, resilient, and enduring, a person who matures into complex womanhood, Polanski's Tess is submissive, enervated, withdrawn, and childlike to the end. Gone is the Tess who feels in her heart that, in succumbing to Alec, she has done no wrong for which she should be eternally condemned; . . . Gone from the film is the Tess who must be driven to the limits of emotional exhaustion before submission. Hardy's Tess, in her relationship with both Alec and Angel, capitulates only after an intense and desperate struggle that also creates a matching tension in the reader .... Gone are the ominous foreshadowing, the grim D'Urberville mansion with the foreboding ancestral portraits on the wall, Angel's hazardous somnambulatory walk in which he symbolically "buries" Tess, and Tess's suicidal despair. Instead, two people sit and talk. Polanski never raises the volume. No change of tempo. Whereas Phase Five of Hardy's Tess is almost unbearable for the reader, Polanski's rendition is languid, flat, even boring.

Although Vedemaitis sounds more like a "new" critic than a character scholar, and although she does not deal directly with Tess's unique problems as a woman or with the possibility that the origin of Tess's tragedy and of her psychology lies in her dysfunctional family, recent feminist scholarship has taken up the "woman problem" regarding Tess, adding important perspective to an understanding of Tess's weakness in the film. Polanski's idea of empathy with the female gender, however, fails to measure up to feminist critical standards any better than it does to the movie critics' standards. Mary Jacobus (1978) firmly emphasizes Tess's "right to be" in the face of oppression, avoiding both Hardy's "moral purity" and Polanski's "vacuous woman" conceptions, while Pamela Jekel (1986) argues that Hardy's Tess "evolves and gives us ample insight into the character of a heroine who emerges as an individual in her own right", an argument that certainly could not be made on behalf of Polanski's Tess.

Three 1990 articles, by Ingham, Blake, and Higonnet, adeptly utilize gender as a critical code, but all three conclude that Tess is a woman with uniquely womanly problems and they all echo Judith Spector's 1986 statement about male attempts to sympathize with female problems-the kind of attempt that perhaps motivates Polanski's Tess undertaking, to the effect that females do a better job on works by those of their own gender:

The study of gender-related aspects of literature by critics who are of the author's same gender can . . . involve an exhilarating feeling of empathy with the text and an eagerness to explain one's insights to others and "opposites."

If Higonnet, for example, finds Hardy's "repressive set of discourses . . inimical to the development and expression of Tess's selfhood," how much more inexcusable is it for Polanski to nearly erase Tess's character entirely? Not only is Polanski's characterization of Tess too weak for an adequate representation of female personhood, but his inadequacy is exacerbated because he, unlike Hardy, is not a Victorian, but is a male living in the modem world and should know better. As Ingham points out, Hardy was somewhat progressive on the "woman issue" for his time, actually beginning to "reform" his conception of women by the time he wrote The Well-Beloved, while, on the other hand, as Veick's 1990 dissertation points out, "Polanski's reading of the novel is reductive, wanting in Tess's tragic qualities".

Actually, Polanski's "vacuous victim" view of Tess seems to follow stale Freudian theory rather than either scholarly character or feminist theory. Inquiry into Tess's nature through a modern psychological analysis of her family background is what is needed to understand her character and to understand what a rather surprising murder is otherwise. Ironically and ingenuously, such psychological inquiry is explicitly provided in the text by Hardy's narrative, affording both reasons for the murder and for its thematic significance. Hardy's text carefully frames a hypothesis that it is not merely Alec's, or any other male's, oppression that is the proximate cause of Tess's criminality, but her "family system." Jerome Bump (1991) has suggested that a modern "family systems" psychology approach may explain D.H. Lawrence's works, while Michael Steig (1968) has cast doubt on the modern utility of psychoanalytic theory, the theory which perhaps underlies Polanski's "oppressive other" film representation of Tess's oppression:

Inferences about the unconscious life of imaginary people involve a confusion of literature and life . . . a fixation on the genital phase of infantile development, with its incestuous attachment [which] seems irrelevant to understanding [Sue Bridehead in Hardy's Jude the Obscure] for the simple reason that we cannot observe the origin of her character in childhood.

Family systems theory avoids the "unconscious life" by dealing directly, as Hardy's narrative does in his text, with overt factual manifestations of family dynamics. Polanski's film omits manifestations of family dynamics. Like Sue and Jude in Jude the Obscure, Tess is the child of an alcoholic family, an acute form of family dysfunction which Hardy, and not Polanski, highlights. Hardy, in effect, fits Bump's description of Lawrence-"a treater and diagnoser of the symptoms and causes of alcoholic dysfunction", while Polanski leaves the observer to infer from a subconscious that is hidden beneath the surface of the film. Many of the adjustment problems supposedly found in adult children of alcoholics are made evident by Hardy's depiction of Tess. Hardy highlights virtually all of the behavioral attributes in Tess that are listed by such "family systems-alcohol" theorists as Bradshaw, for example:

delusion, denial, loneliness (Tess makes few friends), high level anxiety, shame (about her family), faulty communication style (she is evasive, hides true feelings, even has to write out her past), yearning for approval (as her mother taught her), compulsive/addictive (respecting Angel), narcissistically-driven, confused identity (caught between the old and new morality), inhibited trust, possible spiritual bankruptcy (Tess has not internalized her religiononly the resultant guilt).

Such attributes are normally associated with negative alcoholic family child-rearing, the kind of child rearing that is symptomatic of the families in Hardy's novels. Hardy's narrative distinctly shows how John Durbeyfield's alcoholism, lack of ambition, and faulty family leadership doom the family, and, in turn, his daughter Tess's prospects: "John Durbeyfield had more conceit than energy or health, and this supposition was pleasant to him". Durbeyfield's domination of the mother drove her to vacuousness and set the stage for Tess's development. Hardy describes the mother as "light-minded . . . and [she] . . had been discovering good matches for her daughter almost from the year of her birth . . . . The father was in a stupor induced this morning in honor of the occasion". The father was a classic, blown-up drunk, full of hollow intentions, but amounting to nothing but a source of family instability, while the mother, according to Hardy, thought so little of the idea of female personhood that she called a woman's face her "trump card". Hardy describes the workings of the failed "family system" in such detail as to leave no doubt that it is that system which determines Tess's character:

> the wrong man the woman, the wrong woman the man . . . the possibility of retribution lurking in the present catastrophe. Doubtless some of Tess D'Urberville's mailed ancestors rollicking home had dealt the same measure even more ruthlessly .... But though to visit the sins of the fathers upon the children is a mortality good enough for divinities, it is scorned by average human nature and it therefore does not mend the matter.

Polanski fails to sufficiently provide the audience with "text," by dialogue, action or otherwise, to allow any basis for the inference that Tess's criminality results from her up-bringing, despite the fact that Hardy repeats, over and over, the family factor in her character. It is simply not enough for Polanski to imply that Tess is weak because she is a girl when it is manifestly clear, from her own words, that her family made her that way:

Oh mother, my mother! How could I be expected to know? I was a child when I left this house four months ago. Why didn't you tell me there was danger in menfolk? Ladies know what to fend hands against because they read novels that tell them of these tricks; but I never had the chance 'o living in that way, and you did not help me!

The reader, or the filmic re-reader in Polanski's case, must remember that the mother whom Tess addresses is the same mother who was too weak to decide whether Tess should leave home in the first place, who taught her how to be a female object, who delegated the mothering of the Durbeyfield children to Tess while she went to the tavern with her husband, and who taught Tess how to be a "poor me" with so little direction and willpower that she spends her life bouncing from male to male, from job to job, from lie to lie as she descends toward the commission of her criminal act. Kinski does not "act" these phases of Tess's life in the film, because Polanski's mis-reading focuses instead on the male characters' acting upon her.

Polanski misses the point that Tess is not determined by the males, but by a tragic family system that Hardy will not, despite her efforts, allow her to escape from:

She might prove it false if she could veil begones . . . [but] only a young women of twenty, one who mentally and sentimentally had not finished growing, it was impossible that any event should have left upon her an impression that was not in time capable of transmutation.

Hardy ties Tess' character development directly to her father's character so as to make it clear to the reader, in a way that is not clear at all to the film viewer, as she stands, at 97, on the solid, rolling power, majestic English countryside "not sure of her direction. . . still upon the expanse of verdant flames, like a fly on a billiard table", that she, like John Durbeyfield, has "no mind for laborious effect towards such a solid advancement as could alone be effected by a family so heavily handicapped as the once powerful D'Urbervilles were now".

Tess knows, as the relationship with Angel deepens, that she will have to deal with her relationship to her past somehow, but Hardy inserts key passages to specifically indicate that she has irrevocably inherited her parents' indecisiveness:

Don't ask me . . I told you why-partly. I am good not good enough-not worthy enough... Yes-something like that . . . She could only shake her head and look away from him . . . In reality, she was drifting into acquiescence. Every see-saw of her breath, every wave of her blood. every pulse on her ears, was a voice that joined with nature in revolt against her scrupulousness. I shall give way-I shall let myself marry him. I cannot help it.

"The Women Pays" is a chapter that, admittedly, shows how Hardy, like Polanski, felt sorry about Tess's unfortunate dealings with men. The chapter establishes Angel as every bit as cruel and oppressive as Alec, but it is also notable that, in both the novel and the film, in both the text and the acting, Angel is perhaps less aggressive than Alec, inviting thematic generalization about what he means to Tess in light of her background, what her relationship with him means in terms of the plot's progression. Hardy emphasizes this family background theme through narrative between Tess and Angel, while Polanski leaves it out altogether:

Tess: Oh, Angel-my mother says that it sometimes happens so! Angel: Different societies, different manners. You almost make me say you are an unapprehending peasant-women, who have never been initiated into the proportions of social things.... I cannot help associating your decline as a family with this other fact-of your want of firmness. Decrepit families imply decrepit will, decrepit conducts.

In the conclusion, when Angel goes abroad, Tess has a chance to become something on her own but, following her family's example, quickly takes the easy way out and goes back to Alec. While the film adequately portrays her limited resolve to make it in the real world, Hardy does more: Hardy specifically, once again, ties that lack of resolve to the background of her family system: "How she would be able to face her parents? . . . To put an end to myself'. Hardy makes Tess feel shame, a common alcoholic family trait according to therapists John Bradshaw and Alice Miller, in the eyes of her parents, but in the film, Kinski shows so little feeling that she is at most resigned.

The shaming of Tess is crucial for Hardy, for it sets up her subsequent cave-in to Alec, which Hardy suggests is all that she can do because her family has given her no backbone, no capacity for judgment: she "yields to such vague impressions without": "There was not much time for thought or elusion, and she yielded as calmly as she could to the necessity of letting him overtake her". By the novel's end, Hardy has fashioned his notion of necessity-that Tess has no will to do other than what events dictate because of her weak family up-bringing, into the absolute extinguishment of her selfhood: "Adrift, like a corpse upon the current, in a direction dissociated from its living will". Hardy's narrative craftsmanship, absent in any manner or form from Polanski's film, has inexorably led the reader from Tess's past, to her crime, and, finally, to her demise.

The hypothesis that Tess's psychological propensity to murder is the product of her family origins and, hence, is best viewed by a family systems or alcoholic family perspective, is amply supported by Hardy's narrative. Hardy's text reveals evidence that he sympathized with Tess as woman, to be sure, but a fair reading of Tess of the D'Urbervilles cannot rest with a sympathetic gender analysis alone. Therefore, to the extent that Polanski wished to faithfully adapt the novel, he failed by not replicating the evidence of family influence upon Tess's character.

Polanski's vacuous Tess, as played by Kinski, is perhaps a relatively more sympathetic character who is clearly an object of the male character's (as well as Polanski's) "discursive control", with virtually no subjectivity, whatsoever, leaving the audience with only gender stereotyping or conjectural subsurface analytic tools, such as psychoanalytic theory, to explain her.

For Polanski, the audience must do the explaining because he has not employed film technique to harness Hardy's narrative, relying instead on audience sympathy to give rise to a general pro-Tess, pro-female, pro-feminist reception of the film.

The feminist critics cited herein seem basically correct when they assert that reliance of this sort by a male to interpret femaleness is speculative. The truth about Hardy's Tess, and the only reason that she murders, need not be the subject of another male's speculation about her plight as a female or about the male characters' oppressive conduct; the truth is readily available in Hardy's descriptions of family dysfunction found within the literary text.

Chapter 20

Abjection and Degeneration in "Barbara of the House of Grebe"

Thomas Hardy's Gothic tale, "Barbara of the House of Grebe" (1891), dramatizes the horrid consequences of belief in the Victorian myth of degeneration. Only months after writing Tess of the D'Urbervilles, Hardy creates another tragedy in the less well-known "Barbara"; this time tragedy stems from dread of the lower class and of sexually assertive women of any class. The theory of degeneration situates the hatred of the working class and women seen in "Barbara" within the pseudo-scientific debates of the late-Victorian era. Hardy shows how belief in the myth of degeneration could ruin relationships and lives.

Recent studies of degenerationism in history and literature do not discuss Hardy's short stories, but their ideas illuminate "Barbara." Degenerationism posited that groups such as the urban poor, the insane, prostitutes, criminals, and homosexuals adapted to immoral, polluted cities by taking on characteristics of their environment; as a result, they became physically stunted and mentally depraved. Degenerates were thought to pass on their flaws to their children through a kind of Lamarckian evolution that increased aberrations with each succeeding generation.

Facial and bodily deformities might be warnings of degeneracy. But the most dangerous degenerates carried no marks: these decadent artists and writers might seem free from any "taint," helping them to spread their degenerate thinking to the general population through their works (Spackman 1989,

9). Like a disease, degeneracy was thought to be gradually spreading through late-Victorian societies, imperiling their future. Protection of "the race" against decadence was sought through the ostracism of those who weren't respectable, as well as through vigilance about literature and art.

In the 1850s, French psychiatrist Benedict-Augustin Morel developed the theory of degeneration to explain cretinism. An Italian follower of Morel, Cesare Lombroso, applied degenerationism to criminals in a widely read book (Pick 1989, 178-79). Lombroso argued that the "born criminal" is an atavistic throwback to an earlier, more vicious type of human (Hurley 1996, 93); in a later book, Lombroso drew on other studies written from a degeneratist perspective, linking the prostitute to the Hottentot woman as atavistic types (Gilman 1985, 98).

Racism, classism, and sexism intertwined in studies such as Lombroso's: "For the colonial mentality that sees 'natives' as needing control easily shifts that concern to the woman, in particular the prostitute caste" (Gilman 1985, 107). While degenerationism rationalized imperialism, scientific theory helped sell degenerationism to the educated classes. Evolutionary theory, physics, and medicine suggested models of entropy that made degenerationism seem plausible to Victorians (Hurley 1996, 65).

Increasingly, degenerationism made sense to the affluent as there was "a growing sense in the last decades of the century of a lack of synchrony between the rhetoric of progress, the confident prediction by the apostles of laissez-faire of ever-increasing prosperity and wealth, and the facts . . . of poverty and degradation at the heart of ever richer empires". In the 1880s, English psychiatrist Henry Maudsley argued that modern Britain was oscillating between progress and decadence; its development might end up being either regenerative or degenerative.

If crowding in cities continued to spread moral and physical degeneration throughout the population, British society might decay rather than evolve. Maudsley popularized degenerationism for middle-class readers by associating it with both common sense and typical fears (Arata 1996, 16). Through the myth of degeneration, "the conventional and respectable classes could justify and articulate their hostility against the deviant, the diseased, and the subversive" (Greenslade 1994, 2).

No longer would the respectable need to feel guilty about the misery of the urban poor. In other words, degenerationism explained poverty and crime in a supposedly scientific manner rather than as ethical problems needing redress (Pick 1989, 10). Nevertheless, degenerationism was used to justify a variety of middle-class responses to social problems, including philanthropy (Arata 1996, 17).

However, the affluent most often used degenerationism to prove that mass democracy and particularly socialism were dangerous (Pick 1989, 218). Dread of democracy and socialism grew from memories of a century of riots and revolutions in Britain, Europe, and America. It was feared that in the future, widespread degeneracy might lead to mob rule under the guise of democracy or socialism, destroying the middle and upper classes.

Widely translated books about degeneration such as Max Nordau's drew heavily upon nineteenth-century literature for examples of degenerates, including aesthetes (Arata 1996, 28-9). Nordau's ideas about fictional degenerates were then used by London journalists, for example, to explain the accusations of homosexuality against Oscar Wilde (Arata 1996, 3). As for fiction itself, degenerationism influenced novelists such as Rider Haggard and Rudyard Kipling (Arata 1996, 13), Bram Stoker and Robert Louis Stevenson (Hurley 1996, 30), and Emile Zola (Pick 1989, 4).

Degenerative motifs appear most commonly in Gothic novels, as degenerationism "is a 'gothic' discourse, and as such is a crucial imaginative and narrative source for the fm-de-siecle Gothic". In the case of "Barbara," degenerationism is an imaginative source for Hardy's treatment of disfigurement and wife abuse.

The popularity of degenerationism during Hardy's era can be explained ahistorically as well as historically. Abjection explains the appeal of degenerationism from the ahistorical perspective of psychoanalysis. Powers of Horror: An Essay on Abjection describes the abject as "the not-I". The abject is associated with moral and physical decline as well as with death.

Julia Kristeva's theory of abjection explains racial, class, gender, national, and religious hatreds that recur throughout history in new guises. Degenerationism is one manifestation of the tendency to label "others" as abject; degenerationism was used by some well-heeled Victorians to justify acting upon their hatred of those whom they saw as abject.

Using the developmental perspective that characterizes psychoanalytic approaches like Kristeva's, we can see abjection as a lifelong process. Abjection appears early in human development, as the child struggles to create a sense of identity in the face of his or her fear of death. Repulsion towards the mother as nauseatingly linked to decay and death motivates the child's rejection of her. Her exclusion lets the child deny the threat of death, and it fosters the child's narcissism. Labeling the mother as abjectly "other" helps the child erect a sense of self in spite of his or her dread of death. Throughout the human lifespan, the danger to the psyche posed by awareness of death continues to be dealt with through projecting the abject onto a variety of "others."

Kristeva observes that "There looms, within abjection, one of those violent, dark revolts of being, directed against a threat that seems to emanate from an exorbitant outside or inside, ejected beyond the scope of the possible, the tolerable, the thinkable". As the potential for decay exists "inside" of the body, bodily fluids, taboo foods, and sexual acts are sometimes viewed as abject; so are symbols of moral decay such as sins. Marginalized groups, too, are labeled abject since they threaten contagion from "outside."

Such groups may include women, the homeless, the disabled, and Jews. What or who is labeled abject varies according to the prejudices of those who project the abject onto the "other" to suppress recognition of it inside themselves. Despite the variability of regarding what is categorized as abject, the process of labeling the "other" as abject is both universal and ancient, according to Kristeva.

Hardy's story can be understood through considering the intersection between abjection and degenerationism. Both degenerationism and abjection marginalize "others" to build up the confidence of the fortunate (Hurley 1996, 79). In addition, abjection involves revulsion against that which one associates with decay. In late-Victorian England, the decay that triggers the abjective response takes the forms of moral and physical degeneracy. In Hardy's "Barbara," the abject degenerates are working-class men and upper class women by turns, as classism and then sexism fortified by belief in degenerationism are critiqued.

THE DEGENERATE WORKING CLASS HERO

"Barbara" is set late in the eighteenth century. Handsome yet poor, Edmond Willowes elopes with a young aristocrat, Barbara Grebe. Barbara's parents had been pressing her to marry rich Lord Uplandtowers; she runs away with Edmond to escape their arguments. But after several weeks of marriage, Barbara begins to regret the match when she grasps its cost in social terms: her friends greet her coldly now that she is the wife of a nobody. At this point Barbara's disgruntled parents forgive the couple and then send Edmond abroad, as though sensitive to Barbara's growing ambivalence towards him.4 Barbara guiltily hides her snobbery towards her absent husband for over a year until Edmond is maimed while saving strangers from a fire in Italy. His severe disfigurement horrifies Barbara, causing her to reject him.

Barbara had married Edmond because of his exceptional beauty; once accustomed to that loveliness after marriage, she began to search for the revolting qualities that her prejudices tell her he must have as a working man. Those "low" qualities would give her an excuse for distancing herself from him to avoid "contamination" by his degeneracy. "The biologising of class differences was encouraged by the fear of contagion and infection". Barbara responds to the maimed Edmond as though she fears "catching" his ugliness like a cold-ugliness that symbolizes his low status that she has already "caught," to a certain extent, as his wife.

Barbara's overreaction to Edmond's disfigurement implies that, as an aristocrat, she had secretly attributed dreaded qualities to Edmond for a long time. Her gradual revulsion is implied through the narrator's mocking description of her declining interest in Edmond after their wedding, and later through her lack of interest in his affectionate letters from Europe. Edmond's disfigurement increases her distaste as his looks prove that her doubts about him are correct. Persecuting groups tend to attribute to their objects of hatred "disabilities and deformities that would reinforce the polarization against the victim, were they real".

In Barbara's mind, Edmond's repulsive origins are what scar his once lovely face; she projects abjection and degeneracy upon him-poverty, loathsomeness, and death. Barbara "had just that same sense of dismay and fearfulness that she would have had in the presence of an apparition. . he was metamorphosed to a specimen of another species". Maimed, Edmond is an "apparition" indeed: Barbara's fear that he is a monster has come true.

To Barbara, Edmond was of "another species" in the sense of belonging to Disraeli's other, impoverished England even before his accident. As the narrator reminds us at the story's end, Barbara refuses to see that Edmond's nobility of spirit, if not of birth, has been proven by his heroism during the fire. Sadly, his disfigurement causes her to project her fears about the degenerate working class onto him to the point of selfdeceit about his character.

For the affluent, degenerationism "offered a displacement and transference of guilt" (Greenslade 1994, 2). By regarding the disfigured Edmond as a degenerate, Barbara transfers her guilt about her dissatisfaction with their marriage onto him. She need not feel guilty about loathing him if his repulsive looks prove that he actually is unworthy of her. During their last interview, Edmond reinforces her opinion by acting as though he agrees with her transference of blame onto him.

In her pitilessness, Barbara denies the implications for

herself of Edmond's abjection as a supposed degenerate. To see this truth, Barbara would have to recognize the presence of the abject within herself, rather than projecting it onto Edmond. When one sees abjection inside oneself, one knows that "all abjection is in fact recognition of the want on which any being, meaning, language, or desire is founded" (Kristeva 1982, 5).

Barbara is afraid to see an inherent lack or vulnerability in herself, so she cannot accept the embodiment of it in her mutilated husband. Tied to a husband, who signifies entropy and death, she fears that they will take her over. Abjection and the abject are "safeguards" against such fears, that, if acknowledged, may "annihilate" the self (Kristeva 1982, 2).

"These body fluids, this defilement, this shit are what life withstands, hardly and with difficulty" (Kristeva 1982, 3). Edmond's burns disrupt the border between the inside and outside of his body, showing his skeleton. This makes him symbolize the erupting bodily fluids that signify the dedifferentiation of death. Kristeva describes the significance of broken skin such as Edmond's as "It is as if the skin, a fragile container, no longer guaranteed the integrity of one's `own and clean self" (1982, 53). In seeing Edmond as abjectly degenerate, Barbara refuses to accept that the entropy which she associates with the lower orders will erupt from her too at some unpredictable moment; she avoids seeing that all humans of every class must degenerate into the abject through accident, deprivation, disease, aging, or death.

AESTHETIC OBJECT

Upon his arrival in Italy, Edmond had ordered that a statue of him be made for Barbara. At that time, he gloried in being an admired aesthetic object. After the fire, his depression over losing his looks heightens when he realizes that Barbara valued him for his beauty alone. Edmond had taken a traditional "feminine" position that he comes to regret: "Men look at women. Women watch themselves being looked at. This determines not only most relations between men and women but also the relation of women to themselves". What this says about women applies to Edmond too, as the subservient spouse in a cross-class marriage that feminizes him. After the fire, Edmond says to Barbara, "Can you bear such a thing of the charnel-house near you? . . . Your Adonis, your matchless man, has come to this!" Infected by Barbara's prejudice that ties the worth of a working-class husband to beauty, Edmond can't see his own value as a self-sacrificing, scarred hero.

Like the stereotypical upper-class male of her time (and others), Barbara possesses a sense of the erotic that rests on beauty. That is how her class and gender prejudices intersect, causing her to feminize her working-class husband. Barbara's shallowness in desiring a gorgeous consort is consistent with her youth and her babyish facial features that the narrator describes more than once. As the narrator points out, perhaps Barbara's emphasis on a lover's beauty is not that different from how most of us feel; perhaps we would act as cruelly as she does towards a newly ugly spouse whom we hadn't seen for over a year.

In Tales of Love, Kristeva writes, "As soon as the other appears different from myself, it becomes alien, repelled, repugnant, abject-hated". Hardy dramatizes this process of alienation through the burns that ruin Edmond's face, justifying Barbara's sense that he has always been inadequate.

Years later, when Barbara worships Edmond's statue after marrying Uplandtowers, she compensates for her guilt about having rejected Edmond the living man as abjectly degenerate. Early in her marriage to Edmond, Barbara's guilt had been about her repugnance at her husband's "low" ancestry, but after his accident, it is additionally about her looks and health being much better than his. Her guilt intensifies when, after her remarriage, she finds out that Edmond had been as unhappy after their separation as she had feared, and had died lonely and ill years previously. At that point, his naked statue arrives and her obsession with it starts, perhaps as a result of survivor guilt.

What is unusual is that Barbara is a female aristocrat who collects a male art nude. One reason that Uplandtowers is angry at Barbara's infatuation with Edmond's statue is that she has dared to usurp the aristocratic male position of collector of erotic art. Whereas upper-class men could buy beautiful prostitutes, upper-class women had no such option, nor were they thought to need it. Barbara's possession of Edmond the beautiful man and then of his lovely statue can be seen as extensions of the sexual prerogatives of the upper class male of which Uplandtowers feels robbed.

Usually, nineteenth-century art nudes had provided a way for rich men to objectify and own lower-class women. In such representations of naked women, "the subject is aware of being seen by a spectator" for his pleasure (Berger 1972, 49). This representation creates the reassuring illusion that working-class women like to be dominated by upper-class men. Hardy's story transposes genders, yet otherwise adheres to such a representation.6 Edmond presumably had hoped that Barbara's love would be solidified through the pleasure of gazing at his statue and imagining that he gazed back in approval of her ownership of him.

But it is not simply Barbara's ambition to experience "masculine" privileges that underlies her obsession with Edmond's statue. Her attachment to the statue is a way to compensate for the lovelessness of her marriage to Uplandtowers: "The Pygmalion-like episode of the statue suggests that an ideal aesthetic image is preferred to a living body, or to the quotidian banality of sexual intercourse" (Ebbatson 1993, 93). That sex with Uplandtowers is not quotidian, but threatening, is suggested by Barbara's fear of him. She can control the statue of her first husband in a way that she cannot control Uplandtowers; Barbara is freer to feel sexual pleasure through contemplation of the statue than in the arms of her living husband.

Also pertinent to explaining the statue's appeal for Barbara is the idea that "To seduce is to die as reality and reconstruct oneself as illusion" (Baudrillard 1979, 69). That is what happens when Edmond dies and Barbara replaces him with his perfect image. Edmond's image seduces her as his living beauty once did until it began to become too familiar through marriage. Barbara takes the voyeuristic experience of art ownership to an extreme when she repeatedly kisses Edmond's statue. Reflecting upon the statue, Barbara can revel in her pleasure over her former husband's beauty without having to think about his significance as an abject member of the working class.

It appears that, for Barbara, fixity is the statue's greatest appeal-a permanence available only to art objects such as John Keats's Grecian urn. Such fixity counteracts the horrible inevitability of Barbara's own decline into death that Edmond's disfigurement had conveyed. The statue's seeming invulnerability to decay reassures Barbara that she is safe from mortality's depredations. Through her macabre interest in the image of a dead spouse, Barbara recalls the duke in Robert Browning's "My Last Duchess."

Though Barbara does not kill her spouse directly as the duke does, she does so indirectly by causing that depression which, combined with Edmond's burns, makes him susceptible to death from a slight illness. Both the duke and Barbara thrive on control of their spouses. This means control of the duchess's manner in the duke's case, and of Edmond's looks and demeanor in Barbara's. Such absolute control of a spouse cannot be achieved in life; it is only achievable through manipulating artistic representations of the deceased spouse. Ironically, both the duke and Barbara are much happier in their relationships with images of the dead than they were with their living spouses. Browning's and Hardy's analyses of such relationships reveal the murderous sterility of aristocrats' need for control.

Hardy questions what collecting art means not only for the highborn, but for the middle class of his time and ours. He does this through creating a narrative frame in which a surgeon tells Barbara's tale as one of ten stories within A Group of Noble Dames. Told at a dinner of the Antiquarian Society, each of the legends of dead Dames represents an attempt by a different middle-class narrator to know, thus in a sense possess, the ladies involved through taletelling. What do antiquarians do but collect and study remnants from the past-narrative remnants, in this case, of tragic lives. Because of class barriers, the amateur antiquarians would not be allowed the intimacy with the ladies in actual life that they are allowed through the mediation of art and history.

That is also true for the readers of the tales, ourselves, positioned at one further remove from the mythologized ladies.lo Collecting the ladies' tales voyeuristically, we participate in Hardy's dissection of why people label "others" as abject degenerates.

THE STATUE GAME

Reacting to Barbara's obsession with Edmond's statue, Uplandtowers has the statue defaced and painted in lifelike hues so that it mimics the first husband's injuries from the fire. The Earl then places the statue in a wardrobe in front of Barbara's bed, surprising her with it by candlelight. He forces her to view the wrecked image during several successive nights. When the terrorized Barbara finally protests that she no longer loves Edmond but loves her new husband instead, Uplandtowers has the statue removed.

Through the statue game Uplandtowers punishes Barbara for being a degenerate who "fell" twice-in marrying below her to gratify her youthful passion for Edmond, and in being adulterous in that she desires his statue. Through disfiguring Edmond's statue, the Earl revenges himself upon Barbara for her two "falls," and especially for having eloped with Edmond while Uplandtowers was courting her; it offends Uplandtowers that she preferred Edmond's beauty to the Earl's blood. More generally, Uplandtowers hates the female autonomy that such novel preferences as Barbara's demonstrate. In particular, he castigates her for her desire for Edmond as a living and dead man, passion that is forbidden to an upper-class woman.

Even more controlling as a spouse than Barbara was during her marriage to Edmond, Uplandtowers manipulates Barbara through her terror of the disfigured statue. Perhaps Barbara's horror comes in part from the realization that what Uplandtowers did to Edmond's statue, and what she did to

Edmond the living man, Uplandtowers may do to her, now that she is the subordinate spouse. In a sense, Uplandtowers does disfigure her through a series of back to-back pregnancies that eventually kill her. Ultimately, he does reject her, though less definitively than she did Edmond. Her hysterics at the sight of Edmond's mangled statue may come from anticipation of her doom as Uplandtowers' consort.

Another reason for Barbara's fear of the maimed statue is that she wishes to deny her guilt over rejecting Edmond when he became disfigured. Paradoxically, she is afraid for a seemingly contradictory reason: though she knows that she should not have rejected Edmond after he lost his looks, she nevertheless continues to feel revolted by the thought of his ugliness that, for her, is a mark of his degenerate background. Uplandtowers shares her contempt for the class into which she "lowered" herself through marriage. The Earl's mockery of her desire for Edmond through the cruel statue game is a kind of private charivari intended to humiliate her into modesty and subservience. Through the Earl's description of the defaced statue in the closet as a "shrine" and through his laughter at Barbara's hysterical reaction to it, Uplandtowers attempts to humble Barbara. Viewed through the lens of Kristeva's theory, the Earl's laughter can also be seen as a method of displacing abjection from himself (Kristeva 1982, 8).

The Earl's statue game shifts Barbara's position from victimizer to victim as it grinds her fears about Edmond's degeneracy into her psyche yet again. As the widow of a so-called degenerate, Barbara is one too, in her mind and in the Earl's. Through his defeat of Edmond's statue, the symbol of his dead rival, Uplandtowers "asserts the supremacy of the landowning class" over rebels like Barbara and Edmond (Ebbatson 1993, 103). Just as Edmond the workingclass spouse was ruled by an aristocratic wife, so Barbara the aristocrat is manipulated by the crafty Lord whose name connotes his dominance. The narrator describes Barbara's relation to her husband after the statue game as abject, servile, and slavish, emphasizing that she accepts the lowly marital position that Edmond once held. Once Barbara is no longer the collector of art that idealizes members of the lower classes such as Edmond, she becomes an aesthetic object to be collected herself.

THE DEGENERATION OF UPLANDTOWERS

In her study of female masochism in Gothic novels, Michelle Masse argues that Gothic heroines feel "the cultural, psychoanalytic, and fictional expectation that they should be masochistic if they are 'normal' women". Defying this expectation when she weds Edmond and then when she resists the Earl's precedence as her husband, Barbara finally acts masochistic under the rigors of the latter's statue game. That game can be compared to the Gothic beating drama that Masse explores. Masse describes the Gothic dyad of male beater and female victim, in which romance requires female suffering and sacrifice. Surely, the Earl's repeated torments through the statue game are a kind of psychological beating of Barbara that results in her abjection. She learns to seek her beater's attentions, though they torment her. In the light of Masse's analysis, Barbara's sufferings become the expected results of a wife's culturally conditioned "natural" abjection as a "normal" female masochist.

The editors of The Graphic, the periodical for which "Barbara" was commissioned as part of A Group of Noble Dames, forced Hardy to remove the intimate details of physical abuse that dramatized the Earl's cruelty towards Barbara; those details remain absent from the story published in Noble Dames the book. However, George Wing posits that what remains of the brutality of Uplandtowers is "not more than a filament removed from so-called normal posture". Wing is referring to an alleged Victorian norm of mild mental abuse of wives; such a "normal posture" may stem from widespread use of the myth of degeneration to justify placing "uppity" women in abject positions.

Like a stereotypical Gothic heroine, Barbara ultimately embraces her role as the Earl's abject victim. She experiences an intense absorption in her abjection that recalls her previous focus upon prostrating herself before Edmond's statue.

Kristeva writes of the appeal of abjection that it can create "a jouissance in which the Other, in return, keeps the subject from foundering by making it repugnant. One thus understands why so many victims of the abject are its fascinated victims-if not its submissive and willing ones". Barbara is fascinated, submissive, and willing when she gives up her autonomy to Uplandtowers. Abjection appeals to her because it will save her from having to make further, perilous decisions that could cause her to feel the intense guilt and pain that she faced after Edmond was maimed. Not only does Barbara accept abjection as her punishment for rejecting Edmond long ago, but because abjection relieves her from the burden of self-determination.

To make Barbara experience herself as abject and degenerate, Uplandtowers takes on the role of the late-Victorian doctor battling the female patient for control of her psyche, a practice discussed in The Female Malady. It is reassuring for Uplandtowers to pretend that Barbara's interest in Edmond's statue is a sign of mental disease, not the result of her unhappiness in their marriage. One reason she worshipped the statue was to defy the authority of Uplandtowers under the self-righteous guise of a grieving widow rather than the incriminating one of a shrewish wife; Uplandtowers reacts in a similarly sneaky manner to make his tyranny look benevolent. Uplandtowers hopes Barbara will be "cured" of her illicit passion for Edmond by the sight of his ghastly statue.

But the "cure" frightens Uplandtowers as well as Barbara, for the sight of Edmond's disfigured statue causes her to experience "an epileptic fit" (Hardy 1891, 569). Epilepsy was associated with perversion by degenerationists such as Lombroso (Spackman 1989, 30). Barbara's desire for Edmond's statue proves she is unnaturally masculine and perverse, according to the Earl's conservative perspective. Hence, the Earl's "treatment" of Barbara's epilepsy can be seen as coming from a degenerationist point of view. However, the narrator comments that her "cure became so permanent as to be itself a new disease" when describing Barbara's consequent servility towards her husband. In calling the "cure" a "disease," the narrator uses black humour to question the discourse of medical mastery that Uplandtowers exploits for his own ends.

The narrator sees the Earl's "treatment" of his wife as a sign of his perversion, rather than seeing Barbara's seizure as a sign of hers. A further irony is that the narrator is himself a member of the medical profession. His sarcasm suggests that nonprofessionals like Uplandtowers should avoid usurping the doctor's role. However, the narrator's denunciation of the Earl's homemade psychiatric "treatment" of Barbara may be a way to deflect his audience from criticizing his profession's similarly harsh methods for controlling so-called hysterical women.

Barbara's hysteria when Uplandtowers forces her to view the disfigured statue is her defence against the supposedly improper desire she had felt for Edmond, living and dead. The broken Barbara confesses to the inexorable Uplandtowers, "It fills me with shame-how could I ever be so depraved!" In the nineteenth century, doctors saw modesty as a defence against forbidden sexual knowledge or feelings manifested by the hysteric (Ender 1995, 50). Barbara becomes a stereotypically modest, submissive wife to avoid further hysteria, for hysteria's concomitant is the forbidden desire that marks a woman as a destructive degenerate.

Barbara cannot tell Uplandtowers what her hysteria means, because, as Ender explains about the hysteric, "she would show what she cannot show," sexual desire that she is not supposed to feel, and sexual experience that she is not supposed to have had (Ender 1995, 19). Were Barbara to betray such desire, Uplandtowers might treat her even more cruelly. Hence, she exhibits the form of sexuality expected from a wife-passive acceptance of her husband's advances resulting in numerous pregnancies. Hysterical women were thought to be prone to miscarriages (Greenslade 1994, 139): Barbara starts to miscarry and to bear fragile infants under the terror of her husband's "cure" of her worship of Edmond's statue.

Because of her passivity along with her production of children who are too weak to survive, Barbara could be labeled a neurasthenic as well as an hysteric. In the late nineteenth century, neurasthenia was an amorphous term for combinations of symptoms that eluded standard definitions of mental disease. Neurasthenics' characteristic passivity was thought to result from "a decrease in the wattage of the nervous system" caused by modern "turbulence" (Gilman 1985, 204).

Previously, chronic passivity had been thought to result from masturbation (Gilman 1985, 200). However, by the late nineteenth century, "neurasthenia displaced masturbation as the means of presenting the interrelationship of degeneration, sexuality, and society" (Gilman 1985, 204). Neurasthenia thus became the illness "that paradigmatically revealed the degenerative effects of society". From a Victorian perspective, Barbara's permanent passivity after Uplandtowers humiliates her can be seen not just as symptomatic of neurasthenia, but as the result of her forbidden onanistic pleasure in Edmond's statue.

Seen so, her passivity comes from the "turbulence" of ambivalence created by the broken statue: she recalls her guilt over her rejection of the newly maimed Edmond; in addition, the defaced statue triggers her forbidden desire for Edmond simultaneously with her old, contradictory repugnance. Such conflicts that reflect class battles drive Barbara temporarily mad. Despite her degenerationist fear of the lower class, Barbara also suffers from paralyzing self-hatred because she desires one of its members. She finds a refuge from her searing conflicts in the numbness of neurasthenia. However, Hardy shows that Barbara's neurasthenia is caused less by her "degenerate" desire for Edmond than by the Earl's vengeful prodding of her opposing feelings.

Barbara's frequent, failed pregnancies suggest her new, abject status as a disgraced wife. Uplandtowers turns "the once radiant and passionate Barbara into a sickly woman condemned to a cowed life of repeated, unsuccessful pregnancies". That all but one of Barbara's eleven babies dies bolsters Hardy's critique of her second marriage as debased. She is now the vehicle of feminine fluids and transformative powers that take her over in the name of patriarchal succession.

As Edmond was disfigured as a result of being exiled due to class prejudices, so Barbara is disfigured by gender prejudices that compel her to become a monster of thwarted fertility.

Not only Barbara, but all women may be associated with death because of their "messy" childbearing capabilities. Through repeated bereavement Barbara dramatizes that association, mocking the Earl's attempts to create a dynasty that would make his name last. "Blood" loses again, as it did when Barbara chose Edmond over Uplandtowers. As the artist who tries to memorialize Edmond's beauty for all time through his statue fails, so the Earl fails to gain immortality through continuing his family name; Barbara unintentionally revenges herself upon Uplandtowers by producing a living daughter and dead sons. When Uplandtowers dies, his estate goes to a distant male relative, in another example of gender prejudices stealing from a womanthis time, from Barbara's daughter.

The drama of inheritance by "blood" is played out through the Earl's degenerate sexual pleasures. As well as voyeuristic pleasure, Uplandtowers gains a sadistic sexual pleasure directly from Barbara that is suggested by the number and frequency of her pregnancies. In reflecting upon his sexual satisfaction at Barbara's sufferings, we might consider Kristeva's contention that "The erotization of abjection . . . is an attempt at stopping the hemorrhage: a threshold before death, a halt or a respite?" Through making Barbara an erotic object of abjection, Uplandtowers can draw thrillingly close to death while denying its threat.

Unlike Barbara, whose contorted facial expressions, Gothic screams, fainting spells, and epileptic fits express her fears, Uplandtowers hides his feelings in the style of the stereotypical male aristocrat; we can only speculate that the fear of death motivates his displacement of the abject onto his wife and her dead husband. The Earl's coldness suggests that his fears are in fact so great that they have frozen him. His sexual relationship with Barbara is one of loathing that expresses his fear of sexuality's link with death.

Blood, as an abject bodily fluid associated with death, mingles with "blood" as the vehicle of class to explain how the Earl's prejudices stem from fear. The near sterility of his marriage as well as of his personality proves that his obsession with "blood" breeds the degeneracy in himself that he denies. Kelly Hurley argues that degenerationism creates "a gothic nightmare of heredity" in late-Victorian fiction. This nightmare can be seen through the Earl's cruel treatment of his wife that stems from his injured sense of "blood" because she continues to favour a man of no family over him.

ABJECTION, DEGENERACY, AND THE GOTHIC

Hardy's story does not endorse the Earl's definition of Barbara as an abject producer of "unfit" progeny, nor does it support her horror at Edmond's injuries. The old surgeon who narrates the story uses sarcasm to dramatize his disapproval of the two aristocrats' views. Hardy's narrator employs dark humour that distances the reader from Uplandtowers and Barbara, bringing their opinions and actions into question. Wing notes the narrator's "defiant jauntiness" (Wing 1987, 89) and "grim playfulness" (Wing 1987, 81). Mocking his own discomfort with the story, the surgeon considers his tale "a little too professional" (Hardy 1891, 536). Like a surgeon's knife, the narrator's irony dispassionately dissects the twisted aristocratic mentality of Barbara and Uplandtowers.

The use of humour to unveil the meaning of a dark plot is not uncommon in Gothics. Judith Halberstam's ideas about Gothic fiction illuminate Hardy's story, though she does not specifically address it: "Gothic . . . is a textual machine, a technology that transforms class struggle, hostility towards women, and tensions arising out of the emergent ideology of racism into what looks like sexual or psychosexual battles between and within individuals". Halberstam discusses the creation of monsters in nineteenth-century Gothic fiction as a result of the fear of decay associated with marginalized groups: "in the Gothic, crime is embodied within a specifically deviant formthe monster-that announces itself (de-monstrates) as the place of corruption" (Halberstam 1995, 2).

In keeping with the myth of degeneration, "monstrosity was a combination of the features of deviant race, class, and gender". Citing Franco Moretti, Halberstam sees nineteenth-century monsters as symbols of the proletariat.

Although Edmond symbolizes the danger to the upper classes posed by the proletariat, Hardy shifts our sympathy to him. Whereas Edmond's disfigurement makes him a monster in Barbara's eyes, the narrator's irony brings her perspective into question. Since readers don't have to look at Edmond's apparent monstrosity, we can see his nobility in saving strangers from a fire and in forgiving Barbara for rejecting him.

We are also shown enough of the Earl's domestic life to know that Barbara's second husband is the real monster, not her first. The leaking of inner into outer characterizes monsters (Halberstam 1995, 7). Hardy's story moves from the physical leaking of bones into public sight on Edmond's scarred face to the partial unveiling of the Earl's secret cruelty. Through this inversion of expected monstrosities, Hardy questions the myth of working class and "fallen" female degeneration.

However, Hardy's questioning is not unique. Some members of the Victorian middle class regarded the upper class as lazy degenerates. Hardy seems to fall into that camp through making Uplandtowers, not Edmond, the actual monster. Rather than abandoning the myth of degeneration, then, Hardy applies it to a powerful group, the aristocracy. This brings Hardy's story into the Gothic tradition of depicting decaying noble "blood" through skeptical middle-class eyes-here, a surgeon's. Perhaps Sade's observation that the rise of the Gothic is associated with the rise of revolution is pertinent both to eighteenth-century Gothic novels (Graham 1989, 260) and to Hardy's late-Victorian story that criticizes dynastic imperatives. Like Tess, "Barbara" draws upon the Gothic tradition to problematize the Victorian controversy over degenerate "blood."

What Greenslade says of Tess, Jude the Obscure, and The Mayor of Casterbridge is also true of "Barbara": Hardy's texts "take up the cudgels against the myths of degeneration . . . there is a commitment both to the complexities of human experience and to a concern with those sources of ideological power which shape the possibilities open to individuals: determinisms, not merely of biology, of course, but of money, class, status, education" (Greenslade 1994, 10). "Barbara" presents a complex picture of characters' motives, focusing especially upon the simple-minded belief in working-class degeneration shared by Barbara and Uplandtowers, and upon the painful abjection that belief forces onto Edmond and Barbara.

Several generations after Barbara and Uplandtowers die, Edmond's maimed statue is unearthed in their garden. The broken statue surfaces like a decayed corpse that no one recognizes as the symbol of the legions of working class men and of the women from all classes who have been regarded as abject degenerates. In Jude the Obscure, the corpses of Sue's and Jude's children, dead due to prejudice against their sexually "degenerate" parents, come to mind.

To me, reading "Barbara" over a century after Hardy wrote it, the buried, disfigured statue of Edmond suggests the victims of genocide-victims of the theory of degeneration later put into practice by men even more ruthless than Uplandtowers.

Through arbitrarily emphasizing one element in a victim's identity, such men illustrate the workings of abjection and degeneration at their most frightening. Recent studies of degenerationism show that the disparagement of misfits that characterizes both of the Uplandtowers persists through Hardy's time into ours. British degenerationists, including socialists H.G. Wells and Karl Pearson, created the eugenics movement at the turn of the century.

Eugenics fed not only Nazism but also fascist movements in Britain, France, and Italy (Pick 1989, 30, 218). In addition, eugenics was used to justify new laws against immigration in Britain (Pick 1989, 215).

Eugenics arguments persuaded some American states to sterilize inmates of asylums and prisons during the first four decades of the twentieth century. Today a variant of degenerationism underlies the view that American society is decaying due to the influence of non-white immigrants; such fears in California, for example, stimulated the recent passage of laws that eliminated bilingual education and affirmative action.

With an extraordinary ability to prophesy the future based on scrutinizing the past, Hardy allegorizes persecutors' attempts to escape the distressing sense of their own mortality through projecting it upon the supposedly degenerate members of the working class and the female gender (or of whatever marginalized race, nation, religion, or disability): ironically, the humiliation and death of the abject cannot save each newly defined "privileged" group from a similar fate.

Chapter 21

Hardy's The Tragedy of a Life Without Christ

The evangelist Charles Finney stated: "I cannot believe that a person who has ever known the love of God can ever relish a secular novel. Let me visit your...books. What is here? Byron, Scott, Shakespeare and a host of triflers and blasphemers of God." To that list Finney would have undoubtedly added Thomas Hardy the agnostic. Therefore, why read such a writer?

First, there are solid biblical reasons for reading worthwhile non-Christian literature. Frank Gaebelein popularized the maxim: "All truth is God's truth"—no matter what the literary source. The apostle Paul believed this idea, for on at least three occasions (Acts 17:28; 1 Cor 15:33; Titus 1:12) he quoted from secular sources. Paul was obviously versed in more than the Bible.

Second, if we desire to understand the mindset of the non-Christian culture, then we must be aware of the particular philosophies and notions rampant at any given time. Great literature is usually an index to cultural concepts. Third, if we would have a *heart* for unbelievers, then we need to grasp where and how their *head* is functioning. Thomas Hardy himself spoke of the "ache of modernism."

The Christian who has experientially understood that life without Christ is a tragedy should have an ache in his or her *heart* for unbelievers to find the fulfillment that is in Christ. To counter Finney, then, read the playboy Byron's magnificent biblical poem "The Destruction of Sennacherib"; read Sir

Walter Scott, who operated out of a Christian consensus; and read Shakespeare.

B. WHO WAS THOMAS HARDY

If you had literature's leading lights—James Barrie (author of *Peter Pan*), John Galsworthy, Edmond Gosse, A.E. Housman, George Bernard Shaw, Rudyard Kipling, as well as the prime minister of England—as your pallbearers (as Thomas Hardy did), you'd have to be thought rather important. Thomas Hardy (1840-1928) never graduated from college, yet he received honorary doctorates from the universities of Aberdeen, Bristol, Cambridge, and Oxford.

Hardy's five most important novels (in chronological order) are *Far from the Madding Crowd, The Return of the Native, The Mayor of Casterbridge, Tess of the D'Urbervilles,* and *Jude the Obscure*. Hardy also wrote over 900 poems and more than 40 short stories. He was considered the greatest writer of English tragedy in his time. Thus, W. M. Parker (editor of Sir Walter Scott's letters) could call Hardy "the greatest imaginative genius of modern times."

II. THE BIBLICAL HARDY

A. BIBLICAL ALLUSIONS

How many seminary graduates could identify who Ahimaaz and Aholibah are or where they are found in the Bible? How many Bible-literate people could quote from Psalm 102? Do you know where Jared and Mahaleel are in Scripture? All of these items—and (literally) hundreds more—are found by way of biblical allusion in Thomas Hardy's novels.

Thomas Hardy was steeped in classical and biblical literature. Marlene Springer, who wrote a book devoted explicitly to this subject, claimed that as an author, Hardy "out-alluded virtually every allusionist..." This agnostic was virtually a walking Bible concordance! Indeed, I would pit Hardy against any seminary graduate today (and bet big bucks—if I were a betting person) as a sure wager to win any Bible knowledge proficiency test. Hardy read the Bible in both

Latin and Greek. Desmond Hawkins declared that Hardy "was more certainly influenced by [the Bible] than any novelist writing today."[6] I think Hawkins's evaluation would stand undisputed.

The heading to this section of the Journal is "Grace in the Arts." What theologians call "common grace" is functioning in the life of this agnostic to make his pessimistic works so riddled with biblical allusions. Also, God's grace is apparent in allowing this agnostic 88 years of life in which he might even trifle with that grace (2 Pet 3:9).

Thomas Hardy had considerable biblical background. His life-dream as a child was to be a parson. He played the violin in church as a youth. He taught Sunday School. His hero, folk-poet William Barnes, was a Christian.

His best friend was the brother of the Bible commentator H. C. G. Moule, Anglican bishop of Durham. Hardy read numerous theological works up until his mid-twenties, presumably in preparation for the professional ministry. In fact, this agnostic never stopped attending, and taking communion in the Anglican church—even after his first (evangelical) wife died!

Thomas Hardy's works are replete with scriptural allusions. One frequent declaration heard in church history classes is that if our NT had been destroyed, it could almost be replaced by quotations culled from the early Church Fathers.

Almost the same could be said—with forgivable exaggeration—with reference to Hardy's writings.

I have read 9 of his 14 novels and all of his 947 poems. Below are tabulated my count of biblical allusions in 9 of Hardy's major novels.

In the left hand column are listed figures in which Hardy supplies general references to Christian terms, phrases, ideas, and so forth. In the right hand column are listed numbers from each book for sentences containing an allusion where some rather specific Scripture verse or passage can be cited. Naturally, there is some subjectivity involved in the placement of these two sets of figures.

Title	*General Allusions*	*Specific Allusions to Scripture*
Under the Greenwood Tree	74	11
A Pair of Blue Eyes	84	41
Far from the Madding Crowd	154	79
The Return of the Native	124	71
The Mayor of Casterbridge	76	41
The Woodlanders	85	35
Tess of the D'Urbervilles	428	110
Jude the Obscure	456	112
The Well-Beloved	35	18
Hardy's Complete Poems	212	147
TOTAL	1728	665

As can be seen from the statistics compiled above, there are Christian books these days in which one could not find as many references to Scripture as one could find in this agnostic's literature.

The sections in Hardy's books that are a special repository for biblical allusions are those where his rustics speak. These conversations between rural folk are salted with Scripture—sometimes insightful, sometimes confused and superstitious. For instance, when one rural character gets scared, he recites the Lord's prayer, then the Ten Commandments, followed by "dearly beloved brethren," which is what his church experience prods him to remember. One rustic child was erroneously named Cain, since his mother got the name in the Bible story mixed up with Abel's.

One of Hardy's other rustics complains, "I was sitting at home looking for Ephesians, and I says to myself, 'Tis nothing but Corinthians and Thessalonians in this danged Testament". (Perhaps childhood sword drills would have helped him!) Another country fellow speaks erroneously of "King Noah...entering into the ark". Still another rustic figure recites the names of "Matthew, Mark, Luke, and John" when he fears the devil is near him.

At this juncture I would like to provide a brief sampling of some specific scriptural allusions from Hardy's novels:

At the end of *Under the Greenwood Tree* one finds Hardy quoting Jer 2:32 ("Can a maid forget her ornaments, or a bride her attire?") in connection with Fancy Day's vanity over her clothes. "Even to half my kingdom" in *A Pair of Blue Eyes* echoes Mark 6:23. *The Return of the Native* (chap 6) mentions "the witch of Endor [who] called up Samuel." Also in this novel Hardy shows his knowledge of the Greek NT (2 Pet 2:4) by twice using the term "Tartarian." *The Mayor of Casterbridge* refers to "Jacob in Padan-aram" with his ring-straked sheep. In *The Woodlanders* (chap 14) we meet "the sword of the Lord and of Gideon." *Tess of the D'Urbervilles* has one of its characters use Job's words (3:1-3): "I wish I'd never been born." On more than one occasion a character in *Jude the Obscure* cites 1 Cor 4:9 ("we are made a spectacle," etc.). *The Well-Beloved* refers to "the elect lady" (2 John 1; Part 3, chap 5) and "those who knew not Joseph" (Exod 1:8; Part 3, chap 8).

In one case the very name of the novel (*A Laodicean*) reflects biblical language (Rev 3:14). Often Hardy's characters' names reflect biblical borrowing (such as, Bathsheba, Gabriel, Jude, Laban, etc.) and tip us off to the given character's character as well. For example, Bathsheba unintentionally attracts by her beauty, and Gabriel Oak is as sturdy as his name implies.

B. A BIBLICAL PLOT

In *The Mayor of Casterbridge* Thomas Hardy largely modeled his story-plot on the biblical interrelationship between Saul and David. This thesis has been detailed significantly in an article by Julian Moynahan.

The novel itself states that Michael Henchard, the lead

character and mayor, "felt like Saul at his reception by Samuel". The book revolves around the relationship of an older head of government (Mayor Henchard) to a younger man (Donald Farfrae). As the plot progresses, the older becomes jealous of the younger and eventually is replaced as government leader by the younger (as Saul was by David).

Numerous themes in *The Mayor of Casterbridge* clearly parallel the Saul-to-David biblical narrative. First, the older is attracted to the younger particularly by his musical ability. Second, the younger (Farfrae) is described as "ruddy and of a fair countenance" (compare this with 1 Sam 16:12 and 17:42). Third, Henchard is famed for his impulsive moodiness (similar to Saul's mental ups and downs). Fourth, the younger saves the older's reputation from a goliath of failure. Fifth, the older gets jealous of his rival when he hears people praising the younger and wishing Farfrae were in the elder's place.

Thus, Farfrae becomes "an enemy" of Henchard. Moreover Michael Henchard consults a wizard-like weather forecaster in a way similar to that of Saul consulting the witch of Endor. Farfrae, like David, also has opportunities to wreak revenge on the one who hates him, but the younger man refuses the course of vengefulness. In fact, Henchard tries explicitly to kill Farfrae at one point. Also in the novel the hideout of certain bad characters is called "the Adullam of all the surrounding villages" (chap 36). *The Mayor of Casterbridge* concludes just as the book of 1 Samuel does—with the tragic death of its tragic figure. This then is the *biblical* Hardy—the very fabric of his language, the vast amount of biblical allusions, the derived names of certain characters, and the framework of one entire novel are all colored extensively by a mind immersed in the thought-world of Scripture. Tragically, however, such biblical flavoring is far from the whole story. Therefore, we now turn to the *unbiblical* Hardy.

III. THE UNBIBLICAL HARDY

A. HIS ABANDONMENT OF CHRISTIANITY

Hardy's thought-forms were often Bible-tinctured, but his

basic philosophy was anything but biblical. What happened to one who grew up dreaming of becoming a Christian minister and who read theology in preparation for that profession? Unfortunately there is no clear-cut before-and-after traceable in his biography. Nor does there seem to have been a specific crisis marking such a shift in thought. Terry Coleman wrote: "At the beginning of [1861] Hardy was probably still a Christian, and at the end [of 1866] he certainly was not, and of the process by which this charge came over such a mind we know nothing."

While it isn't quite true to say "we know nothing," we certainly have no definitive data on a distinct turning-point in Hardy's turning away from Christianity. Robert Gittings observed that "until the age of 26 [Hardy] still considered entering the Church [ministry]." While we may not be able to pinpoint some watershed experience in which Hardy abandoned orthodox Christianity, there are clearly some contributing causes for his forsaking the faith.

The first of the contributing causes to Hardy's apostasy is a hard one to pin down with definitive evidence, yet I suspect that every Hardy biographer would concur that some mysterious romantic attachment was at the root of bitterness in Hardy's life. Biographers have suggested at least five different love affairs in Hardy's early life. One researcher, Lois Deacon, postulated on the basis of plausible evidence that Hardy had had a five-year affair with Tryphena Sparks, whom he thought to be his cousin.

Then he discovered that Tryphena was the illegitimate daughter of his own sister, who herself was the illegitimate daughter of his mother. Thus, he broke off an engagement. Some interpreters even claim they had an illegitimate child together who is represented by the character called Little Father Time in *Jude the Obscure*. Whether Lois Deacon's specific hypothesis is factual or not, something very unaccountable and suppressed in Hardy's relationship with women seems necessary to account for his turning sour on life as well as this theme in his writing.

Second, Hardy's best friend (and mentor)—Horace Moule,

the brother of evangelical commentator H. C. G. Moule—committed suicide. Moule's father and his brothers are to some extent the prototype for Angel Clare's father and family in *Tess of the D'Urbervilles*. In this book the clerical father is described as "an evangelical of the evangelicals" (chap 25) and an "unimpeachable Christian" with a "Pauline view of humanity" (chap 26). Nevertheless, Horace Moule, a Cambridge graduate, became an alcoholic and committed suicide. This tragedy unquestionably had a devastating effect upon Thomas Hardy.

Third, Hardy was influenced by "the yeasty ideas of his formative years," such as "evolution [and] the new morality." Darwin's *Origin of the Species* was published when Hardy was nineteen years old. Hardy read Darwin, Spencer, Comte, and Schopenhauer. A nature "red in tooth and claw" (to borrow Thomas Hobbes's phrase) is a major theme in Hardy's novels.

Fourth, some scholars have asserted that (like the painter van Gogh) Hardy was rejected upon application to Cambridge University as Jude Fawley was in *Jude the Obscure*. Such a bitter rejection might partly account for his anti-Christian attitude. Fifth, one occasion may have cemented Hardy's convictions away from Christianity. Leslie Stephen, editor of Cornhill Magazine, was influential in Hardy's writing experience.

In fact, Hardy described Stephen as "the man whose philosophy was to influence his own…more than that of any other contemporary." Stephen called on Thomas Hardy "on 23 March 1875 to witness his renunciation of the holy orders [to the Anglican ministry] he had taken in 1855…" By affirming Leslie Stephen on that occasion, Hardy was issuing a sort of declaration of agnosticism.

B. HIS POISONED PHILOSOPHY

To say that Hardy is not known for his novels ending "happily ever after" is an understatement! In his writings "all things work together" for the worst—to parody Rom 8:28. In *The Woodlanders* Grace Melbury watches her truest love, Giles Winterbourne, die. She was "bitter with all that had befallen her—with the cruelties that had attacked her—with life—with Heaven" (chap 43). Schoolmaster Phillotson remarks, "Cruelty is the law pervading all nature and society; and we can't get out of it if we would" [*JO*, Part 5, chap 8]. In *Desperate Remedies* Mr. Springrove says, "There's a back'ard current in the world, and we must do our utmost to advance in order just to bide where we be."

Most readers of Hardy label him a pessimist. His books tend to get more bitter in the consecutive order of their writing with the bitterest novels (*Tess* and *JO*) coming at the end of his novel-writing career. Hardy consistently denied that he was a pessimist, preferring to call himself a "meliorist," that is, one who was neither an optimist nor a pessimist, but believed the world could be made *better* if we all worked at it. Sheila Sullivan said Hardy was "prepared to face the worst an indifferent universe might have to offer, but who believed nevertheless that the will to live persists, and that no life is entirely without its consolation."

C. HIS PHILOSOPHICAL PREDICAMENT

If there is a God, then God can be blamed for the tragic mess on this planet (some would reason). However, if there is no God, who or what is there to blame for such rotten happenings? This dilemma tends to be Hardy's philosophical predicament. To let God be or not be—that is the question (à la Shakespeare's Hamlet). Somewhere G. K. Chesterton (the Anglican debater-turned Roman Catholic) takes Thomas Hardy to task for playing both sides of the fence. If there is no God, why spend your time railing in the direction of heaven?

This dilemma emerges in a conversational interchange between Sue Bridehead and her first husband (to whom she eventually returns), Richard Phillotson (in *JO*). She admits that her penchant for not wanting to sleep with her lawful husband is wrong, yet she exclaims: "It is not I altogether that am to blame!"

Philottson then responds, "Who is then? Am I?" To his remark Sue counters, "No—I don't know! The universe, I suppose—things in general, because they are so horrid and cruel!" (*JO*, Part 4, chap 3). Thus, the big question is: Who do you blame if you're an agnostic?

D. HIS INVENTED IRONIES

In one's fiction a writer can control his or her world. Thus, through the mouths of his characters, Hardy inevitably reflects his own pessimistic world-view. Many writers have used a technique called *deus ex machina* (woodenly rendered, a "god out of a machine"). This technique was literally used in ancient drama when a mechanical device would be employed in order to let a "god" down on stage to serve as a rescuer from the characters' predicament.

Thomas Hardy used almost a reverse approach to the *deus ex machina* technique. He invented ironical incidents in order to show a perverse world-order in operation. For instance, an inexperienced sheepdog (in *FMC*) drives Gabriel Oak's entire flock over a precipice, thereby bankrupting Oak and altering the course of Gabriel's entire life. Or, Tess sticks a future-determining note under Angel Clare's door—only to have the paper stick under the carpet so that Angel never reads her moral confession. Thus, on one small act hinges huge significance for Tess. Marlene Springer said that Hardy "saw all of life as a collage of ironies."

There are three classic cases of these inserted ironies where Hardy seemed to be taking his best and most brutal potshot at the orthodox Christian view of God. All three involve Christian hymns. In *Tess,* before her family is about to be evicted from their home (due to poverty and Tess's refusal to succumb to her relentless seducer, Alec D'Urberville), Tess asks her little brothers and sisters to sing. They select a hymn they knew entitled "Joyful"! Thus, Hardy gets in his digs at Christian joy when life is caving in around the sexually-faithful Tess.

There is a second hymn referred to in *Tess*. It is also sung on a heart-wrenching occasion (Chapter 51). The hymn runs:

"Here we suffer grief and pain;
Here we meet to part again.
In heaven we part no more."

There is a chime of compassion in the Christian's heart as the agnostic Hardy comments after the hymn: "If she could only believe what the children sang." Yes, if only... Probably the bitterest ironical twist in Hardy's novels appears in his last and, by common consent, bitterest book, *Jude the Obscure.*

Jude and Sue have several children together. They also unofficially adopt the child by Jude's first (legal) marriage. Because of his gloomy disposition, the child is nicknamed "Little Father Time." When the family has a desperate time securing a room together (because Jude and Sue have never been legally married), Little Father Time bewails the news that there is yet another child on the way.

More children, more problems. Because this originally unwanted child is so morose, he hangs the other two children and then commits suicide himself. Martin Seymour-Smith quotes Ian Gregor as calling this incident the "most terrible scene in Hardy's fiction—indeed it might reasonably be argued in English fiction." Ironically, however, just as the horrendous hanging and suicide are discovered, a nearby church organ peals out a rendition of the seventy-third psalm: "Truly God is loving unto Israel." Consequently, Hardy takes his *hardiest* knock at the Christian concept of a loving God in a cruelly destructive world. Thomas Hardy was the obverse to Robert Browning's optimism: All's *wrong* with the world!

E. HIS AGNOSTIC APPRAISAL

Hardy's pen was dipped in acid. A significant part of his own life-story is reflected in *Jude the Obscure.* Like Jude, Hardy had been a stonemason's apprentice. Like Jude, Hardy had been enamored of the famous university—which closed its doors to him. Like Jude, Hardy had his lifelong sexual struggle of flesh versus spirit. Like Jude, Hardy had wanted to be a ministerial student and later rejected Christianity. And—like Jude—Hardy had faced the "arrows of outrageous fortune."

As a result of his rejection of Christianity, Hardy adopted an embittered, agnostic stance—claiming not really to believe in a God, yet relentlessly flailing away at Someone or something out there. In country music vernacular, he kept singing a "Somebody-done-somebody-wrong song."

The author's appraisal—in the form of agnosticism—of what was going on in our world took the form of using roundabout phrases for the Supreme Power that Christians call "God." Thus, Hardy will speak of an "unconscious will' or an "Immanent Will" or "the Prime Cause." In *The Woodlanders* Hardy uses the expression "the Unfulfilled Intention." This "Prime Force" is without moral value and is oblivious to people's pain. Once one has abandoned the supernatural, all that is left is the natural world. Consequently, Hardy's "Unfulfilled Intention" in nature is described in *The Woodlanders* (chap 7). Here the trees are suffocated by "huge lungs of fungi." Hardy writes: "The leaf was deformed..., the lichen ate the vigour of the stalk, and the ivy slowly strangled to death the promised sapling." Nature does not present a pretty picture in Thomas Hardy's books.

For Hardy, what happens to inanimate nature also happens to human nature. One of the saddest passages in literature is the concluding summary in *Tess of the D'Urbervilles*. For several hundred pages the reader has looked over the shoulder of Tess while she is raped, is abandoned by her too-good legal husband, is forced to wander and take menial, starvation-level jobs, is pestered repeatedly by her old seducer, and waits on her abandoning husband to return from South America. Finally, Tess breaks. In order to keep her maternal family from starving, Tess finally returns to her original, wealthy seducer, Alec, only then to have her sickening husband show up. Then Tess murders Alec out of love for her husband. Consequently, Tess is hanged. This scene Hardy milks for all it's worth by proclaiming that "the President of the Immortals" had finally done savagely toying with Tess—a "moral woman" (so Hardy proclaims her).

A Christian reader resultantly feels that beneath Hardy's text there is a subtext that constantly suggests: I want you Christians to see your malevolent "God" for all He's worth. In *The Woodlanders* one female character bewails: "if heaven would only give [me] strength—but heaven never did."

Thus, the Hardyan conclusion (in *Tess*, chap 37) is:

"God's not in his heaven;
All's wrong with the world."

Chapter 22

A Lesson Learned from an Agnostic

There is a scene in Hardy's *A Pair of Blue Eyes,* which may epitomize Hardy's dilemma probably better than any other. The scene also reveals precisely the predicament of a world that has forsaken the true God who has uniquely revealed His love in Jesus Christ. In *A Pair of Blue Eyes* two men are in love with one woman—Elfride. While Elfride is watching for the ocean steamer that is bringing one of them home (Stephen Smith, to whom she first promised marriage), she has fallen in love with the second one, Henry Knight. While Henry and Elfride scan the horizon, he slips and falls over a precipice. Henry hangs on for dear life.

While Henry is hanging on for his life, his eyes turn to see a trilobite fossil embedded in the cliffside (symbolizing the recent emergence of a Darwinian world-view). Obviously the skeletal remains can do nothing to save Knight from his life-threatening predicament. In other words, evolution provides no salvation, no ultimate answer.

Knight's rescue finally comes when Elfride moves away from the scene and removes all of her (extensive Victorian) underwear so as to weave it rapidly into a rescue-rope. It is sensually suggestive. (Thus, the only salvation in this pessimistic post-Darwinian world is the sex-and-love relationship between the genders, Hardy implies.)

This scene speaks volumes. What's left to make life tolerable in a Darwinian world? With a supernatural genesis abandoned and no supernatural afterlife guaranteed, Hardy logically proceeds to the natural genesis of human life—namely, sexual romance. (We have not explored this major Hardyan sub-theme here, but Hardy has been called "the father of the modern sex novel" although his writings on this score are relatively tame by comparison with today's uninhibited pornographic explicitness.)

Without the invasive grace of God, what does an unbeliever have to live for? As T. S. Eliot put it in *Sweeney Agonistes*:

"Birth, and copulation, and death.
That's all the facts when you come to brass tacks:
Birth, and copulation, and death."

I believe that reading an agnostic such as Thomas Hardy should make a believer's heart bleed for the raw and pained condition of a thinking-and-feeling unbeliever. The deplorable end-run of Hardy's philosophy is fleshed out by his own tragic character, Little Father Time, who committed suicide.

No wonder Hardy spoke of "the ache of modernism." Should we not feel for those who live unhappily now and, unless they put their faith in Jesus and His atonement, will live *unhappily ever after*? Like Thomas Hardy, his character Angel Clare had forsaken his evangelical roots. Therefore, Angel Clare experienced the "chronic melancholy which is taking hold of the civilized races with a decline of a belief in a beneficent Power."

One of the most poignant passages in Hardy is when the about-to-be-hanged Tess says to her lover Angel Clare: "Do you think we shall meet again after we are dead?" (*Tess*, chap 58). To this question Angel, the modernist or religious liberal, has nothing to say. What a contrast with the apostle Paul, who buoyantly asserted that while "*they*...have not hope," "*we* believe that Jesus died and rose again," and so *we* shall "meet the Lord in the air. And thus *we* shall always be with the Lord" (1 Thess 4:13, 14, 17). Thomas Hardy the agnostic is a parable of the tragedy of a life without Christ.

Bathsheba Everdene, who has inherited a large farm from her uncle, becomes the centre of attention for three men. After a chance meeting with a gentle sheep farmer, Gabriel Oak,

Gabriel proposes marriage to Bathsheba, but is refused, as she does not consider him a proper suitor. Gabriel loses most of his herd and becomes a faithful shepherd for Bathsheba. She then meets a neighboring well-to-do farmer, Mr. Boldwood, who impresses Bathsheba. She later capriciously sends him a valentine, which excites Boldwood, and he later proposes marriage. Bathsheba puts him off, but it is assumed that she will succumb.

In a subplot, a marriage between Bathsheba's servant, Fanny Robin, and the dashing Sergeant Troy is stopped because of a misunderstanding. Troy turns his attentions to Bathsheba and impresses her with his dazzling sword practice. Troy gains her hand in marriage, leaving Boldwood heartbroken. Meanwhile, the hapless Fanny dies in the workhouse, and her body is brought back to Bathsheba's farm. Bathsheba discovers the corpse of a baby, Troy's child, beside that of Fanny.

Troy then disappears, and when his clothes are discovered on a beach, it is presumed that he has drowned. Boldwood reappears on the scene, and Bathsheba agrees to marry him out of a sense of remorse. Troy, however, unexpectedly returns and is killed by the distraught Boldwood, who is later tried and found insane. Bathsheba is at last ready to see the true worth of Gabriel, who has faithfully waited like the Oak of his last name, and the two are married.

A facile interpretation of *Far from the Madding Crowd* would be that true love triumphs over adversity. Since Hardy's ending, however, has often been criticized as contrived, other dominant themes in the novel should be explored. The "Wessex" setting is almost a theme in itself, with the changeless rhythms of nature and agrarian life set against the vicissitudes which confront the characters. It is noteworthy that the most positively portrayed characters are those closest to the earth, such as Gabriel and the peasants who work the soil.

The timelessness of the setting is contrasted with the struggles that the characters face against time and chance. Had Bathsheba not sent the valentine, had Fanny not missed her wedding, for example, the story would have taken an entirely different path. Another important theme is that virtue will ultimately be rewarded. Bathsheba's final acceptance of Gabriel is a form of redemption for her earlier willful behaviour. The development of Bathsheba's character reinforces the ideas that vanity is futile and that rebellion will ultimately be put down for the good of the community. While Bathsheba ultimately is portrayed as a reformed character, the reader may find that her old feisty self was truly more interesting.

Far from the Madding Crowd was the first Hardy novel to receive considerable critical attention. It was widely reviewed in England and also marked an important stage in the growth of Hardy's international reputation; the Paris journal *Revue des deux mondes,* for example, made it the occasion for a long survey-article on Hardy's work to date. After the appearance (anonymously) of the first installment, the *Spectator* observed that "If *Far from the Madding Crowd* is not written by George Eliot, then there is a new light among novelists." Critics during a number of decades have noted that the early serialization of the novel presupposed certain conventions, which could account for the melodramatic nature of many of the scenes.

Study of Hardy's manuscript has shown that he had to make extensive alterations in the portions of the novel referring to Fanny Robin and her illegitimate child. Hardy was widely read and respected at the turn of the twentieth century, but a perception that his work was mostly for a popular audience discouraged serious criticism for several decades. In 1940, a seminal issue of the *Southern Review* devoted solely to Hardy precipitated a rebirth in Hardy criticism. Early modern critics tended to praise *Far from the Madding Crowd*'s evocation of rural life or its universality of theme.

By the 1960s and 1970s, Freudian and feminist criticism predominated. In the 1980s and 1990s, critics used a wide variety of critical approaches to *Far from the Madding Crowd.* While some reviewers continued to adopt a New Critical stance, most were influenced by deconstructive or New Historical techniques. A few of the themes critics exploited were the forms of love in the novel, its subtexts, Hardy's narrative techniques, the relationship of *Far from the Madding Crowd* to Hardy's own life experiences, and the novel's treatment of gender and power. Reviews of film and television adaptations of the novel formed a wholly separate genre of criticism.

On financial terms quite disadvantageous to himself, Hardy persuaded the publisher William Tinsley to issue his novel *Desperate Remedies* in 1871. Published anonymously, this rather melodramatic work received a harsh review in *The Spectator*, which essentially destroyed any chance of its being taken up by the circulating libraries which were then the key to a novel's success. *Under the Greenwood Tree*, the first of his novels to draw upon the scenes, characters, and folkways of his Wessex youth, appeared, also anonymously, the following year, to a more welcoming reception.

With *A Pair of Blue Eyes* (1873), published under his name, Hardy achieved not only the three-volume format favored by the circulating libraries but also something perhaps even more important for the widespread circulation and financial success of his work, serialization of the novel in a leading magazine prior to publication in book form.

With the success in 1874 of *Far from the Madding Crowd*, the first of his novels that can fairly be described as great, Hardy felt securely enough established in his writing career to abandon architecture and to marry Emma. Over the next twenty-three years, he published another ten novels. Many of them contain memorable characters and striking descriptive passages, and three of them are acknowledged to be among the masterpieces of English fiction: *The Mayor of Casterbridge* (1886), perhaps his finest novel, which describes in shatteringly tragic terms the rise and ruin of a strong but fatally impulsive man; *Tess of the d'Urbervilles* (1891), whose frank presentation of a trusting young woman's ruination by the men in her life caused the serial publication to be "mutilated," in Hardy's term, and drew outcries from reviewers for its presumed immorality and the unrelenting bleakness of its vision; and *Jude the Obscure* (1896), a dark and pessimistic novel that is his most controversial work, through whose tormented protagonist Hardy explores issues of idealism and human weakness, and questions the strictures of traditional morality. Painful to read, it is impossible to forget.

It is sometimes claimed that it was Hardy's disgust over the hostile reception of this novel that led him to abandon fiction once and for all, but the reality appears to be somewhat more complex. There is no doubt that he was offended by the attacks upon him, but, despite his refusal to pander to the market and his use of the novel form for profound and often troubling meditations on the human condition, he had always regarded novel-writing essentially as a profession, one which, like any other occupation, could be confining as well as fulfilling. He had always been remarkably, at times astonishingly, amenable to suggestions from his publishers, and it was a strain to have to submit his work to the evaluations of limited and ignorant reviewers and to the shallow and fickle tastes of the reading public, both of which groups seemed, at the end of the nineteenth century, resolutely determined to avoid any presentation of life that was not sweet, sentimental, and simplistically optimistic.

Thus, in the opinion of many, the adverse reaction to *Jude* was essentially an impetus, if not a pretext, for a decision that Hardy was secure enough financially and more than ready psychologically to make. After living in various places in England during the first decade of their marriage, Hardy and his wife had in 1885 moved into Max Gate, a home they had built for themselves in Dorchester. In his mid-fifties, he had completed successful careers as an architect and a novelist (one final novel was published in book form in 1897, but it had already appeared as a serial five years earlier).

He was settled in his personal circumstances and liberated from the pressures of earning a living, and could turn his full attention to what had been his first and was still his greatest enthusiasm, poetry. The most complete edition of Hardy's poetry contains 947 lyrics composed over two thirds of a century, a body of work that demonstrates an amazing consistency of tone and technique, coupled with an even more amazing variety of metrical and stanzaic patterns. As has been observed, it seems as if he is at pains to give every poem its own individual shape and form. The subtlety and range of his metrical experiments, added to his deliberate plainspokenness and refusal of large rhetorical gestures, have often led to the erroneous assumption that Hardy was a clumsy craftsman, when he was in fact a master technician who had honed his art through decades of patient practice.

There is in his work, as there would almost have to be in so vast a collection, a considerable range of moods and subjects, including the humorous dialogue of "The Ruined Maid," the philosophical musing of the sonnet "Hap," the affectionate but somewhat rueful recollection of "The Oxen," and the austere comment on the sinking of the *Titanic* in "The Convergence of the Twain." Nonetheless, there is a distinct sensibility at work in his verse: most typically, his poems seek to capture moments that are seemingly small in event but large in their undercurrent of powerful feeling, which is often a sense of loss, whether of lost loves, missed opportunities, or recollections of the dead.

Calm and quaint-seeming on the surface, Hardy's poetry—a poetry of brief, straightforward treatments of isolated facets of experience—seems intent upon avoiding greatness, as greatness is commonly measured in poetic terms. As such, it constitutes a body of work as radical as anything that would be attempted by his modernist successors.

In his final decades, the controversies surrounding his work receded, and Hardy quietly accumulated honors and established himself as a grand old man of English letters. His marriage had for many years been difficult: Emma was, as he was frequently made to understand, his social superior, and his philosophical investigations and agnostic, if not atheistic, leanings grated upon her conservative religious sensibility.

Their relationship was further strained by his forming of strong emotional bonds with several other women, including a cousin, Tryphena Sparks, who had refused his proposal of marriage because of their blood connection, but whom Hardy continued to love both before and after her death in 1890, three days before her thirty-ninth birthday. Emma's death on

November 27, 1912, brought about a surge of powerful feelings in Hardy that led to a number of passionate and regretful poems, some of which are among his finest. In February 1914, when he was seventy-three, Hardy married thirty-five-year-old Florence Dugdale.

Despite the disparity in their ages, and Florence's jealousy of Hardy's feelings for Emma, their relationship seems to have been overall a happy one. Hardy spent a good portion of his last years dictating (or ghost-writing) large parts of her two-volume biography of him, and was preparing his final collection of poems for publication when he died on January 11, 1928.

Hardy has few equals in his combination of seriousness and skill, and has long been recognized as one of the very greatest of British novelists, for his detailed depiction of a now-vanished way of life, his extraordinary delineation of the subtleties of human personality, and the overwhelming power of his presentation of tragic destinies. Recent decades have seen the growth of his reputation as a poet, to the point where he is esteemed equally highly in both genres. Writing in 1972, Donald Davie asserted, with considerable justice, that Hardy had been *the* dominant influence on British poets for the previous fifty years.

And a quarter of a century later, James Gibson concluded: "Although Hardy has always been better-known as a novelist it should not be overlooked that his first wish was to be a poet, that he took up novel-writing only because he could not earn a living as a poet, that he returned to writing poetry as soon as he had an assured income from his novels, that in later life he more than once pointed out that he had spent more years in writing poetry than in writing novels, and that he frequently said that it was as a poet that he wished to be remembered. Nothing would have pleased him more than to know how widely read his poetry is today, so many years after his death."

The first book-length studies of Hardy were written principally by other poets, including Lionel Johnson, Lascelles Abercrombie, and Edmund Blunden, but over the past century attention to his work has been fairly well divided between the poetry and the fiction. His fiction is thoroughly steeped in the customs and the landscapes of his native Wessex, so much so that there have been several books of photographs intended to acquaint his readers with his part of the world, and it has also been the subject of a good deal of Sociological and Historical interpretation. Hardy was a very uneven writer: several of his novels are brilliant, imperishable masterpieces, while several others hardly bear scrutiny.

This unevenness also extends to his skills in characterization: some of the figures in his novels are shadowy representations or near caricatures, but his best and most significant characters are intensely convincing Psychological studies.

Hardy went as far as was permissible in his time—and in some cases a good deal further—in his presentation of the sexuality of his characters and their relationships to their socially imposed sex roles, and Gender criticism has focused on such characters as Tess Durbyfield and Jude Fawley in the novels that bear their names, Michael Henchard in *The Mayor of Casterbridge*, and others (as in Susan Beegel's essay "Bathsheba's Lovers: Male Sexuality in *Far from the Madding Crowd*"). Aligned with his progressivism in this area were his dissent from traditional religious beliefs and his questioning spirit, exhibited in both his fiction and his poetry. These, along with his framing of his characters' lives in the larger continuum of time and history, have been the occasion for Mythological inquiries into his work.

In that Hardy was a relentless experimenter with form and technique in his verse, a considerable amount of analysis of his poetry has been in the Formalist mode. Given the unusualness, perhaps the uniqueness, of his poetic and his method, which can be seen as a questioning of the traditional assumptions about the nature and intent of poetry, his poems can serve as an excellent basis for a Reader-Response-discussion.

Chapter 23

Poems of Thomas Hardy

Thomas Hardy was both a great poet and a great novelist. Although, as Laurence Lerner and John Holstrom point out in *Thomas Hardy and His Readers,* Hardy "was a classic of the English novel long before he died," he was not celebrated as a poet of the very first rank until after his death. Helmut E. Gerber's brief synopsis, in the first volume of *Thomas Hardy: An Annotated Bibliography of Writings about Him,* gives some indication of the evolution of Hardy's reputation: "In the first period, 1871-1896, Hardy established himself with critics and general readers as an important novelist, but recurring storms of controversy made his life difficult at times. During the second, 1897-1928, Hardy the poet and dramatist lost some of this 'celebrity,' but by the time of his death in 1928 he had gained a measure of national respect tendered to few English authors of the last one hundred years.

The third period, 1929-1939, was a time of falling reputation for Hardy. In the fourth, 1940-1969, beginning with a centenary celebration curtailed by the incipient World War, the rediscovery of much that had been undervalued and the reassessment of Hardy the man and artist proceeded without pause."

This brief summary, however, only partially suggests the controversy that has enveloped judgments of Hardy's works, both his poetry and prose. If there is at present a "Hardy industry" producing dozens of books and hundreds of articles, it arose, in part, as Jean Brooks suggests in *Thomas Hardy: The Poetic Structure,* because Hardy's "place in literature has always been controversial, [and] constant reassessment is essential to keep the balance between modern and historical perspective." Lerner and Holstrom's collection of reviews written about Hardy's works during the author's lifetime demonstrates the kinds of responses his novels engendered initially. But characteristics of Hardy's works that may have disturbed his contemporaries prompting an anonymous reviewer of Hardy's novel *Jude the Obscure* (1895) to entitle his article "Jude the Obscene"—may not trouble modern readers.

As Albert J. Guerard indicates in *Thomas Hardy*: "We are in fact attracted by much that made the post-Victorian realist uneasy." Even today, however, Hardy's works evoke an especially powerful subjective response in critics. Brooks believes that the "strong disagreements about what is 'good' or 'bad' in Hardy's work prove only the relativity of judgement and the vitality of the author." As Donald Davie suggests in *Thomas Hardy and British Poetry*, "Each reader finds in the poems what he brings to them; what he finds there is his own pattern of preoccupations and preferences. If this is true of every poet to some degree, of Hardy it is exceptionally true."

The variety of opinions about Hardy's works has been expressed by several of the most famous modern writers; Lerner and Holstrom record that Henry James, writing about *Tess of the d'Urbervilles* (1891) to Robert Louis Stevenson, asserted: *Tess* "is vile. The pretense of 'sexuality' is only equalled by the absence of it, and the abomination of the language by the author's reputation for style." In *After Strange Gods* T. S. Eliot commented: "[Hardy] seems to me to have written as nearly for the sake of 'self-expression' as a man well can; and the self which he had to express does not strike me as a particularly wholesome or edifying matter of communication."

By contrast D. H. Lawrence, in his perceptive "Study of Thomas Hardy" included in *Phoenix: The Posthumous Papers of D. H. Lawrence*, claimed that the writer's "feeling, his instinct, his sensuous understanding is ... very great and deep, deeper than that, perhaps, of any other English novelist." Moreover, Virginia Woolf, in *The Second Common Reader*, declared: "Thus it is no mere transcript of life at a certain time and place that

Hardy has given us. It is a vision of the world and of man's lot as they revealed themselves to a powerful imagination, a profound and poetic genius, a gentle and humane soul." Quite clearly, then, the quality of Hardy's writing has been variously assessed; but as Irving Howe notes in *Thomas Hardy,* any "critic can, and often does, see all that is wrong with Hardy's poetry but whatever it was that makes for his strange greatness is hard to describe."

The variation in responses to Hardy's work is due in part to the writer's extraordinarily prolific output. In the twenty-six years between 1871 and 1897, he wrote fourteen novels, three volumes of short stories, and several poems that would be published later. Not even illness curtailed his productivity: *A Laodicean* (1881) was dictated to his wife when Hardy was bedridden with what Michael Millgate in *Thomas Hardy: A Biography* speculates was kidney stones complicated by typhoid fever. From 1898 until his death in 1928 Hardy published eight volumes of poetry; about one thousand poems were published in his lifetime.

Moreover, between 1903 and 1908 Hardy published *The Dynasts*— a huge poetic drama in 3 parts, 19 acts, and 130 scenes. In a canon of this size, some works will not measure up to the highest standard. Indeed, only five or six of the novels and some frequently anthologized poems are familiar to most American readers. Although criticism of Hardy's works varies considerably, certain subjects recur in commentary discussing both the novels and the poems.

First, there is the question of Hardy's style. Eliot's opinion of the writer's techniques has been discussed since it was first published in 1934's *After Strange Gods:* "[Hardy] was indifferent even to the prescripts of good writing: he wrote sometimes overpoweringly well, but always very carelessly; at times his style touches sublimity without ever having passed through the stage of being good." Hardy insisted that he purposely created the strange effects that critics have labeled as lapses.

His technique, Hardy explained in his autobiography, engendered in critics "the inevitable ascription to ignorance of what was really choice after full knowledge. That the author [Hardy] loved the art of concealing art was undiscerned." Brooks notes: "Time has revealed Hardy's antirealistic devices to be imaginative truths about cosmic Absurdity rather than the author's incompetence."

Second, Hardy's subjects have drawn much critical attention. Many of his early critics disapproved of certain topics or motifs that run throughout Hardy's novels, poems, and stories. Guerard identifies some of these: "The inventiveness and improbability, the symbolic use of reappearance and coincidence, the wanderings of a macabre imagination, the suggestions of supernatural agency; the frank acknowledgement that love is basically sexual and marriage usually unhappy; the demons of plot, irony and myth." The contemporary reader, on the other hand, may not be disturbed by these particular issues but may find others more difficult to accept.

In Hardy's time, as now, readers complained of what they perceived in the author's tone and stance as pessimism, a word he especially disliked to have applied to his works. This complaint charges that the novels are too gloomy and that most end unhappily. Although modern readers would phrase their responses differently, an anonymous 1892 reviewer of *Tess of the d'Urbervilles* expressed feelings that are echoed today: "Nor do we believe that any person reads novels to reform himself—he reads them for pleasure.... In this view the story of Tess appeals to human sympathy very strongly and directly; it harrows our hearts, it arouses our anger, it fills us with indignation, and it leaves us depressed and sorrowful.... No way out of shame and sin has been shown us, and we already knew the way to death.... A sense of this superb workmanship is the only pure pleasure the book affords; every other effect is as black as night, as cheerless as a tomb, as hopeless as the scaffold."

Hardy's long career spanned the Victorian and the modern eras. He described himself in "In Ten Ebris II" as a poet "who holds that if way to the Better there be, it exacts a full look at the Worst" and during his nearly eighty-eight years he lived through too many upheavals—among them the Boer War and World War I—to have become optimistic with age. Nor did he seem by nature to be cheerful. J. Hillis Miller, who in *Thomas Hardy: Distance and Desire* sees the writer as a "spectator," suggests, "The tone of voice natural to a spectator who sees things from such a position imparts its slightly acerb flavour throughout his work as a compound of irony, cold detachment, using reminiscent bitterness, an odd kind of sympathy which might be called 'pity at a distance,' and, mixed with these, a curious joy, a grim satisfaction that things have, as was foreseen, come out for the worst in this worst of all possible worlds."

Miller believes that Hardy's stance had its roots in his early childhood, reflecting what many contemporary critics have come to recognize: in spite of Hardy's frequent denials, his works are strongly autobiographical and reveal events and feelings of his youth and early manhood. Born in 1840 in the English village of Higher Bockhampton in the county of Dorset, Hardy died in 1928 at Max Gate, a house he built for himself and his first wife, Emma Lavinia Gifford, in Dorchester, a few miles from his birthplace.

As a youth, Hardy traversed the distance on foot between Bockhampton and Dorchester, where he attended school; as an adult he frequently traveled from Dorchester to Bockhampton to visit his family, especially his mother, Jemima Hand Hardy, whom Robert Gittings in *Young Thomas Hardy* calls the real guiding star of his early life. Until he was in his seventies, Hardy usually stayed from April to July of each year in London, where he attended the theater, concerts, operas, his clubs, and the many gatherings of his literary associates and aristocratic friends. But Dorset was his home; his family, the people of his childhood, his memories, the land itself with heath and river—all these made him a rooted man.

Living in Dorset, one of the poorest and most backward of the counties, Hardy was exposed to patterns of rural life little changed in hundreds of years, which he described in his essay "The Dorsetshire Labourer" (1883) and explored through the rustic characters in many of his novels. A local dialect similar to German was spoken in the vicinity at least by the older inhabitants. Stonehenge was only the most famous of the many remains of the past with which the English south abounded. There Hardy could explore and contemplate Druid and Roman, ancient and medieval ruins.

For Hardy, the Napoleonic Wars constituted the great event of the historical past; Dorset tradition, which he imbibed, told of the fear of Bonaparte's invasion of England. Hardy's novel *The Trumpet Major* (1880) and his epical, poetical drama *The Dynasts* reflect a lifetime of involvement with this historical material. The author interviewed elderly soldiers who had fought in the Napoleonic campaigns so that, as Richard H. Taylor notes in his introduction to *The Personal Notebooks of Thomas Hardy,* "impressions of the Napoleonic era were passed down to Hardy by word of mouth"; Hardy also visited the field of the battle of Waterloo, where Napoleon's forces were defeated.

But if Hardy were alive to the past, he was also sensitive to the future, at least as a writer; scores of younger authors, including William Butler Yeats, Siegfried Sassoon, and Virginia Woolf, visited him, and he discussed poetry with Ezra Pound. Furthermore, Hardy spoke eloquently against some of the horrors of his present, notably the Boer War and World War I, in such works as *"Drummer Hodge"* and *"In Time of 'The Breaking of Nations,'"* to name only the best known of his many war poems.

Strongly identifying himself and his work with Dorset, Hardy saw himself as a successor to the Dorset dialect poet William Barnes, who had been a friend and mentor. Moreover, Hardy called his novels the Wessex Novels, after one of the kingdoms of Anglo-Saxon Britain. He provided a map of the area, with the names of the villages and towns he coined to represent actual places—for example, Hardy's fictional Casterbridge is Dorchester, Budmouth is Weymouth, and Melchester is Salisbury—and he helped his friend Hermann Lea to locate scenes from the novels for Lea's book *Thomas Hardy's Wessex,* published in 1925. Interest in Hardy country has remained high, and the literary pilgrims to Dorset have contributed to what Gerber, in the introduction to the first volume of his bibliography, calls the "'Hardy of Wessex' cult."

In spite of what turned out to be a highly productive career as both novelist and poet, Hardy had not decided initially to become a writer. After his schooling he was apprenticed, at the age of sixteen, to the Dorchester architect John Hicks. In Hardy's choice of architecture, he seemed to have continued in the line of work pursued by his father and grandfather; both men were stonemasons and builders. Like his father, too, Hardy played the violin and accompanied the senior Thomas Hardy at country dances.

During the years of his apprenticeship Hardy was not only studying architecture and playing the violin but satisfying his curiosity in other ways. At sixteen he took pains to witness the hanging of a young woman. His description of her rain-drenched body dangling from the rope had, according to Gittings, "distinctly sexual overtones." The incident satisfied voyeuristic tendencies and echoed in his writing. Guerard suggests that Hardy's presentation of almost pathologically unaggressive male characters reveals "unconscious autobiography" and equates the "unaggressive spectator" with the "neurotic voyeur."

Hardy recreated the spectacle of the execution in his conclusion for *Tess of the d'Urbervilles* in which Tess is hanged; and the event remained vivid in Hardy's memory: Gittings notes in *Thomas Hardy's Later Years* that when the writer was in his eighties, "his mind and his tongue reverted to some of the less seemly obsessional topics of his youth. One was the hanging and public execution of women."

Hardy's other interests during the time of his apprenticeship seem to have been decidedly intellectual in nature. He awakened early in the morning to read Latin or Greek before his walk to John Hicks's office, a pattern of study his fictional character Jude was also to follow in *Jude the Obscure*. Hardy was aided in his studies by his friend Horatio Mosley, known as Horace Moule, eight years his senior.

As H. C. Webster notes in *On a Darkling Plain*, Hardy's friendship with Moule "was primarily responsible for his early contact with the thought of his time." As a result he read the *Origin of Species* by Charles Darwin, whose funeral Hardy was to attend, and Herbert Spencer's *First Principles,* John Stuart Mill's *On Liberty,* and Ernest Renan's and John Colenso's biblical criticism. Moule, however, was a deeply troubled man; his suicide in 1873 was a "cataclysmic event" in Hardy's life, according to Gittings in *Young Thomas Hardy:* following Moule's death Hardy was unable to portray in his novels "a man who was not, in some way, maimed by fate."

After his apprenticeship to Hicks ended in 1862, Hardy was employed by Arthur Blomfield, a distinguished London architect, and spent the next five years in London continuing his extensive reading and his architectural work but also availing himself of the opportunities that London afforded to a young man of literary, musical, and artistic talents. But London could also satisfy Hardy's taste for the bizarre and macabre.

One day when he was overseeing the removal of coffins from the graveyard of Old St. Pancras Churchyard prior to church restoration, Hardy observed an open coffin with one skeletal body and two skeletal heads, a sight which made a vivid impression on him and subsequently on his writing. Richard C. Carpenter, in a 1960 *Modern Fiction Studies* essay, traces the grotesque in Hardy's novels- "the kind of situation, scene, or image which yokes man and his environment together in strange relationships."

The "gurgoyle" that spouts torrents of water and washes away the flowers planted on a freshly dug grave in *Far from the Madding Crowd* (1874) or the clergyman who is late to perform a wedding ceremony and is found wandering in a graveyard because he thought he was to officiate at a funeral in *Two on a Tower* (1882) are only two of many examples of Hardy's use of the grotesque, what can be called his nightmare vision.

Much is known about the places Hardy visited and what he observed during these London years and the years immediately afterward when he returned to Dorset because of ill health and continued his architectural work there. Much is also known about his intellectual growth, about the books he read. In *Thomas Hardy: A Study of His Writings and Their Background,* William R. Rutland cites the Bible, the Romantic poets—especially Percy Bysshe Shelley, John Keats, and William Wordsworth—and the Dorset poet William Barnes as early influences on Hardy.

Adding to the writers whom he read under Moule's tutelage during the years of his apprenticeship, Hardy turned to the classics, reading Homer, Sophocles, Euripides, and Aeschylus, whose recurring theme "call no man happy while he lives" Rutland believes to have had a strong influence on the development of Hardy's "twilight view" of life. Hardy also studied Virgil, Horace, and Catullus among the Latin writers.

Many critics point to an influence of German philosopher Arthur Schopenhauer on Hardy, although Hardy himself dismissed such speculation; both critics and the author are partially correct. Hardy was forty-three in 1883 when Schopenhauer's *The World as Will and Idea* was first translated and published in English, and the English writer had already published nine novels. Naturally, his views, his stance, his cast of mind were by then well developed. On the other hand, Schopenhauer's and other German philosophic works were almost certainly absorbed and incorporated in Hardy's view.

Indeed, Rutland shows how Hardy grappled with the German philosophers and demonstrates their influence on the evolution of *The Dynasts.* Nonetheless, as Miller notes in *Thomas Hardy: Distance and Desire:* "[It] is impossible to demonstrate, however, that any one of these sources is uniquely important in determining Hardy's view of life. He read many of the writers who formulated the late Victorian outlook, and his notions were undoubtedly also acquired in part from newspapers, periodicals and other such reading."

No matter how "philosophic" his novels seem, Hardy was not a philosopher, as he clearly revealed in his preface to *Jude the Obscure:* "Like former productions of this pen, *Jude the Obscure* is simply an endeavour to give shape and coherence to a series of seemings, or personal impressions, the question of their consistency or their discordance, of their permanence of their transitoriness, being regarded as not of the first moment." John Holloway notes in *The Victorian Sage: Studies in Argument* that Hardy's novels and works in general are impressionistic; they are not philosophic documents, not arguments.

In spite of the destruction of many of Hardy's notebooks, critics can trace his intellectual growth and development. About his private life, however, the writer was extremely reticent, indeed, secretive. Gittings says in *Young Thomas Hardy* that Hardy was "determined to set up a barrier against biography." The two-volume official biography—*The Early Life of Thomas Hardy,* published in 1928, and *The Later Years of Thomas Hardy,* published in 1930—listed Hardy's second wife, Florence, whom he married in 1914 after the death of his first wife, Emma, as the author of the two volumes, commonly labeled "The Life."

However, in 1954 Richard L. Purdy, in *Thomas Hardy: A Bibliographic Study,* revealed that the majority of "The Life" had actually been composed by Hardy himself. Although Florence added the last four chapters and some other material after Hardy's death, "The Life" is, with some qualifications, an autobiography written in the third person. Autobiographical and biographical material is of great significance to an understanding of Hardy's work because it has become increasingly clear that, in spite of the writer's denials, his novels are very strongly autobiographical. His poems, on the other hand, have always been more intimately and directly connected with their author; the subjects alone make this link inevitable.

The great poems of 1912 to 1913 were written after the death of Emma on November 27, 1912. Some of these works are dated as early as December, 1912, a month after her death, and others were composed in March of the following year, after Hardy had visited St. Juliot, Cornwall, where he first met Emma. Some poems bear initials identifying the person or persons referred to; certain travel poems clearly mark places Hardy visited; several poems are dedicated to writers Hardy knew, such as George Meredith, Algernon Charles Swinburne, and Leslie Stephen; and among his greatest works are occasional poems—for example, *"The Convergence of the Twain"* on the sinking of the Titanic in 1912—and his war poetry.

Moving beyond obvious connections between the author's life and his verse, scholarship of the 1960s and 1970s has ever more explicitly revealed the autobiographical basis for much of the poetry. Davie notes that "whatever the rights or wrongs of using biographical information to assist explication of other poets, in the case of an author so secretive as Hardy it has already proved itself indispensable." The writer's extraordinary ability to retain a moment, an impression, a seemingly trivial event in his memory for forty years and then to bring it forth in verse is attested to by J. O. Bailey in *The Poetry of Thomas Hardy*. Bailey writes that Hardy seemed "to think of the past as present and of the dead in their graves as somehow alive." As Kenneth Marsden declares in *The Poems of Thomas Hardy,* the writer's "chief resource [was] memory and his chief modes, meditation and reminiscence."

Hardy's extraordinary memory of events of the past should not obscure the fact that, as Gittings notes in *Young Thomas Hardy,* "if one were to believe 'The Life,' Hardy had no contact at all with young women from the time he was sixteen to the age of twenty-nine, when he met his first wife." Lack of first-hand information about his relationships with women has encouraged speculation and conjecture.

In *Providence and Mr. Hardy,* Lois Deacon and Terry Coleman contend that Hardy was in love with his cousin Tryphena and had a child with her. Gittings—as well as other biographers—agrees that Tryphena was very important to Hardy, but does not support the theory about the child; he does believe that Hardy loved not only Tryphena, but two of her sisters as well, and that this situation was reflected in his novel *The Well-Beloved* (1897), in which the hero is in love with a woman, her daughter, and her granddaughter at intervals of twenty years. In spite of Hardy's apparent attraction to other women throughout the years, Emma Lavinia Gifford, Hardy's first wife, was the most significant of his attachments, both for his life and for his art.

Hardy met Emma in 1870 when he was sent to St. Juliot, Cornwall, to plan and oversee a church restoration. It was to the early days of their courtship that the poet so frequently turned in the memorial verses which Carl J. Weber in *Hardy of Wessex* declares may "outlive anything else that Hardy has done." Emma strongly supported Hardy's decision to give up architecture and turn to writing, for at the time they first met, he had a number of poems to his credit and was working on his first novel. Hardy's career as a novelist technically began in the 1860s. His first novel, *The Poor Man and the Lady,* was completed in 1867 but was never published, although George Meredith, who read it for the publishing house of Chapman & Hall, recognized the writer's talents. Sections of it, however, were cannibalized for use in *Desperate Remedies,* published anonymously in 1871 after Hardy helped defray the costs by giving the publisher Tinsley seventy-five pounds. This book is a love story and mystery thriller. Howe says that the novel reveals a "repeated upsurge of barely controlled psychic materials."

Hardy, in years to come, learned to control and to refine his material, but even in this apprentice work certain characteristics of his best novels are found. H. C. Duffin, in *Thomas Hardy: A Study of the Wessex Novels, the Poems and "The Dynasts,"* notes the erotic situation around which almost all Hardy's novels are built, a situation also reflected in most of his short stories and many of his poems. As Pierre d'Exideuil suggests in *The Human Pair in the Works of Thomas Hardy,* the writer "sees in love at once the creative and motor force, [and] accords it first place among human preoccupations." Lawrence, in his study of Hardy, describes this theme as the characters' "struggle into love."

In *Desperate Remedies* the heroine Cytherea Graye has two suitors—Edward Springrove, whom she loves, and Aeneas Manston, to whom she is strongly attracted. This situation, a heroine with two, or perhaps three, lovers occurs frequently in Hardy's works. One of the writer's earliest admirers, Havelock Ellis, noted in an 1883 *Westminster Review* article this "persistent repetition of the same situations."

Although *Desperate Remedies* seemed barely under the author's control, Hardy's next novel, *Under the Greenwood Tree* (1872), is a model of form. Taking its title, as Geoffrey Grigson explains in his introduction to the 1974 Macmillan edition of the novel, "from the broadside ballad of 'Under the Greenwood Tree,' in which countrymen and country girls ... have rural fun under the greenwood tree," the narrative is composed of four parts representing the seasonal divisions of the year. In Douglas Brown's view expressed in his *Thomas Hardy*, the value of the agricultural life is here elaborated by the novelist for the first time.

Although "the old, stable order is passing," Brown notes, the "loss, the dismay, is not yet tragic, and the deliberate framing of the tale to suggest hope balances the insistence upon dying traditions." The love story, in which the heroine, Fancy Day, is attracted to two men, is only in part a private affair, for the novel conveys a constant sense of community. As Perry Meisel suggests in *Thomas Hardy: The Return of the Repressed*, the love story is symbolic of broader social forces. The theme of betrayal, which came to dominate Hardy's work, is sounded here, but *Under the Greenwood Tree* is his sunniest novel.

His next novel, *A Pair of Blue Eyes*, published in 1873, is of special interest because it presents a slightly fictionalized account of Hardy's first meeting with Emma. But the best of his early novels, and the one that has received the greatest critical attention and acclaim, is *Far from the Madding Crowd*. However, as astute a reviewer as Henry James, whose *Nation* article is reprinted in Lerner and Holstrom's collection, was not favorably disposed: "Everything human in the book strikes us as factitious and insubstantial; the only things we believe in are the sheep and the dogs."

The publishing history of *Far from the Madding Crowd* is significant. During the nineteenth century novels tended to be serialized in magazines before being published in volume form. Magazine editors were highly concerned that nothing in the serial version of the novel be offensive to their primarily female readers or to an editor's idea of what material was appropriate for women. Hardy, as well as William Makepeace

Thackeray, Charles Dickens, and other writers, submitted to this procedure.

In the case of *Far from the Madding Crowd,* Hardy was asked for a novel by Leslie Stephen, editor of *Cornhill,* a prestigious magazine whose first editor was Thackeray. Stephen's invitation to Hardy was, according to Millgate, an "extraordinary moment for a hitherto unknown writer." Moreover, Stephen—editor of the *Dictionary of National Biography* and the father of Virginia Woolf—eventually became Hardy's close friend and admired associate. Stephen's influence on the writer was greater than that of any other contemporary, according to Millgate, and one of Hardy's loveliest poems is the sonnet he wrote on Stephen's death, *"The Schreckhorn."*

The problems of censorship implicit in serialization for a family magazine did not disappear simply because Hardy and Stephen were friends, although the difficulties were eased. Stephen suggested changes which the novelist made, knowing that when the book was published in volume form he would be able to restore the original version if he chose. In *Thomas Hardy from Serial to Novel,* Mary Ellen Chase traces some of the changes appearing in the serial publication, alterations which, on occasion, completely undermined the novel in question.

Although Hardy gave vent to his frustration with censorship in his essay *"Candour in English Fiction"* (1890), the problem was one that continued to plague him: "What this practically amounts to is that the patrons of literature,... acting under the censorship of prudery, rigorously exclude from the pages they regulate subjects that have been made, by general approval of the best judges, the bases of the finest imaginative compositions since literature rose to the dignity of an art."

Sensible and intelligent readers and critics certainly understood the seriousness with which Hardy wrote, yet some prepared to burn Hardy's books on the grounds that they pandered to lascivious tastes, degraded the institution of marriage, or were antireligious. As virtually all Hardy biographers note, he was extremely sensitive to criticism and very vulnerable to attacks, even by readers who appeared to be deranged. *Far from the Madding Crowd* is called by Dale Kramer in *Thomas Hardy: The Forms of Tragedy* "the non-tragic predecessor."

The novel ends happily when the steadfast hero, Gabriel Oak, marries Bathsheba Everdene, the woman he has loved and served for many years, although the darker side of life is never at far remove. Once again the heroine is given a choice of men—Oak, Farmer Boldwood, and Sergeant Troy—who are very different from one another. Kramer declares that this situation is based on the idea of dichotomy: "The assumption of the aesthetic in the novel is that any and all reactions to situations will be between two extremes, or on one of two extremes."

Brown also responds to this division, but sees it in terms of Bathsheba's major choice between Troy, who is an outsider, and Oak, who knows such enduring things as the land, his sheep, the weather, the cycle of the seasons: "value inheres in the persistence itself. Oak embodies that persistence." Hardy's skill in describing the countryside, the farms, and the setting of the novel is emphasized by Joseph W. Beach in *The Technique of Thomas Hardy:* "we know by evidence of all our senses that we are dealing here with 'substantial things.'"

Bathsheba is the most memorable of the heroines of Hardy's early novels, and he lavished care on his portrayal of her. However, in her flightiness, her inability to run her farm without Gabriel Oak's help, her general dependence on men, and her attraction to Sergeant Troy—who is handsome, dashing, and skilled with his sword, but a womanizer—some critics have seen a depreciation of women. J. I. M. Stewart writes in *Thomas Hardy: A Critical Biography,* "If Hardy does shake a slightly obsessed fist in *Far from the Madding Crowd* it is neither at Crass Causality nor at the decay of the times but at Woman"; Hardy is afflicted, Stewart suggests, by "sexual pessimism and [an] inclination to misogyny."

Hardy's women have fascinated critics of the novels. Samuel C. Chew suggests in *Thomas Hardy: Poet and Novelist* that "Hardy's women are all of one type, differing only in degree." Although many other critics hold similar views, few state them so absolutely. Guerard, for example, sees Hardy's women as "charming, impulsive, and dangerously contradictory"; they fall into several categories ranging from those who are fickle to those who are pure. Howe notes that Hardy liked women and that he was "thoroughly traditional in celebrating the maternal, the protective, the fecund, the tender, the lifegiving."

Lascelles Abercrombie declares in *Thomas Hardy: A Critical Study* that for the writer the "first requirement of feminine nature seems to be, on the whole, the *maintenance* of personal integrity (this desire typifying itself in purity, chastity, virginity)." With the exception of Arabella Donn in *Jude the Obscure* and a few less important characters, most of Hardy's women are young and sexually inexperienced, of marriageable age, and eager to attach themselves to some man. Since most either have no parents or highly unreliable ones, the heroines are looking, as Ruth Milberg-Kaye writes in *Thomas Hardy—Myths of Sexuality,* for "substitutes for the fathers they miss, and most discover that the ideal Hardy hero is a perfect paternal substitute, although not an adequate lover."

Hardy's men, on the other hand, fall into two general categories: the dependable, enduring, somewhat stolid, and sexually unaggressive men, such as Gabriel Oak, who tend to idealize women; and the rakish, devilish, sexually aggressive users of women, such as Sergeant Troy, to whom the heroines are inevitably attracted. Howe suggests that although Hardy valued the virtues associated with passivity, his creativity was stirred by assertiveness. Guerard feels that Hardy liked pathologically unaggressive men: "Those who do seem normally aggressive, or of normal sexuality, are either grotesquely unreal" or are rakes or stage villains. Lawrence suggests that this division of character represents a split between the spirit and the flesh and that Hardy believed "that which is physical, of the body, is weak, despicable, bad"; at the same time, according to Lawrence, Hardy maintains an "unconscious adherence to the flesh."

The composition of Hardy's *Far from the Madding Crowd,*

Millgate contends, can be seen in retrospect as "marking the end of the earliest, happiest, and in certain respects most generously creative period in his career." Webster notes that from 1878 on Hardy "became increasingly melancholic." With the exception of *The Trumpet Major*, the novels that followed are darker, more ironic, bitter, tragic. During the years between 1874, which saw the publication of *Far from the Madding Crowd*, and 1886, when *The Mayor of Casterbridge* appeared, Hardy wrote one of his best-known works, *The Return of the Native* (1878), and a number of lesser-known novels that are useful in tracing Hardy's development as a writer but of somewhat limited interest to a general readership.

Unlike the other novels written during this second period, *The Return of the Native* breaks new ground. In it Hardy described the various forces—personal and elemental—that seem to be beyond the characters' control. He wrote of the destructive relationship between a mother, Mrs. Yeobright, who, according to Millgate, resembles Jemima Hardy, and her son, Clym Yeobright; this sort of attachment Hardy never explored in writing again in any detail. He portrayed sexual involvements—Clym and Eustacia Vye, Damon Wildeve and Eustacia Vye—that are resolved only when the lovers, Wildeve and Eustacia, drown.

He showed the power of the land itself, Egdon Heath, which, according to Brown, "nourishes the very vitality and stability it would threaten to destroy." A growing sense that man is driven by impulses that are not under rational control asserts itself more strongly here than in Hardy's previous novels; Beach describes this theme as the "tragedy of irreconcilable ideals": "What happens is subordinate to what is felt."

Webster believes that *The Return of the Native* represents a "sudden break from the effort to balance social and cosmic evils." These dichotomies are still present in *The Return of the Native*, but, as Ian Gregor notes in *The Great Web: The Form of Hardy's Major Fiction*, they are now somewhat different: "The characters tend to perceive they are acting in two plots, one of their own devising, one of vast impersonal forces, but in this novel they see no relationship between the two." Even the ending of the novel is problematic. For one thing, the marriage of Diggory Venn to Clym's cousin Thomasin—Wildeve's widow—was not a conclusion Hardy wanted; he claimed that it was contrived to satisfy readers' desire for a happy ending. Of more importance, however, is the ambiguity of Hardy's view of his protagonist Clym Yeobright at the end of *The Return of the Native.* Has Clym achieved a modest success or is he a minor failure? Has he gained wisdom or is he deluded? Are such terms meaningful in these circumstances? These are questions with which critics have grappled.

Although in *The Return of the Native* Hardy explores what Millgate suggests is a "road he had not taken," in the novel he returns to his childhood, to the memories of his mother, and to Egdon Heath, the expanse of heathland between Dorchester and Warham.

In *The Mayor of Casterbridge* (1886), on the other hand, Hardy treats the Dorchester of the 1820s, thirty years and more before his youth and years of apprenticeship there. While writing this novel Hardy returned both to the actual Dorchester that was to be his home until his death, and to Casterbridge, the fictional Dorchester of his imagination; the novelist prepared by reading the *Dorset County Chronicle* for 1826, the era portrayed in *The Mayor of Casterbridge.*

He noted in the novel's preface three historical events which came together for him in the composition of the novel: "They were the sale of a wife by her husband, the uncertain harvests which immediately preceded the repeal of the Corn Laws, and the visit of a Royal personage to the aforesaid part of England."

But in *The Mayor of Casterbridge* Hardy also developed themes already in evidence in *The Return of the Native.* Starting from the German Romantic poet Novalis's dictum "Character is fate," Hardy traced in the person of Michael Henchard the rise to and fall from power of a man who, from the very beginning of the novel, carries the seeds of destruction within himself. His tragic plight, according to Brooks, is threefold: "cosmic (representative of man's predicament in an uncaring universe), social (showing the plight of a rural community when old methods are swept away by new) and personal."

Of central interest to critics of *The Mayor of Casterbridge* is the character of Henchard, a man capable in a moment of drunken abandon of selling his wife and young daughter, Elizabeth-Jane, to the highest bidder; in repentance for his inhumanity, Henchard vows to give up alcohol for twenty-one years, and with the strength gained from guilt and sobriety, he goes on to become mayor in the town of Casterbridge, only to be supplanted by a Scotsman named Donald Farfrae. Judgments of Henchard range from that of Beach, who believes that Henchard's vanity is everyman's vanity and that to condemn him is to condemn ourselves, to that of Miller, who speculates that Henchard's soul casts a shadow between himself and all others he meets.

The unique position of *The Mayor of Casterbridge* in Hardy's canon is suggested by the writer's preface to the novel: "The story is more particularly a study of one man's deeds and character than, perhaps, any other of those included in my Exhibition of Wessex life." Gregor believes the *Mayor* to be a "rare novel" in the history of English fiction because "it must be one of the very few major novels ... where sexual relationships are not, in one way or another, the dominant element."

Critics view the novel as reflecting change. For Kramer, one feature of *The Mayor of Casterbridge* is "the presentation of an individual struggle as but one occurrence of timeless rhythm, the cycle of change within the organization of society." Farfrae, who supplants Henchard, can, Kramer suggests, "be toppled by a man" just as he upset Henchard. Brown, on the other hand, sees the conflict between the two men as the "struggle between the native countryman and the alien invader."

Gregor believes that the conflict is both public and private and "finds dramatic expression in the idea of generation," which connotes both history as well as development. Gregor finds change, the movement from youth to adulthood and maturity, emphasized in the novel's final sentence: "And in being forced to class herself [Elizabeth-Jane] among the fortunate she did not cease to wonder at the persistence of the unforeseen, when the one to whom such unbroken tranquillity had been accorded in the adult stage was she whose youth had seemed to teach that happiness was but the occasional episode in a general drama of pain."

Although both Roy Morrell, in *Thomas Hardy: The Will and the Way,* and Gregor stress the importance of reading this sentence in its entirety, its final part—"happiness was but the occasional episode in a general drama of pain"—has been frequently used as a clear and simple thematic expression of Hardy's view of the human condition.

Webster declares that the novels written after *The Mayor of Casterbridge* come "closer to striking a mean between what is comprehensible (natural law) and what is incomprehensible ('Chance')" because they are more balanced between optimism and pessimism than the earlier works. Certainly *The Woodlanders,* published in 1887, does fit Webster's characterization. In his 1960 *Modern Fiction Studies* essay, Robert Y. Drake, Jr., describes *The Woodlanders* as a "traditional pastoral" and states that the novel ends on a happy note. Little in the novel is determined by forces outside the characters; what happens to them is, for the most part, not a matter of chance, but of choice.

In *The Woodlanders* the heroine, Grace Melbury, marries Edred Fitzpiers, a doctor who is above her in station, rather than the man who has loved her for years, Giles Winterbourne. Fitzpiers falls in love with Grace when he sees her face in a mirror. He explains that love is innate; all it needs is a face—an image—on which to be projected. Fitzpiers says: "I am in love with something in my own head, and no thing-in-itself outside it at all." Many of Hardy's characters, especially the men, fall in love in this way, reflecting a tendency toward idealization that Miller has studied in Hardy's novels.

The Woodlanders suggests, however, that "loving kindness, unlike love," is based upon understanding people's "true shape": "The woman herself [Grace Melbury] was a conjectural creature who had little to do with the outlines presented;... a shape in the gloom, whose true quality could only be approximated by putting together a movement now and a glance then, in that patient attention which nothing but watchful loving-kindness ever troubles itself to give."

This conflict between the self-involvement of love and the generosity of loving-kindness is most fully worked out in Hardy's next novel, *Tess of the d'Urbervilles* (1891), which bears the subtitle *A Pure Woman Faithfully Presented.* Tess Durbeyfield, the novel's title character, has left her lover, Alec d'Urberville, and borne him a child who dies; some years later, she is deserted by her husband, Angel Clare, when she tells him about her former lover. Throughout the novel, each of her lovers sees Tess as a projection of himself and makes no attempt to see her as she is.

Hardy's attempts to allow the reader to see Tess as she is and as no one in the novel is able to see her—may account for the diversity of critical views about the character. P. N. Furbank, in spite of his enthusiasm for the novel, suggests in his introduction to the 1974 Macmillan edition that "Tess is so many things that we may forget what she is not—I mean, a rounded character in the nineteenth-century novelist's sense. She is so vivid to us, we know so exactly what she looks like and what her voice sounds like, that we credit her with more coherence as a character than she possesses."

Milberg-Kaye contends that there is "something of a made-up quality about her.... She is incomplete, made up of bits and pieces, because Hardy wanted to do more with her and have her stand for more than his representation of her warrants." Another way of looking at this problem is suggested by Bernard J. Paris who, in an essay collected in The Victorian Experience, observes that Hardy seems "particularly blind to the contribution which their [the characters'] neuroses make to their unhappy lives." And a number of critics have identified masochistic impulses in Tess.

Tess is drawn to two men who are very different from one another. Alex d'Urberville is, as Guerard notes, a stage villain, and Angel Clare, as his name implies, is spiritual to a fault; according to Lawrence, Hardy himself was "something of an Angel Clare." Angel, however, unlike Alec, is able to mature and develop. In *Ethical Perspectives in the Novels of Thomas Hardy,* Virginia R. Hyman declares that during Angel's reunion with Tess his perception of her "utter reliance upon him arouses his own feelings, which are, at last, adequate to the situation: 'Tenderness was absolutely dominant in him at last.'" He is now able to protect Tess, although what she has done—her murder of Alec—is far worse than what he had deserted her for in the past—her affair with Alec.

Although Angel supports her, the law finds her guilty, and Tess is hanged. In the last paragraph of the novel, Hardy writes: "'Justice' was done, and the President of the Immortals, in Aeschylean phrase, had ended his sport with Tess." Hardy's involvement with Tess (he called her "my" Tess, and Paris says that her creator was in love with her), the intensity with which she is portrayed, and the sympathy Hardy evokes for her plight create the novel's special quality. Stewart declares that "*Tess of the d'Urbervilles* is not merely an emotional novel; it is one of the greatest distillations of emotion into art that English literature can show."

Tess of the d'Urbervilles initially aroused much strong opposition, but the truly vitriolic responses were reserved for *Jude the Obscure.* Titles of review articles, as reprinted in Lerner and Holstrom's collection, included not only "Jude the Obscene" but also "Hardy the Degenerate." However, writers Havelock Ellis and H. G. Wells were strong supporters, recognizing the novel's great powers. Hardy responded briefly to his severe critics in the 1912 preface to *Jude the Obscure* and ironically noted an unexpected consequence of the attacks: "the experience completely curing me of further interest in novel-writing." Much critical discussion of the novel centers on the three major characters—Jude Fawley, Sue Bridehead, and Arabella Donn. Stewart contends that in this "innovatory novel" there is much literary stereotype—an honorable man, Jude, falls for an earthy, sexual woman, Arabella; disgusted by her, he turns to her opposite, a spiritual type, Sue. In his afterword to the New American Library edition of the novel, A. Alvarez suggests that the women are projections of Jude's inner needs. Jude and Sue, on the other hand, were seen by Hardy as counterparts, images of one another.

As Frank R. Giordano, Jr., notes in his 1972 *Studies in the Novel* essay, *Jude the Obscure* is a *Bildungsroman,* a novel of development. It is the only novel of Hardy's that traces, albeit briefly, a child's development from youth to adulthood. The reader follows Jude's study of the classics, his desire to go to Christminster (Oxford), his attraction to Arabella, his yearning for Sue, and, after Sue's departure, his self-destructive urges and early death. Lawrence writes that Jude becomes "exhausted in vitality, bewildered, aimless, lost, pathetically nonproductive." And Stewart says that perhaps "no work of the English imagination since *Samson Agonistes* at once suggests so much power and so much fatigue." When he finished *Jude the Obscure* in 1895, Hardy seems to have come to the end of what he had to say in the novel and to have explored all the problems he felt were within the scope of his fiction. Liberated from the novel, he turned to poetry, devoting considerable effort to *The Dynasts.*

According to John Wain's introduction to the 1965 St. Martin's Press edition of the dramatic poem, in composing *The Dynasts* Hardy took "one of those sudden jumps which characterize the man of genius.... He wrote his huge work in accordance with conventions of an art that had not yet been invented: the art of cinema." *The Dynasts,* following this view, is "neither a poem, nor a play, nor a story. It is a shooting-script." Walter F. Wright suggests in *The Shaping of "The Dynasts"* that the work "epitomizes his [Hardy's] world view after he had secured from the philosophers the metaphorical structure for expressing what he had long felt to be true."

In *The Dynasts* Hardy confronted the problem of reconciling determinism and man's capacity for making moral choices, as Wright points out. What, in short, is Hardy's philosophy? Bailey describes three stages in the writer's philosophic development: the first, influenced by Darwin, expressed the view that "natural law rules the world"; the second, influenced by Schopenhauer, "tended to personify natural law as the Universal Will or an Unconscious Mind capable of being waked to consciousness through human agency"; and the third, Hardy's "evolutionary meliorism," presented the hope that human action could make life better.

But how is the Universal Will or the Immanent Will, which is unconscious, to become conscious? As Rutland notes, there is conflict between the "limited and fallible, but conscious and directed, will of the individual towards ordered well being; and the unlimited and all-powerful but unconscious and senseless, urge of an 'Immanent Will' to continuing but purposeless existence." Hardy's answer to this problem is to be found in the concluding verses of *The Dynasts*, which Bailey calls a "paean of hope": "But—a stirring thrills the air / Like to sounds of joyance there / That the rages / Of the ages / Shall be cancelled, and deliverance offered from the darts that were, / Consciousness the Will informing, till It fashion all things fair!" A work of such size and scope as *The Dynasts*, which was published in three parts over five years, engendered varied, and sometimes bewildered, responses. But by 1908, with the publication of the third part, most reviewers were enthusiastic.

In his remaining years, Hardy turned almost exclusively to poetry. Samuel Hynes, in *The Pattern of Hardy's Poetry*, points to two productive poetic periods: the 1860s, and 1910 to 1920. In the latter period, Hardy most fully developed his poetic talents. He published eight volumes of poetry, beginning in 1898 with *Wessex Poems*, containing lyrics dating from the 1860s, and ending with *Winter Words*, published in 1928 and including poems written during the last year of his life.

When Hardy died in 1928, his ashes were deposited in the Poets' Corner of Westminster Abbey and his heart, having been removed before cremation, was interred in the graveyard at Stinsford Church where his parents, grandparents, and his first wife were buried. Although his family were understandably distressed by these somewhat bizarre arrangements, this double burial—a reflection of the duality of the public and the private man—seems quite fitting for Thomas Hardy. Writer. Worked as an architect in Dorchester and London, beginning as an apprentice.

Bibliography

Thomas Hardy: A Biography Revisited, Michael Millgate. (Oxford Univ Press, 2004).

Thomas Hardy and Contemporary Literary Studies, Ed. Tim Dolin & Peter Widdowson. (Palgrave Macmillan, 2004).

Seeing Hardy: Film and Television Adaptations of the Fiction of Thomas Hardy, Paul J. Niemeyer. (McFarland & Co., 2003).

In the Steps of Thomas Hardy, Anne-Marie Edwards & Michael Edwards. (Jones Books, 2003).

Thomas Hardy, Patricia Ingham. (Oxford Univ Press, 2003).

Thomas Hardy A to Z: The Essential Reference to His Life and Work, Sarah Bird Wright. (Facts on File, 2002).

The Life of Thomas Hardy, Paul Turner. (Blackwell Pub, 2001).

Thomas Hardy: The Novels, Norman Page. (Palgrave MacMillan, 2001).

Thomas Hardy: His Life and Work, F.E. Halliday. (House of Stratus, 2001).

The Achievement of Thomas Hardy, Phillip Mallett. (Palgrave Macmillan, 2000).

The Cambridge Companion to Thomas Hardy, Ed. Dale Kramer. (Cambridge Univ Press, 1999).

Thomas Hardy's Major Novels, Julie Sherrick. (Rowman & Littlefield, 1998).

Thomas Hardy in Our Time, Robert Langbaum. (St. Martin's Press, 1997).

Thomas Hardy: A Literary Life, James Gibson. (St. Martin's Press, 1996).

Thomas Hardy and the Church, Jan Jedrzejewski. (St. Martin's Press, 1996).

Thomas Hardy: The Ranging Vision. Noorul Hasan. (North-Eastern Hill Univ Pub, 1996).

Thomas Hardy on Stage, Keith Wilson. (Palgrave Macmillan, 1995).

The Decline of the Goddess: Nature, Culture, and Women in Thomas Hardy's Fiction, Shirley A. Stave. (Greenwood Press, 1995).

New Perspectives on Thomas Hardy, Charles P. Petit. (Palgrave Macmillan, 1994).

Thomas Hardy and the Proper Study of Mankind, Simon Gatrell. (Univ Press of Virginia, 1993).

Thomas Hardy, Charles Lock. (Palgrave Macmillan, 1992).

A Critical Introduction to the Poems of Thomas Hardy, Trevor Johnson. (Palgrave Macmillan, 1991).

Thomas Hardy's Tragic Poetry: The Lyrics and The Dynasts, Katherine Kearney Maynard. (Univ of Iowa Press, 1991).

Thomas Hardy, Harold Bloom. (Chelsea House Pub, 1987).

Thomas Hardy's Jude the Obscure, Harold Bloom. (Chelsea House Pub, 1987).

Brodie's Notes on Thomas Hardy's *"Tess of the D'Urbervilles"*, Graham Handley. (Macmillan, 1986).

Study of Thomas Hardy and Other Essays, D.H. Lawrence. (Cambridge Univ Press, 1985).

A Thomas Hardy Dictionary: The Characters and Scenes of the Novels and Poems Alphabetically Arranged and Described, F. Outwin Saxelby. (Greenwood Press, 1985).

Masters of World Literature: Thomas Hardy, Irving Howe. (Palgrave Macmillan, 1985).

Thomas Hardy's England, Jo Draper & John Fowles. (Little, Brown & Co., 1984).

Thomas Hardy's Later Years, Robert Gittings. (Granite Impex ltd., 1984).

Thomas Hardy and Women: Sexual Ideology and Narrative Form, Penny Boumelha. (Harvester Press, 1982).

Thomas Hardy: The Sociological Imagination, Noorul Hasan. (Humanities Press, 1982).

Thomas Hardy: A Biography, Michael Millgate. (Random House, 1982).

The Short Stories of Thomas Hardy, Kristin Brady. (Palgrave Macmillan, 1982).

Thomas Hardy: Psychological Novelist, Rosemary Sumner. (St. Martin's Press, 1981).

Thomas Hardy, Lance St. John Butler. (Cambridge Univ Press, 1978).

Young Thomas Hardy, Robert Gittings. (Penguin, 1978).

Thomas Hardy: The Poetry of Necessity, James Richardson. (Univ of Chicago Press, 1977).

Thomas Hardy After Fifty Years, Lance St. John Butler. (Macmillan, 1977).

A Commentary on the Poems of Thomas Hardy, F.B. Pinion. (Macmillan, 1976).

Thomas Hardy: The Poetry of Perception, Tom Paulin. (Macmillan, 1975).

Thomas Hardy and History, Reginald James White. (Macmillan, 1974).

Thomas Hardy and Rural England, Merryn Williams. (Columbia Univ Press, 1972).

Thomas Hardy: His Career as a Novelist, Michael Millgate. (Random House, 1971).

Thomas Hardy and His Readers: A Selection of Contemporary Reviews, Laurence Lerner. (Bodley Head, 1968).

The Later Years of Thomas Hardy, Florence Emily Hardy. (Macmillan, 1930).

The Early Life of Thomas Hardy, Florence Emily Hardy. (Macmillan, 1928).